Political Parties and the Maintenance of Liberal Democracy

Kelly D. Patterson

Columbia University Press
NEW YORK

Columbia University Press
Publishers Since 1893
New York Chichester, West Sussex

Library of Congress Cataloging-in-Publication Data

Patterson, Kelly D.
Political parties and the maintenance of liberal democracy / Kelly D. Patterson.
p. cm.—(Power, conflict, and democracy)
Includes bibliographical references and index.
ISBN 0–231–10256–9 0–231–10257–7 (alk. paper)
1. Political parties—United States. 2. Political parties—United States—Platforms. 3. Party discipline—United States. 4. Presidential candidates—United States. 5. United States. Congress—Leadership. 6. Political leadership—United States. I. Title. II. Series.
JK2261.P318 1996
324.273—dc20
96–8617
CIP

Casebound editions of Columbia University Press books are printed on permanent and durable acid-free paper.

Printed in the United States of America
c 10 9 8 7 6 5 4 3 2 1
p 10 9 8 7 6 5 4 3 2 1

Political Parties and the Maintenance of Liberal Democracy

POWER, CONFLICT, AND DEMOCRACY
American Politics Into the Twenty-first Century
Robert Y. Shapiro, Editor

To Jeanene, Andrew, and Kate

Power, Conflict, and Democracy: American Politics into the Twenty-First Century

Robert Y. Shapiro, Editor

As it examines the political processes and major trends in politics that will affect the workings of democracy and policymaking in the United States as it moves into the twenty-first century, this series focuses on how the will of the people and the public interest are promoted, encouraged, or thwarted. It aims to question not only the direction American politics will take as it enters the next century, but also the direction American politics has already taken.

The series treats such diverse topics as the role of interest groups and social and political movements; openness in American politics; important developments in institutions such as the executive, legislative, and judicial branches at all levels of government as well as the bureaucracies thus created; the changing behavior of politicians and political parties; the role of public opinion; and the functioning of mass media. Because the characteristics of pressing problems drives politics, the series also examines important policy issues in both domestic and foreign affairs.

Presented are all theoretical perspectives and the uses of different methodologies and types of evidence that answer important questions about trends in American politics.

Contents

Preface

Thanking a number of institutions and individuals for assistance in the completion of such a large project is quite commonplace. I feel a particular need to conform to this custom because I am indebted to so many. Generous funds were provided by the Eisenhower World Affairs Institute, Franklin and Marshall College's Hackman Fellowship and the Department of Political Science, and the College of Family, Home, and Social Sciences at Brigham Young University. Without their belief in this project, undertaking such a labor-intensive effort would have been impossible. I would also like to thank the Congressional Fellowship program of the American Political Science Association. The opportunity to view presidential campaigns from inside Congress was an extraordinary bonus.

Of course funding is only the first step. Many research assistants devoted their time, energy, and attention to this project. I enjoyed my association with them more than I enjoyed seeing the project completed. Charles E. Trobman, Todd C. Marshall, Brian Davis, Brooksany Barrowes, Amy Bice, and Erika Rahden loaned their considerable research talents for months at a time. Owen Abbe, Michael E. Hendron, and Vaughn Hromiko were particularly valuable to the completion of this book. Their extraordinary computer skills, determination, enthusiasm, and attention to detail significantly improved the research. My heartfelt gratitude goes to them all.

Intellectually and academically I owe debts to many. Charles V. Hamilton first piqued my interest in governance. His efforts were bolstered by the genius of Robert Y. Shapiro, who actually seemed to understand the details of the research and the implications of its findings long before I moved a cursor across a computer screen. John T. Young, Paul S. Herrnson, and Stephen H. Wirls provided friendship and intellectual guidance. They have taught me what it means to be a colleague. David B. Magleby has reinforced the lessons I learned from the others. I sincerely hope that all political scientists have such supportive department chairs at least once during their career. Finally, the people at Columbia University Press have been wonderful. Working with professionals such as John Michel and Polly Kummel, who are gracious and kind, is quite refreshing. I would also like to thank the anonymous reviewers who read the manuscript; their comments and suggestions are greatly appreciated.

I thank my parents, Dale and Arlene Patterson, for always encouraging me to follow my dreams. Their belief in education as a lifelong enterprise has never wavered.

My family has been patient and understanding during a project that has undoubtedly taken me away from them for far too many hours. My wife Jeanene has been consistently optimistic and supportive. Andrew and Kate have always been a source of happiness and inspiration. Their arrival in our home has taught me the wisdom of patience and persistence. It is to Jeanene, Andrew, and Kate that I dedicate this book.

Kelly D. Patterson
Provo, Utah

Introduction

Political Parties and the Question of Democracy

The election of 1992 dramatically illustrated Americans' growing dissatisfaction with the more recent practices of democratic politics. The voters' rage converged on the glaring ineptitude of democratic institutions and the scandals that plague them. Indicators of wrath were widely and plainly evident: on November 3 a record number of voters turned out, the largest percentage of eligible Americans to vote since the election of 1964, and an incumbent president was unable to win 40% of the popular vote, something that had not occurred since the defeat of Herbert Hoover in 1932. Sixty-five members of the House, a postwar high, had decided to retire rather than face what most of them believed would be severe retribution at the ballot box.

Public opinion polls recorded the depth and intensity of the anger. Large majorities expressed disapproval with the job that Congress was doing, and the approval rating enjoyed by individual representatives dropped to barely 50%.[1] The presidency did not fare much better. As Bill Clinton began his tenure as president, only 51% of voters approved of the way he was handling his job.[2] To make matters worse the dissatisfaction did not evaporate as Clinton settled into his job. He ended the first one hundred days of his presidency, a time traditionally dubbed the honeymoon, with the lowest approval rating ever registered for a new president.[3]

Certainly the voters' disapproval was exacerbated by the constant finger-pointing and bickering among the major political players. The Democratic-controlled Congress and Republican president George Bush blamed each other for perpetuating the institutional "gridlock" that left unresolved the many policy crises confronting the nation.[4] Even Clinton, while still campaigning as the Democratic presidential candidate, could not resist assigning blame to the poor relationship between the institutions that form the foundation of American democracy.

But the changes ushered in by the 1992 elections were only the prelude to a much more historic series of events. Indeed few, if any, individuals were prepared for the stunning transformations wrought by the 1994 midterm elections. The Republican Party gained control of the House of Representatives, the Senate, and a majority of statehouses and governorships. Republicans gained control of the House for the first time in forty years, and for the first time since 1860 a standing Speaker of the House was defeated at the polls. And for the first time since Reconstruction a majority of representatives from the South were Republican. In 1992 pundits were quick to contend that the voters simply rejected all political incumbents; perhaps the most amazing statistic to emerge from the 1994 elections was that not one Republican incumbent for the House or the Senate lost.

The elections of 1992 and 1994 amplified the clamor for political change growing out of citizens' dissatisfaction with American politics. Citizens wanted change—not just a variation in policy but a fundamental change in the way in which the institutions of American democracy operate. Measures establishing term limits for members of Congress appeared on the ballots of twenty-two states from 1991 to 1994, passing in all but two, Washington and Utah. In the state of Washington, Thomas Foley, the Speaker of the House, waged a vigorous 1991 campaign to defeat term limits. In Utah voters rejected the term-limits initiative because it included a cumbersome and expensive runoff provision. Utah voters still favored the concept of term limits by a 2 to 1 margin.[5]

Another sign that change was in the air was that most, if not all, candidates in 1992 and 1994 touted several reform measures, ranging from campaign finance to budgetary items. Indeed the Republican candidates for the House of Representatives sought to seize the reform agenda by publishing their *Contract with America,* a series of promises that the Republicans promised to vote on in the first one hundred days of a Republican majority.[6]

Individuals inside and outside government insisted on substantial reform of government agencies and reorganization of Congress. In 1993 only 7% of the population expressed "a great deal" of confidence in the people running Congress. Only slightly more—12%—said they had "a great deal" of confidence in the executive branch. Significantly the two popularly elected institutions did much worse than the Supreme Court in this area. Thirty-one percent said they had a "great deal of confidence" in the people running the Supreme Court.[7] Clearly individuals are dissatisfied with the performance of democratic politics.[8]

Displeasure with democratic politics is not bad per se. A reasonable amount of skepticism is often a necessary self-corrective for some weaknesses of democratic governance. However, too much displeasure is certainly unhealthy for the polity, especially when it is increasingly manifested in calls for wholesale reform of the institutions that structure the conduct of politics in this country. Such dissatisfaction is particularly dangerous, and potentially fatal, when it results from confusion about the way in which democracy operates.

Any description of today's political situation that urges caution strikes most people as somewhat odd; after all, in today's society commentators and citizens alike never entertain the notion that they might be confused about the principles of democracy. Instead most individuals believe they are irritated only by the seemingly shoddy and lackadaisical performance of democratic institutions. These feelings are supposed to justify the calls for reform that have become so commonplace; whether these feelings are connected to larger questions about how the American version of democracy operates is popularly viewed as irrelevant.

Of course the calls for institutional change emanate from a number of quarters. All are concerned with making the American form of democracy workable, even if little attention is given to what is meant by *workable.* But the most prominent and influential people encouraging change are the many intellectuals and academics who populate American universities and Washington, D.C., think tanks. Their recent concern with American democracy centers on their belief that the government of the United States cannot perform effectively. They see substandard performance in such diverse quarters as the production of public policy and the inclusion of citizens in the democratic process. The titles spawned by this concern surely testify to the growing belief that American democracy teeters on the brink of the abyss.[9]

When coupled with the news industry's need to sensationalize happenings in American government, a burgeoning market of ideas is sustained by those willing to comment on the disappointing, if not inferior, practices and performances of the American political system. But the reporting routines of the modern mass media consistently neglect, by chance or design, to place the commentary and opinions in a context that allows citizens anything more than a visceral reaction to what is being portrayed.[10] For instance, reporting on the budget stalemates that periodically afflict Congress and the president often centers on the personalities of the politicians. The reporting hardly ever mentions that the conflict traces its roots to the constitutional separation of power that parcels out political responsibility to different institutions. Popular outrage with democratic practices is often the result. Public opinion polls chronicle the outrage, and the news media report their findings. Consequently, people who do not necessarily understand or appreciate constitutional relationships clamor for constitutional changes. Such clamoring can pose serious challenges to the stability of the polity.[11]

Much of the discussion of reform centers around the weakened state of political parties. The general argument states that the decline of political parties, in all of their various manifestations, has produced the unsatisfactory performance of American political institutions, thereby damaging American democracy. If only institutional or constitutional reforms were adopted, the argument continues, the impending crisis of legitimacy and performance facing American democracy could be averted. But this argument embraces various assumptions about democracy and its links to political parties that need to be examined.

Democracy and Political Parties

The possibility of misunderstanding democracy is very real. *Democracy* is a vastly complex term; volumes have been written about its various meanings and how those meanings have been translated into specific regimes. To make matters worse modern political discourse does not respect the complexity of the debate. Political campaigns, and the reporting generated by these campaigns, are not concerned with the often subtle distinctions that have marked serious debates about the nature of democratic regimes. When you add to this debate the hybrid nature of the American system, a system that combines liberal and republican values, the occasions for misunderstanding or even distorting the operation of American democracy multiply.[12] These occasions have led one prominent political theorist to observe that we live in an "age of confused democracy."[13]

Properly defining and understanding democracy is crucial because any judgment about democracy's performance is largely a function of the way in which democracy is defined—meaning that our estimations about performance and vitality are largely shaped by the definition of democracy. For example, if the definition of democracy stresses purposeful and substantial participation for a majority of citizens, American democracy cannot receive a favorable evaluation. Other definitions may stress other values or features, but the point remains: the definition structures the evaluation.

The plethora of viable definitions does not mean that democracy can be anything. Particular properties make regimes democratic, and being clear from the outset about what these properties are is important. However, if the meaning of the term is confusing or emphasizes the wrong components, evaluations of its performance will be largely inadequate. Inadequate evaluations are not dangerous per se. But well-intentioned individuals are quite likely to act on these evaluations. Cries for reform and change flow from citizens' level of dissatisfaction with the system of government. If citizens have an unclear or incomplete understanding of democracy, their expectations of its performance will be unrealistic. Unrealistic expectations in turn create the serious hazard that large numbers of citizens might embrace certain reforms. If the reforms are based on a faulty understanding of democracy, the reforms may make the situation even worse by damaging the culture that sustains the performance of democracy over the long run.

The chances for confusion are even greater when the evaluation of political parties is attached to the discussion of democracy. Scholars of political parties have always been ambivalent about the actual contribution that political parties make to the maintenance or even enhancement of democracy. Some studies have portrayed political parties as downright incompatible with democracy because of their oligarchic tendencies. Two of the most prominent scholars on political parties, Moisei

Ostrogorski and Robert Michels, despair that democracy can ever be realized unless parties are either completely overhauled or abandoned entirely.[14] Other scholars characterize political parties as necessary evils to be tolerated because, despite their shortcomings, they could produce important benefits. E. E. Schattschneider, who argues that "democracy is unthinkable save in terms of political parties," is probably the best example of this school of thought.[15] Schattschneider's bold proclamation about political parties and democracy is rare in the modern literature on political parties, largely because he was both a political scientist and a political theorist who was interested in the larger question of how democracies are maintained.

However, the common thread in all these scholarly efforts is the recognition that political parties have a special relationship, for good or for ill, with democracy. The reason for this special relationship is clear: political parties perform a number of visible and latent functions. The debate is over whether the functions that parties do perform, and the manner in which these functions are performed, promote the particular virtues necessary to the maintenance of liberal democracy. These questions can be answered only in a framework that asks serious questions about the nature of democracy. For this reason modern scholars of political parties must come to grips with democratic theory.

The discussion thus far assumes that we can fashion a workable definition of democracy and identify its main components. It also assumes that these components, once properly identified, clearly betoken the tasks that parties should be performing. For only after we have identified democracy and its constituent elements can we judge adequately whether political parties, in their present form, nourish democracy. This determination requires thinking about "how the theory [of democracy] relates to, and passes into, practice."[16] As Giovanni Sartori states, "The artifact 'democracy' has to be conceived and constructed before being observed" (p. 18). Consequently Sartori's theory of democracy is extremely useful to those who study political parties. His examination of the constituent components of democracy and the way in which they pass into practice provides the framework for a realistic evaluation of the performance of modern political parties.

Sartori begins his theoretical development by looking at the concept upon which the entire notion of democracy rests: the people. The obvious need to interpret a concept like "the people" does not make the task any easier, for the principle can be construed in a number of ways. Sartori argues that, when discussing democracy, only one principle merits serious consideration: the limited majority (p. 22). The principle of limited majority states "that no rights of any majority can be absolute" in the sense that the rights of a majority are without limits (p. 24). The ability to replace one majority with another majority "turns out to be *the* democratic working principle of democracy" (p. 25). Any other definition of the term does not guarantee that a majority can be replaced, and without the ability to replace a majority, democracy ceases to be a democracy.

By establishing the principle of limited majority as the foundation of the definition of democracy, the attention we pay political parties should focus on the manner in which a political party organizes to capture control of the mechanisms of government, that is, we should focus on the way in which political parties can court voters in order to convert minority positions into majorities.[17] Properly understood, *conversion* implies competition, and a competitive party system is one in which "party leaders confront one another *indirectly*: They vie with each other with an eye to the voters—and this entails far-reaching consequences."[18] The actual legislative performance of victorious parties becomes secondary to the larger question of democracy. Competition directly benefits democracy by making the limitation of power possible. Emphasizing competition and conversion does not make the performance of parties, once in government, irrelevant. Rather, the party's role in the conversion from minority to majority speaks more directly to the question of the vitality of democracy.

The second and rather novel feature of Sartori's theory of democracy revolves around the reinvigoration of a vocabulary that expresses the politically possible. These days too much of academic and political discourse, especially discourse involving the question of democracy, appropriates a vocabulary that belies democratic reality. Sartori argues that "utopianism consists of *practical contradictions* whose logical formulation is this: One cannot obtain *more* of two things that require *contrary actions*."[19] However, the debate over democracy in the United States today contains serious proposals that could never seriously be realized.

This observation applies specifically to the debate over the role to be played by political parties in democratic governance. Political parties are asked to be the means by which citizens are provided with meaningful modes of participation and elites are provided with effective control of government institutions. These cross-pressures expose the extent to which the vocabulary describing political reality lacks an awareness of the politically impossible. The current debate about governance and participation manifests an irrational acceptance of the unreal, a belief that two contrary actions—intense and meaningful citizen participation and effective control of government—will actually give us more of each of these two important values.[20] At the very least merging political theorizing with the study of political parties should illuminate the zero-sum character of the different values pursued by those who seek to reform the political parties. As it stands now, the debate over the performance of democracy and the modern party system makes promises that are impossible to keep. It raises expectations that cannot be fulfilled.

The third component of Sartori's theory of democracy is the concept of autonomous public opinion. Autonomous public opinion is public opinion formed under two conditions: "a system of education that is not a system of indoctrination," and "an overall structure of plural and diverse centers of influence and information."[21] In other words, significant competition exists within the marketplace of ideas that affect public opinion. Autonomous public opinion also means that the elected representatives can use the will of the people, expressed in frequent elections, as an accurate guide.[22] Elected representatives have strong incentives to pay close attention to public opinion, and these incentives are much stronger than the reasons for their allegiance to a particular party. As another author has emphasized, "The government floats in public opinion; it goes up and down on great long waves of it that often have little to do with parties."[23] It follows that as candidates compete with each other through party labels, the parties bolster democracy not only because of how they will act in government but because of the competitive way in which they structure the information used by voters to form public opinion.

Once again including autonomous public opinion in a theory of democracy directly influences the evaluation of political parties' effectiveness. Such a theory of democracy relegates political parties to the status of one among many competing groups, all of which seek to provide information to citizens. As I will argue later, the apparent and stark dilution of the strength of parties in the formation of public opinion poses a problem only if effective control of government by political parties is made the sine qua non of party effectiveness. Otherwise the decline in the importance that voters ascribe to political parties in forming and evaluating policy alternatives is of secondary concern for the maintenance of democracy. Even the decline of party identification is less important. The theory of democracy specifies only the need for robust competition between the parties in order to ensure that no one group dominates information and that the majority could become a minority.

These three features, when combined in a theoretical whole, lead to a definition of democracy that emphasizes the conditional and limited nature of power held by those who rule in a democratic polity. As Sartori states, democracy "is a system in which no one can choose himself, no one can invest himself with the power to rule and, therefore, no one can arrogate to himself unconditional and unlimited power."[24] Power is limited by the ever-present possibility of converting minorities into majorities, which is exclusive to the electoral sphere. Therefore to the extent that parties are critical to the question of democracy, their electoral activities are much more important than their governing activities. We should give much more weight to their organization for purposes of competition than their activities and organization once in government. After all, the theory of democracy demands that we distinguish between decision-making principles and electoral instruments. Electoral instruments jump-start the principle of limited majority, whereas decision-making rules are simply the means for acting on the decisions made in the electoral sphere. Although decision-making rules strongly shape the kinds of decisions that are made, they are not a decisive factor in determining whether a regime is democratic.[25]

A practical theory of democracy such as Sartori's—which emphasizes decisions made in the electoral sphere and the competition that can reverse those decisions in the next election—points toward the most fruitful area in which to study the intersection of democratic theory and political parties. Such a theory demands caution when discussions of the health of democracy separate governance from electoral considerations.

Political Parties and Governance

The odds of misunderstanding democracy and its performance are particularly great when studying the relationship between political parties and the process of governing. First, as I discussed earlier, any evaluation of governing contains implicit assumptions about democracy and how it ought to work. Second, the causal relationships of the various elements of political parties and their effect on creation of public policy are not obvious. Designing a research project that can accurately measure the effects, no matter how remote, that parties do have on public policy is difficult.

However, studies have shown that relationships between the electoral activities of parties and the broader policy environment do exist. Therefore, when a study seeks to examine how political parties relate to overall governability, its focus cannot be a single feature of the party system. As David, Goldman, and Bain observe, "Neither the party system nor the nominating system can be studied in isolation; the practical requirements of the party system have determined many aspects of the nominating process, and vice versa."[26] Furthermore "such relationships exist because the nominating process is not an end in itself. It is preparatory to an attempt to win an election, which in turn is preparatory to an attempt to operate a government." For these reasons they suggest that "there are relationships between the manner in which a party nominates its candidates, the manner in which it campaigns for their election, and the manner in which it governs—or even the extent to which it can be said to govern—if it succeeds in electing its candidates" (p. 6).

The foregoing discussion suggests the importance of studying the policy promises that candidates, especially presidential candidates, make in the electoral environment and the way in which various interests are mobilized to support the adoption and implementation of these promises. Several facets of the party system, then, need to be considered, including the evolution of the methods for nominating candidates and the relationship between the candidates and those individuals who will participate in the governing process after the general election. Furthermore the relationships must be considered in the context of a particular theory of democracy, because only in such a context can the normative judgments about performance and vitality assume any real meaning. Therefore any study that purports to examine political parties and their relationship to democratic governance faces the daunting task of looking at both the broader party system and the theory of democracy that sustains it.

This book accepts such a challenge. Although some may disagree with my overall conclusion, I hope that the theory, methods, and evidence will bring a measure of clarity to the discussion of political parties and the degree to which their operation helps to sustain American democracy. For if we are not clear about the question of democracy and the importance of political parties, we end up with a spate of unproductive efforts to reform what may not need to be reformed.[27]

This study examines specific links among the nominating, electoral, and governing coalitions. Furthermore it contends that these links have not eroded as the political parties have declined. By selecting various manifestations of these coalitions, reconstructing the links that may exist between them, and observing the changes in these links over time, we can test whether the decline of the parties has actually produced certain effects. For example, party platforms can symbolize the positions of the nominating coalition because they are a compilation of the issues favored by various party leaders, coalitions on issues, and the candidates themselves. The policy positions of the presidential candidate represent the electoral coalition because they signal which groups are important to the presidential candidate and suggest the size and the extent of the electoral coalition that the candidate hopes to assemble. Finally, the policy positions of the party leaders represent one important segment of the governing coalition. Although any governing coalition has other components, its agreement with congressional party leaders on specific issues must be regarded as a critical contributor to its success.

I believe the creation and maintenance of the first two coalitions have a significant effect on the operation and effectiveness of the governing coalition. For this reason assessing a president's potential for governing requires evaluating the connections between all three coalitions. Moreover we cannot examine the connection between these coalitions as if the success or failure of one administration reflects some underlying weakness in the party system. Surely some administrations are better at producing and maintaining these coalitions than others. A longitudinal analysis allows us to take into account the variations that occur across different administrations while identifying those properties that are common to all administrations.

To examine these connections between parties and governance I compare the policy positions of presidential candidates during elections from 1952 to 1992 to the positions outlined in party platforms and to those of party leaders in Congress. Comparing the party platforms to the positions taken by candidates is one method of probing the connection between the nominating coalition and the electoral coalition. Furthermore comparing the policy positions of the presidential candidates to the publicly stated positions of both parties' congressional leaders yields considerable evidence about the relationship between the presidential candidate's electoral coalition and other vital components of the governing coalition.

In chapter 1 I review the literature on the decline-in-party thesis and its relationship to the question of governability. Much of the argument concerning the crisis in American politics can be traced to the perception of the role that political parties are supposed to play in American politics. The fragmentation and ineptitude thought to surround political parties fuel the widespread perception that the links that bind the entire political system in a governable whole have broken. In chapter 1 I review the coalition theory that ties the system into this governable whole and use it as a theory for generating hypotheses that I test in subsequent chapters.

Chapter 2 explores the effects that changes in the electoral system have had on the nominating and electoral coalitions. Specifically I examine how a shift from one party era to another is manifested in relationships between the nominating and electoral coalitions, including how the reforms have modified the functions of the national conventions. These functions include the nominating of the candidates and the drafting of the platforms.

I also compare the policy positions of the presidential candidates from the eleven elections held between 1952 to 1992 to the positions contained in the party platforms. I divide the comparisons into the two different party eras represented in the eleven elections. The elections of 1952 to 1968 are from the period some have labeled the brokered convention era. The elections from 1972 to the present represent the system of popular appeal because of various reforms that have increased the participation of the public. I have analyzed the two eras separately because they differ in their levels of public participation, the rules that govern the national conventions and delegate selection processes, and the role played by the media. The hypothesis tested in chapter 2 is that, as the party system shifts from one type to the next, the relations between the presidential candidates and their coalitions should also change.

Chapter 3 addresses issue types and their relevance to campaigns and governance over the last forty years. I examine the types of issues stressed over time and argue that the policy types are not neutral in their effect on a candidate's appeal to voters or in their relationship to a candidate's ability to govern. Theories of issue types predict that presidents have more influence in some issue arenas than in others simply because different issues give rise to different politics. For example, presidents normally do not have as much influence in distributive arenas as they do in redistributive. I look at the proportion of issue types stressed over time to see whether presidents rely more on distributive issues to assemble nominating and electoral coalitions, even though chances for success in these arenas diminish once the president begins the task of governing. The existence of more distributive issues would be an indicator of how the new requirements for winning office handicap a president when attempting to govern.

In chapter 4 I examine the role of party leaders in Congress and their rates of agreement with the issue positions of the presidential candidates. I compare the public positions of the congressional leaders to the stances of the presidential candidates to ascertain the possibilities for creating governing coalitions after the electoral season and to determine the extent to which these possibilities may have diminished over time.

The final chapter examines the concept of governability and the various theories of democracy attached to it. I also examine whether the American party system is well served by the recent reforms of the political parties. I probe the recommendations made by those who argue for specific reforms to rejuvenate the political parties and examine whether these reforms are compatible with certain theories of governability.

Political Parties and the Maintenance of Liberal Democracy

1

Party Performance and the Decline-of-Party Thesis

Rancorous partisan disputes and seemingly intractable social problems have cast serious doubt on American democracy's ability to meet the challenges of governing in a modern global economy. The general argument is that the decline of political parties is responsible for the tumultuous political times, and each segment of the party—electorate, organization, and government—shoulders some responsibility.[1]

Following this reasoning, the decline of political parties is connected to the general problem of governability. Little scholarly work in the field of political parties, interest groups, the media, and American institutions is comprehensive enough to make inferences about the extensive connections between these significant components of American democracy and whether the way in which they relate to one another has come to be a detriment of American democracy. The framework for linking the failure of the three forms of the political party (electorate, organization, and government) to the failure of democratic governance is a theory of coalition formation and linkage.[2]

Modern Political Parties and the Record of Disappointment

Political parties have borne much of the criticism for the shoddy performance of the American political system. Indeed some have laid the blame for poor performance squarely at the feet of the political parties. However, the recent spate of criticism is simply the continuation of a well-honed American tradition. Throughout the last two hundred years political parties have never enjoyed a particularly favored status. At one point political parties were regarded as dangerous factions that threatened the republican form of democracy created by the Constitution. Some analysts even maintain that the founders of the Republic actually established a constitution that would prevent the development of political parties.[3]

Today political scientists seem to be the only friends that political parties have. And most of them would truly like to see parties fare much better. Even though political scientists have long argued that political parties play a vital role in democratic politics by aggregating the interests of voters, providing citizens with access to modes of political participation, and furnishing participants with cues that help to simplify and structure their political world, most citizens and elites look at the parties with suspicion, if not contempt.[4]

But even political scientists cannot resist the temptation to criticize, mostly because the parties' performance in government is viewed as so inadequate. According to a popular argument, political parties are supposed to bring a measure of cohesiveness to an otherwise fragmented system of policy making by generating policy programs and forming the majorities that ensure passage of legislative programs.[5] The political scientists deem this function to be the most crucial that American parties can perform, given the dispersion of power among the three national branches of government. Many political scientists regard the integration and coordination of policy making as so important that they openly wonder whether American democracy can survive without effective and disciplined parties. For this reason many observers lament the perceptible weaknesses of political parties and clamor for a modification of the electoral system. The intent of these changes is to restore parties to their former position of power and prestige, if ever they had one, by allowing them to perform the interest-aggregating function in government more efficiently.[6]

But on almost any measure you can select, someone has evaluated the political parties since the early 1980s and found them wanting. Such exercises have produced a number of books and articles devoted to each facet of the failure. Usually the decline of political parties is described in the following manner:

> There is remarkable agreement among the political science profession on the proposition that the strength of American political parties has declined significantly over the past several decades. Regardless of how one measures partisanship—by personal party identification within the electorate, by party discipline in Congress, or by the vitality of party machinery—there is massive evidence attesting to the weakened condition of the parties in the United States.[7]

Many observers accepted the description uncritically during the 1970s and early 1980s. Even more important, acceptance of this thesis has emboldened some to make connections between the wretched state of political parties and the future of democracy in the United States. Given the generally negative evaluations of party performance, their predictions about the future of American democracy could hardly be optimistic. Looking at this literature is critical because its conclusions strongly shape the characterizations and predictions about the current state of American democracy.

In the United States political parties assume a variety of shapes and forms. Probably the most frequently discussed or studied form is the "party in the electorate." A majority of voters identify with either the Republican or Democratic party, and candidates for office compete in primary elections for the right to run under the banner of the party. In the absence of a major party's label, attempts for public office—the case of Ross Perot notwithstanding—are largely futile because the structure of the electoral system discourages multiple parties by rewarding only one party. The multiplicity of elective offices and the lack of a highly informed electorate in the United States exacerbate the need for a major party's label. Voters use party labels in order to make choices with a minimum of effort.[8] In the absence of knowledge about candidates and issues a voter's party identification serves as a conspicuous standard that ultimately helps the voter to judge the candidates. Therefore the candidate who seeks office under the banner of a major party has an advantage.

Lately, however, as table 1.1 shows, an increasing number of voters have identified themselves as "independents" rather than as members of a major party.[9] Martin Wattenberg argues that this decline in parti-

TABLE 1.1 *Voters' Decline in Party Identification, 1952–1992*

	1952	'54	'56	'58	'60	'62	'64	'66
Democrat	47%	47%	44%	49%	45%	46%	52%	46%
Independent	23	22	23	19	23	21	23	28
Republican	28	27	29	28	30	28	25	25
	1968	'70	'72	'74	'76	'78	'80	'82
Democrat	45%	44%	41%	38%	40%	39%	41%	44%
Independent	30	31	34	37	37	38	34	30
Republican	25	24	23	22	23	21	23	24
	1984	'86	'88	'90	'92			
Democrat	37%	40%	35%	39%	35%			
Independent	34	33	36	35	39			
Republican	27	25	28	25	26			

SOURCES: Reprinted by permission of the publisher from Harold W. Stanley and Richard G. Niemi, *Vital Statistics on American Politics*, 4th ed. (Washington, D.C.: Congressional Quarterly Press, 1994), 158.

sanship is not the result of an increase in negative attitudes toward the parties but more from an increase in the number of individuals who view political parties as less relevant to the realm of politics. The increase in the number of independents simply reflects the growing number of people who are neutral in their attitudes toward the parties.[10]

This trend is said to have serious consequences for the effective operation of the party system in the United States. If fewer and fewer individuals strongly identify with one party, voters must base their decisions on other criteria. Some of these criteria are characteristic of an age dominated by television and radio. A candidate's appearance, a slick advertising campaign, a catchy slogan, or even simple name recognition are all potential substitutes for the party label.

Some argue that the decline in partisanship ultimately affects the way in which the party performs in government because winning candidates tend to enter Congress and the presidency with weak commitments to their political parties.[11] Similarly Wattenberg theorizes that "if members of the electorate cast their ballots on the basis of factors other than partisanship, then those public officials who are elected can be expected to act more as individuals and less as members of a collective body committed to common goals."[12]

Today's individualistic predilections of House members are enshrined in the Preamble to the *Preamble and Rules of the Democratic*

Caucus. The Preamble states that "the following cardinal principles should control Democratic Action: a. In essentials of Democratic principles and doctrine, unity. b. In nonessentials, and in all things not involving fidelity to party principles, entire individual independence."[13] The tension between the "cardinal principles" of "unity" and "entire individual independence" is usually resolved in favor of individual independence, simply because individual independence allows the members to pursue their careers free of excessive institutional interference.[14] Indeed a person can be expelled from the Democratic Caucus only by a two-thirds vote, a high threshold for a body designed to control "Democratic action."[15]

The roots of the disarray among party officials and the weak commitment of voters are in the reforms undertaken during the Progressive era by those who sought to remake the party system in the image of a more participatory form of democracy.[16] Distinct party eras arise from the clash of values emphasized by participants as well as reformers. In this case values prevalent during the age of party machines receded as the reforms of Progressives gained widespread adoption. Consequently a new political era, complete with new participants and forms of participation, emerged. Indeed the values and participants can be so unconventional that they give rise to clear distinctions between the beginnings and ends of the assorted party systems.

For example, party systems are continuously divided into different periods according to the methods used to select presidential nominees. According to these analyses, the disparities in the methods used for nomination in the different eras can have widely varying results. Because of the many differences in each era the role played by rank-and-file members, party leaders, the media, and even the type of candidate that will benefit will vary from period to period.[17] Furthermore the type of policy-making system should also vary by party era because the different rules shape and inform the activities of the political actors.

The period from 1832 to 1968, the brokered convention system, was characterized by nominations that revolved around the national conventions of the political parties. Presidential primaries were used sparingly—and even then their chief function was to illustrate to party leaders and other national convention delegates that the candidate was capable of gaining broad support in the electorate.[18] For example, in 1952 General Dwight D. Eisenhower selectively entered primaries to demonstrate his popular appeal, a move that helped him to deprive Ohio's senator Robert Taft of the nomination. On the Democratic side, however, Senator Estes Kefauver of Tennessee entered several primaries and fared extremely well in all; yet even this demonstration of popular support was not enough to give him the nomination. Eventually the Democrats selected Governor Adlai Stevenson of Illinois, who had stated on numerous occasions that he did not even want the nomination, a scenario hard to imagine in today's primary-dependent environment.

In 1960 Senator John F. Kennedy of Massachusetts relied on primaries to show that his religion would not be a major stumbling block in the general election. And, finally, in 1968 Senator Eugene McCarthy of Minnesota and others altered the character of the general election by using presidential primaries to end-run the party leaders who already had made commitments to President Lyndon Johnson.

With presidential primaries of limited effectiveness for securing the presidential nomination, the important decisions about candidates were largely made at the national party conventions during this period. Here state and national party leaders evaluated candidates and selected the person they believed would have the best chance of uniting the party and leading it to victory in the general election. Because of the "closed" nature of national conventions during the age of limited primaries, the party platforms and the policy positions announced by the presidential candidates were in substantial agreement. Party leaders were routinely involved in both drafting the platform and selecting the nominee.

Given that party leaders were extremely interested in the performance of the party and its platform, they were unlikely to select a nominee who offered policy programs that differed dramatically from the established party program. To capture the nomination a candidates had to demonstrate to party leaders that their agenda conformed to the ideals and preferences of the dominant wing of the party. The need to conform to the party's traditional positions in order to capture the presidential nomination would seem to ensure considerable agreement between the platform and the candidate during the era of the brokered conventions.[19]

Dissatisfaction with the lack of rank-and-file participation in convention activities provided the impetus to reform important segments of the American party system. The most obvious manifestations of this dissatisfaction were the turmoil and bitterness that surrounded the Democratic convention of 1968 and the resulting clamor for reform of the presidential nominating system, which was heeded by the political parties, particularly the Democratic Party. In the wake of the 1968 debacle the Democrats formed the Commission on Party Structure and Delegate Selection, which later became known as the McGovern-Fraser Commission after its two vice chairmen.

One of the many subjects of the McGovern-Fraser Commission's report concerned the guidelines with which the state party organizations would have to comply before the 1972 convention. The most widely publicized feature of these reforms involved the banning of two customs for selecting delegates to the national convention: the party caucus and the delegate primary.[20]

The party caucus usually consisted of precinct-level meetings of party officers and members to elect delegates to a county or state convention. Eventually the highest level of this process selected the delegates to the national convention. Each state that used this method had a unique system. For example, states varied in the number of stages between the local and state levels. As the oldest system for choosing delegates to the national conventions, the party caucus enjoyed wide use.[21]

The other method prohibited by the McGovern-Fraser Commission was the delegate primary. In the delegate primary individuals campaigned for the position of delegate. The names of the individuals campaigning for the position were the only names to appear on the ballot. Furthermore those individuals seeking to become a delegate were not compelled to declare their candidate preferences.[22] This method favored prominent local politicians or other well-known persons who possessed enough appeal and name recognition to win the primary election.

Instead of these two methods the commission mandated that the state party organizations use either the "participatory convention" or the "candidate primary" to select delegates for the 1972 convention. The participatory convention was analogous to the party caucus, with the exception that the convention had to be accessible to any party member.[23] The commission issued directives that included the provision for adequate public notice "of the time, places and rules for the conduct of all public meetings" and for furnishing "information on the ballot as to the presidential preferences of (1) candidates or slates for delegate or (2) in the States which select or nominate a portion of the delegates by committees, candidates or slates for such committees."[24] These directives were meant to correct abuses of the system that were all too frequent. Kenneth Bode and Carol Casey provide a particularly flagrant example:

> In Virginia, . . . mass meetings—the equivalent of precinct caucuses—constituted the first step of the process, and the only step generally open to rank-and-file Democratic participation. In 1968, the rules said that these were to be held sometime in April at a time and place determined by city and county committees and that notice was to be given in local newspapers. Seeking to turn out their supporters to these meetings, McCarthy organizers found that the typical notice was a small announcement in the legal section of the newspapers. Not infrequently, the mass meetings were convened on party-sponsored buses on the way to the state convention.[25]

The directives issued by the McGovern-Fraser Commission were intended to eliminate such conspicuous abuses.

The second acceptable method of selecting delegates for the convention was the candidate primary. In this method usually only the name of the candidate was featured on the ballot, but in some instances the name of the delegate appeared alongside the candidate's.[26] The candidate primary was intended to increase the participation of rank-and-file Democrats and provide a more efficient means of expressing their preferences. In any event the guideline guaranteed the division of "delegate votes among presidential candidates in proportion to their demonstrated strength."[27]

Another important guideline issued by the commission concerned the adequate representation of minorities. The commission declared that the state parties must "add the six basic elements of the Special Equal Rights Committee" to the party rules and begin procedures to achieve them. The six elements consisted of statements forbidding discrimination on the basis of race, color, creed, or national origin, requiring publication of times and places of meetings, and expressing support for the fullest and widest participation of all people in the Democratic Party. Furthermore the guidelines mandated that state parties, in order to correct past discrimination, should "encourage minority group participation, including representation of minority groups on the national convention delegation in reasonable relationship to the group's presence in the population of the State."[28] The

TABLE 1.2 *Composition of Delegates to the National Conventions, 1968–1984*

	1968		1972		1976		1980		1984	
	D	R	D	R	D	R	D	R	D	R
Female	13%	16%	40%	29%	33%	31%	49%	29%	50%	44%
Black	5	2	15	4	11	3	15	3	18	3
Under 30	3	4	22	8	15	7	11	5	8	*
Median age (in years)	(49)	(49)	(42)	*	(43)	(48)	(44)	(49)	*	*

*Data not available

SOURCE: Reprinted by permission of the copyright holder from William Crotty and John S. Jackson III, *Presidential Primaries and Nominations* (Washington, D.C.: Congressional Quarterly Press, 1985), 108.

immediate result was greater participation by youth, women, and minorities at the 1972 Democratic convention (see table 1.2).

Other important guidelines issued by the commission were intended to prohibit certain practices once used to dilute the influence of certain groups or candidates within the party. State party bosses could use these practices, such as proxy voting and the unit rule, in highly selective ways to determine the outcome of primary contests. Another example cited by Bode and Casey describes a caucus meeting in Missouri at which "McCarthy supporters found themselves in a majority at the meeting, on the verge of electing some delegates. Suddenly, the party official chairing the caucus unpocketed 492 proxy votes—three times the total number of people in attendance—and cast them as a unit for his own slate."[29]

In order to comply with these guidelines by the Call for the 1972 Convention, state party organizations sought an uncomplicated method of legitimizing their delegations. The need to comply forced more states to adopt presidential primaries between 1968 and 1972 (see table 1.3). The number of primaries increased again between 1972 and 1976. The immediate result of these changes was a rather significant increase in the number of delegates who were selected through the presidential primaries.

In the wake of these reforms the political parties could do little to slow the disintegration of bonds linking the congressional candidates, the presidential candidates, and the parties. The expansion of the primary system to most states made it not only possible but likely that a presidential candidate would capture the delegates necessary for nom-

TABLE 1.3 *Number of Presidential Primaries, 1964–1976*

Year	Number of States with Primaries	Percentage of Delegates Selected in Primaries	
		Democrats	Republicans
1964	17	50.8	49.9
1968	17	48.7	47.0
1972	23	66.5	58.8
1976	30	75.8	70.2

SOURCE: Reprinted by permission of the publisher from John H. Aldrich, *Before the Convention: Strategies and Choices in Presidential Nomination Campaigns* (Chicago: University of Chicago Press, 1980), 57.

ination before the convention even convened. And primaries have become the dominant means for candidates to capture the nomination. Consequently the candidate and the managers of the personal campaign organization have replaced the party organization and its leaders. In 1960 only sixteen states held presidential primaries. By 1980 presidential primaries had spread to thirty-six states, and the presidential choices of approximately 75% of the Republican and Democratic convention delegates were determined in presidential primaries.[30] For this reason the chance of ever returning to a system of brokered conventions—in which party leaders and their state organizations exclusively determine the outcome—seems small.

The Republican Party also initiated reforms, although it did not experience the same pressures that the Democratic Party felt. The Republicans created two commissions to deal with reform: the Delegates and Organization Commission (1969–1972), and the Rule 29 Commission (1972–1974).[31] Both commissions made recommendations that were similar to those made by the McGovern-Fraser Commission. But the Republican Party did not impose these recommendations on the states.[32] Consequently the Republican Party was not forced to make a hasty transition from a closed to a more participatory system, although it eventually did so because some states with Democratic-controlled legislatures tried to change the state election laws to require greater participation. Eventually the Republican Party adopted many of these reforms in an effort to conform with the more participatory mood of the nation. But the national Republican Party granted and continues to allow a great deal of latitude to the state party organizations.[33]

Clearly the intent of the guidelines from the McGovern-Fraser Commission and the Republican commissions was to make the nominating system conform to the standards of a participatory democracy, where unnecessary barriers between voters and government are removed.[34] All indicators suggest that the reformers succeeded.

The presidential candidates now press their campaign directly to the people through television and other forms of the mass media without the mediation of party bosses. The reforms, particularly the institutionalization of the presidential primary, have redistributed the political resources from state party leaders, placing them squarely in the hands of the candidates and their personal organizations. State party leaders no longer wield exclusive control over their state delegations. Nor is the aid to campaigns once provided by big-state governors and big-city mayors so crucial.[35] Candidates now file and exercise strict control over their delegate slates. Long gone are the days when a party boss like James Michael Curley, former mayor of Boston and governor of Massachusetts, could have his delegate slate thoroughly defeated in a primary and still appear at the convention as "Alcalde Jaime Miguel Curleo, a FDR delegate from Puerto Rico."[36]

The reforms have had a dramatic effect on every facet of the presidential nominating system. One particularly notable change has occurred in the type of candidates seeking the nomination. Indeed the term *availability* in today's system bears little resemblance to its meaning under the old nomination system. Traditionally it suggested the support of party leaders and delegates who believed that the candidate possessed all the characteristics to lead the party to victory in the general election. Implicit in this concept were a number of factors that made a politician an attractive candidate for the nomination.[37]

Recently, however, candidates have been able to pursue the nomination with little regard for the attitudes of party leaders and no particular need to conform to the old standards of availability. Availability now simply means having the desire, time, and money to pursue the nomination through an increasingly protracted campaign season. In 1992 Bill Clinton was a long shot at best when he began his bid for the nomination. He survived a grueling primary schedule and a number of serious scandals. Party leaders probably would have pulled the plug on the bid long before the convention, but the candidate's perseverance is all that matters now—a point that has been underscored in the last two presidential contests: Bill Clinton in 1992 and Gary Hart in

1988. Hart, who had earlier dropped out of the presidential primary amid reports of an illicit affair with a model, reentered the race for the Democratic nomination. Richard Lamm, former governor of Colorado, described Hart's reentry as "the ultimate nightmare for any political party."[38] *Newsweek* went on to report that "the problem for Lamm and others is that it doesn't really matter what *party leaders* think about Hart; there *are no* real Democratic Party leaders, and there haven't been for years. Governors, senators, mayors and other officials wield little clout in presidential contests" [emphasis added].[39] Therefore political parties find it nearly impossible to perform any kind of quality control.

All this means that candidates in today's system bear little resemblance to the candidates of yesteryear. Today's would-be presidential nominees come from the electorally diminutive states of Arkansas, South Dakota, and Idaho; indeed candidates who seek and win the nomination may represent only a faction of the broader party coalition. In the words of Stephen Wayne, the reforms "have enlarged the selection zone of potential nominees."[40]

Moreover the campaigns that presidential candidates conduct can be successful without the influence of party leaders in key states. Candidates staff and manage their own campaign organizations in each state, and the inclusion of party leaders is left to the discretion of the candidate. The candidates' autonomy from party leaders is enhanced by their ability to appeal directly to the voters through television and other forms of the mass media.

Public financing of presidential campaigns has accelerated the extensive disintegration of bonds between parties and candidates. Public financing has made presidential candidates much less dependent on the financial backing of political parties. A presidential aspirant raises money, is responsible for spending that money, and assembles a campaign organization with that money. Of course political parties receive a special status because they are allowed to spend money in concert with presidential candidates. But this amount is a small percentage of what the candidates spend,[41] and it is not clear that even the large sums of "soft money" that political parties pump into campaigns provide them with the means to control candidates.

Finally, new campaign technologies—the use of mass media, direct mail, polling techniques, and accounting devices—allow candidates to campaign with little need for the traditional forms of organization provided by political parties. According to Frank Sorauf, "Political parties have historically dealt largely in nonfinancial resources and have never successfully made the transition to the cash economy of the new campaign politics."[42] The labor-intensive forms of campaigning that parties performed so well in times past have been eschewed by candidates in favor of techniques that rely on the technology of the modern media. The national parties are trying to catch up, but their efforts have not made candidates more dependent on them.[43]

Campaign finance laws also encourage candidates for Congress to raise their own money, generally independent of any help from a formal party organization. National party organizations can play a significant role, even though the amount of money that they are able to contribute is a small percentage of the overall amount raised by congressional candidates.[44] But with the proliferation of political action committees (PACs) many sources are available to raise the large amounts of money necessary to finance congressional campaigns in the United States. The cost of running for office is astronomical. In the congressional elections of 1992 the average House incumbent spent nearly $595,000, an increase of 41% over 1990's average.[45] In the same election the average challenger raised about $269,000, not nearly enough to test the well-funded incumbents.[46]

Today all congressional candidates must raise a substantial amount to finance the expensive technologies needed to win in the era of open politics. Television and radio ads are extremely expensive, as is polling, but the cost does not seem to deter the candidates. Although the effectiveness and ethics of these new modes of campaigning are still being debated, try convincing a politician seeking reelection that these technologies are not necessary. Because most campaign money is raised and spent independently of the political parties and because the electorate's party identification has declined, congressional campaigns tend to emphasize the candidate's characteristics more than the candidate's party affiliation.[47] Thus the new style of campaigning for office weakens bonds between a party and candidate.[48]

Similarly it is the candidates for Congress, as well as the candidates for state and local offices—not the political parties—who decide who will stand for office. Because of the wide acceptance of the direct primary, recruiting candidates to run for office has become chiefly a process of self-selection. The formal party organizations have little influence over who seeks to contest for an office under their political banner.[49] When the candidates are largely elected on their own efforts and independent of the party organization, they owe little, if anything, to the party when they arrive in office.

This independence is thought to be largely responsible for preventing the political parties from becoming the institutional means for creating stable majorities. According to William Crotty, "Any change that alters the effectiveness of the parties carries important institutional implications, for it is largely through the parties that Congress generates whatever *coherent* policy making it can muster."[50] Thus political parties do continue to have a substantial effect on policy making in the U.S. Congress; although the recent changes may have muted their overall effect, many hold out hope that parties can be revitalized to the point where they largely shape relations between the White House and Congress.

Despite the parties' apparent decline in other spheres, their presence in Congress is pervasive. Briefly stated, political parties "determine who runs Congress and how."[51] An overwhelming majority of the members of Congress belong to a major party, and both the House and the Senate are organized along party lines. The party that holds the majority in the chamber determines who that chamber's leaders will be, who the committee and subcommittee chairs will be, and which party will have the majority on all these committees and subcommittees. The task of the political parties, particularly the majority party, is to organize and control the business of Congress. In the House of Representatives the majority party is responsible for selecting the Speaker of the House, the majority leader, and the majority whip. Although the Speaker is elected by a vote of the entire House, the vote is always strictly along party lines.

Political parties also determine the leadership in the Senate, although the Constitution mandates that the vice president is the president of the chamber. The Constitution also states that the president pro tempore presides in the absence of the vice president. But the real leader in the Senate is the majority leader. Selected by the party that maintains a majority in the Senate, the majority leader schedules legislation and chairs important party committees. Like the Speaker of the House, the majority leader in the Senate wields tremendous influence.

Despite the resources available to these several party leaders and the pervasiveness of party organizations in Congress, strict party government remains beyond the grasp of the U.S. system. To be sure, party leadership can be, and is sometimes, quite effective.[52] But from the standpoint of responsible party advocates, the overall cohesiveness of parties leaves much to be desired.[53]

The first reason for this lack of party government concerns the potency of the resources at the disposal of party leaders. Today's Congress has no sure-fire methods for disciplining recalcitrant members of the party. Party leaders once could have withheld committee assignments or support for a piece of legislation in order to discipline a maverick member.[54] But changes in Congress since 1970 have made managing Congress much more difficult. On the heels of the Watergate scandal and the resignation of President Nixon voters sent 118 new Democrats to the House in 1974 and 1976. In the words of Tip O'Neill these elections "brought in a whole new breed of legislators."[55] According to the former Speaker, these individuals "were a highly sophisticated and talented group," but "they were also independent, and they didn't hesitate to remind you that they were elected on their own" (p. 283).

The effects of this influx of independent and talented new members were realized immediately. According to O'Neill, "With such a large group of outspoken new members, Congress became more difficult to control than ever before. Party discipline went out the window" (p. 283). These first-term members used their large numbers to speed up the reorganization of the House by creating committees and subcommittees that would allow them to have an immediate effect on legislation and that would strengthen Congress relative to the executive office.[56] These members of Congress further used their influence to oust three senior members from the chairs of their respective committees.[57]

The rise of individualism in Congress coincided with the decline of political parties in other areas, leading some to believe that the two were linked. The conventional wisdom generally accepts as gospel that all these elements taken together—the changes in electoral procedures, differing presidential and congressional coalitions, and the complex structure of Congress—hopelessly complicate the formation of responsible and constructive party government. Those who ascribe to this theory cite the quality and effectiveness of the legislative process as evidence of ungovernability.

For example, in the modern Congress proposals are more likely to be so amended and diluted that the original intent of the legislation is lost.

To enact legislation with far-reaching consequences "the House leadership [is] forced to incorporate many . . . demands, the ultimate outcome being a weakened, patchwork version."[58] Moreover policy formulated in a fragmented legislature inevitably produces contradictions because coordinating all the committees and subcommittees in the many policy areas is so difficult.[59] The support of Congress for the National Institutes of Health and the subsidizing of the tobacco industry is an example of the results produced by the many cross-pressures.[60]

But the argument that the American party system is in a decrepit state, and that this wretched condition is responsible for the problems of governance, is challenged by a growing body of literature that casts some doubt on the occurrence of party decay.[61] A number of articles now attest to the continuing strength and vitality of local, state, and national political parties.[62]

Moreover counterreformers, reacting to the trends encouraged by the changes to the parties and Congress in the early 1970s, have sought to reverse the decline by providing political parties with an opportunity to form coalitions that are ideologically cohesive and institutionally powerful.[63] Since 1985, for example, the Republican and Democratic parties have tried to centralize their resources and use them more efficiently to achieve collective goals in congressional campaigns. The wings of the national parties (the Republican National Committee, National Republican Congressional Committee, Republican Senatorial Committee, Democratic National Committee, Democratic Congressional Campaign Committee, and Democratic Senatorial Campaign Committee) amass millions of dollars to contribute to their candidates.[64] In the 1992 congressional elections the Republican and Democratic parties spent $43 million on House and Senate races.[65]

What is significant about such spending is that it represents an attempt by the party organizations to maximize party interests (a larger number of seats in Congress). By efficiently distributing resources so that money is spent on the campaigns that need it most, the parties seek to maximize their collective interests at the expense of individual candidates whose main interest is simply reelection at any cost. Furthermore the two parties have been recruiting candidates and providing them with the training and professional services necessary to conduct a modern campaign.[66] The political parties hope to recruit, develop, and elect candidates who are more dependent on the political party than the incumbent members of Congress.

Such efforts are not always rewarded because party control is still difficult to exert once the individual candidate arrives on Capitol Hill to assume congressional duties. With all the perquisites available to members of Congress, most can quickly moderate excessive dependence on the party organization without suffering electoral repercussions. Thus attempts to form links between the formal party organization and the party in government may be too weak to result in effective party government.

The debate over the effectiveness of parties in the policy-making process certainly extends beyond the confines of the congressional party system and includes the kinds of efforts made by the president to generate and enact policies. Without question, the presidency is unique in the American constitutional order because of the amount of power concentrated in the office; consequently presidential leadership in governing is seen as paramount. Many observers believe that with strong leadership from the president the U.S. government would fare better; thus they advocate reforms designed to enhance presidential performance, most of which involve concentrating even more power in the office. If such power is used wisely, the argument goes, the deadlock that has increasingly characterized American government can be averted.[67]

However, others assert that, because of the increasing factionalization of the political system and the inability of the political parties to form binding and enduring coalitions of the electoral and governing arenas of the American political system, the president becomes entangled in a web of diffused power that permits effective leadership to occur only rarely.[68] A decline in the power of political parties ultimately means that the president has one less resource available for enacting items on a legislative agenda. Furthermore, if the candidates selected by the campaign process have significantly different opinions on issues and even stress issues different from those stressed by people responsible for enacting the president's programs, the policy gridlock predicted by those who lament the transformation of political parties may actually occur.

What is not yet obvious in the debate over the decay or revitalization of political parties is the specific effect that continuing changes in the party system have on the possibilities for effective governance in the short run and the maintenance of liberal democracy in the long run.

Parties and Governance American Style

The argument that ties the condition and the performance of the party system to the question of democratic governance implicitly accepts a theoretical framework that stresses the importance of coalitions. The resources necessary to govern in a system of diffused power are marshalled through the creation and maintenance of coalitions. When coalitions between various political arenas cannot form and abide, the conditions for democratic governance are fleeting at best. Indeed the theory of democracy described in the Introduction also accepts, if even indirectly, the tremendous importance of coalitions for democratic governance. Without elections *and* the means for converting the results of those elections into public policy, how can a system retain its democratic character?

A discussion of the connection between political parties and governing begins with mobilizing groups and interests in the electoral environment (nominating and general campaigns) and ends by including those interests in governing activities. The empirical component of this discussion demands the identification of those who have influence in both campaigns and public policy and the means by which they exert this influence. This endeavor involves more than tracing the money trail in campaigns and the lobbying that takes place after—two activities that coincidentally are the focus of a number of studies that conclude that democracy in America is on its final leg.[69] Coalition theory approaches the problem by underscoring the necessity of assembling various interests to win the party nomination and ultimately the presidency. Significantly coalition theory contends that the origins of successful democratic governance lie in the electoral arena, which shoulders much of the burden for maintaining democratic regimes in democratic theory.

For several reasons the types and intensity of the interests that form nominating and electoral coalitions have a significant effect on the ability of the president to govern successfully.[70] First, the individuals and groups involved in the campaign usually assume important posts in the policy-making organizations of the executive branch. At the very least these groups and individuals become involved in campaigns to advance or oppose particular policy positions—to which the candidate often gives heed in exchange for continued support.

The electoral success of the president and the backing he receives from Congress are not unrelated. If a president runs well in a particular congressional district, the representative from that district will be more disposed to help the president.

The electoral and governing coalitions have other links as well. The issue agenda the candidate assembles and features during the campaign is a critical component of the agenda the president pursues upon entering office. Campaigns provide other sources of ideas for the issue agenda, including party platforms and public opinion.[71] Issues stressed during the electoral season are not the sole sources of ideas for the president's agenda, but they are crucial.

Finally, the president must constantly maintain the coalitions that put him in office. Reelection incentives often compel presidents during the governing stage to make decisions that preserve and even strengthen the coalitions that served them during the nomination and electoral stages of the campaign.[72]

Coalition theory specifies that a candidate must complete two tasks before the governing process can begin in earnest, and the recent decline in the strength of political parties described earlier jeopardizes the adequate completion of both tasks. The first task is to develop a nominating coalition to secure the party's label. This activity normally includes gathering both elite and popular support. Before the reform of the political parties this activity usually focused more on political elites and the delegations they controlled and relied much less on attracting popular support.

Today candidates spend more effort to capture delegates through popular primaries than to sway the opinions of political elites, although the task of manufacturing a nominating coalition still involves to some extent the solicitation of both elite and popular support. Candidates nowadays can convert into presidential primary votes the resources that elites provide, but the elites no longer control the actual delegates as they did in earlier eras.[73] Moreover nominating coalitions secured in this fashion are not as reliable and stable. Voters can forsake candidates much more easily than political elites ever could. Despite these difficulties, a candidate still must assemble a winning nominating coalition, no matter how precarious the task.

The second task consists of fashioning an electoral coalition. A successful electoral coalition is significantly broader than the nominating coalition in order to secure the electoral votes needed to win the presidency. At this stage the candidate plots and implements a strategy to attract certain groups, states, or regions to create an electoral coalition that wins a majority of the electoral votes. The decline of the political parties also has complicated this chore. Candidates must solicit votes from nearly every state because political parties are not a reliable means for delivering the votes. Candidates who made unpopular promises while courting groups during the nominating stage must now try to explain them to a much wider, and often less receptive, audience.

Successfully assembling the nominating and electoral coalitions is simply preparatory to the much more formidable task of assembling the final coalition: the governing coalition. The governing coalition must be formed from a number of diverse political arenas: congressional leaders, rank-and-file members of Congress, the bureaucracy, foreign governments, the political party, and other interested observers, including regular citizens.[74] Furthermore the dramatic changes in American politics have expanded the number of arenas a president must seek to influence. These new arenas include "the media, political interest groups, . . . [and] the institutional presidency."[75]

The translation of nominating and electoral coalitions into support for governing is "the key requirement for presidential success. . . . Translation occurs when the actions involved in electing a president also put into position people needed by the president to govern."[76] Lester G. Seligman notes that "a president's influence depends on the stability and breadth of support his governing coalition provides."[77] The source of the influence of the governing coalition is "the breadth and stability of the presidential candidate's core of support, crystallized in the coalitions that nominated and elected him" (see figure 1.1).[78]

Coalition theory is relevant to the discussion of the role of political parties in democratic governance for several reasons. First, it emphasizes what happens in the electoral arena. Elections imply a degree of popular control and are largely viewed as the primary means for conveying the general will of the people to the government.

Second, coalition theory takes elections seriously as a point of departure for evaluating governability. It recognizes that rules and

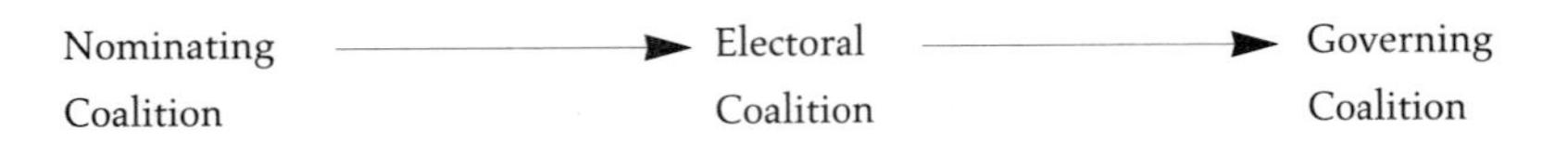

FIGURE 1.1 Three Phases of Coalition Building

procedures for assembling coalitions can have long-term consequences for the performance of government institutions that are dependent on elections. Evaluation of governability requires properly placing it in the context of democratic elections and the many constraints that these elections impose on governability. Elections significantly constrain what can be done in the governmental sphere. During elections candidates make promises, coalitions form around those promises, and the promises recruit individuals to the campaign. All these features are necessary for winning office, and they dramatically shape how the candidate will ultimately govern. So long as elections remain the means by which power is secured, candidates cannot ignore or turn their backs on promises, coalitions, or individuals. To do so would cripple the governing effort because presidents are held accountable for promises, if not by voters, then by the groups courted by these promises or by the press. Furthermore those who govern need the support of coalition members to persuade representatives and senators of the importance of backing certain promises.

Finally, individuals recruited during the campaign are a handy source of reliable and loyal aides. For the most part they can be counted on to devotedly pursue the candidate's interests and agenda once in office.

These coalitions, and therefore presidential success, are not created in a vacuum. Rules, both formal and informal, govern the party system. The party system that fosters the creation of these coalitions has a substantial effect on the performance of the president and, by extension, democracy, even though that connection is difficult to ascertain and is often forgotten, especially by political pundits. In analyzing presidential performance these connections seem distant and removed from the daily task of governing. A president is usually allowed to stand and fall on his own, regardless of the strength of the coalitions the president brings to the White House.

The obvious point to be made here is that to the extent that the party system and the way a president acts are connected, party politics and the performance of the democratic regime are connected. Performance in office can be measured in terms of policy performance or a more esoteric measure such as the creation of legitimacy and stability. But political analysts too often make a connection between the party system and presidential performance, or other less visible measures, without grounding the discussion in democratic theory. Indeed the criticism of the current performance of the American political and policy-making system misses a significant step in logic. Democracy must be clearly defined; only then can standards for evaluating the parties be properly constructed. Suitable answers to the questions of whether the parties are properly performing their tasks and whether changes in the constitutional order are necessary to improve their performance can be obtained only by taking the question of democracy seriously. Most analysts work backward; they see the dissatisfaction with American politics or the complex policy-making process and conclude that the parties must not be doing the job properly, probably because they are weak.

Ample evidence suggests that the decline of political parties may not produce the deleterious effects that some observers have predicted. Studies show that rates of presidential fulfillment of campaign promises have remained virtually the same since 1912. From 1912 to 1948 presidents fulfilled their campaign promises 72.3% of the time. From 1952 to 1976 the rate of fulfillment was 75.1%.[79] This stability in the fulfillment of promises has occurred despite the substantial changes in the party system.

Moreover different methods of measuring rates of fulfillment produce the same result: presidents perform effectively across different party eras. Although Lyndon Johnson was the most successful of modern-day presidents in delivering on his campaign promises, Jimmy Carter and Ronald Reagan do not seem to have suffered terribly because of the decline of the parties. Their fulfillment rates of 56% and 64%, respectively, are comparable to the 61% rate posted by John F. Kennedy and the 70% success rate enjoyed by Johnson but still equal to or greater than the 56% of Richard Nixon.[80]

We can base similar conclusions about governance and the American system on studies of divided government. Divided party control has not affected the ability of American institutions to enact significant laws and conduct vigorous investigations and oversight. Remarkably the ability is constant, not only across divided party eras but also across the decline-in-party era. If the decline of political parties holds significant ramifications for governance, we should have felt them during the long period of divided party control. The conclusion is that "political parties can be powerful instruments, but in the United States they seem to play more of a role as 'policy factions' than as, in the British case, governing instruments."[81] Perhaps as "policy factions" political parties in the governing sphere are indeed impervious to the major shocks experienced by the American party system since the 1950s.

These studies cast serious doubt on the contention that the decline of political parties, in all their forms, inevitably leads to a decline in governability.[82] Those who argue that party decline means a decline in governability have failed to explore the subtle connections between political parties and governance on two levels. First, they must ask normative questions about whether the links that are maintained across party eras are effective and conform to the prevailing attitudes about democracy. Such an exercise should include the reasons that particular standards are used and others are excluded.

Second, they must use the context of these standards to explore the empirical connections thought to exist between different elements of the party and the governing system. The theory of coalitions that links the activities of political parties in the electoral sphere to governance yields a number of testable hypotheses with regard to governance, some of which I have alluded to here. But critics of the American political system too often fail to consider these hypotheses, for reasons discussed in chapter 5, in light of the normative questions about democracy that they raise. Students of political parties must settle on a theory of democracy that permits them to take the links between coalitions seriously. As it stands now, the theory of democracy used by most political scientists still relies heavily on a notion of party government that "plays a role in political science somewhere between a Platonic form and a grail."[83] Rethinking notions of democracy and governance places the current state of political parties in a new light.

2

Presidential Issue Stances and Party Platforms: Party Cohesion or Disintegration?

Party organizations and the partisan orientations of voters still affect elections for lower offices, but the national parties rarely act as intermediaries for the voters and the presidential candidates.[1] Of course political parties have not been entirely replaced, but the media, interest groups, and individual candidates' organizations are now more influential in national campaigns.

The inclusion of these additional players undoubtedly has complicated the task of assembling electoral and governing coalitions from nominating coalitions. But have changes in the system of nominating presidential candidates precluded the formation of overlapping nomination and general election coalitions? Part of the answer to this question can be found by assessing the extent to which the party platforms and the presidential candidates' policy positions agree.

Drafting the Platform in the Pre-Reform Era

In the pre-reform era the drafting of the political platforms followed predictable patterns, recognizing of course that "power relationships within a party in a presidential year may alter the influence of a particular element in the drafting process."[2] In the early stages numerous organized groups appeared before the platform committee to enumerate the goals and issues that they believed should be incorporated. But this procedure did not mean that creating the platform was a completely democratic activity. In actuality a small group of individuals drafted the platform. For the party in power the platform was usually the task of the White House and its staff. For the party out of power platform drafting typically fell to a small staff comprised of delegates from the platform committee and professional staff from the national party committees. The goal of this drafting committee was to assemble a document acceptable to the full platform committee.

Most conflicts occurred at the full committee stage, with the various factions within the party struggling to have their preferences incorporated in the final version of the platform. Yet the committee members also recognized the importance of creating a document that unified the party; consequently they made strenuous efforts to forge compromises that allowed the full committee to give the platform a unanimous recommendation.[3]

With a unanimous recommendation from the platform committee the platform usually was sent to the floor for approval by the full convention. If no one offered platform amendments from the floor of the convention,the convention needed only a single voice vote to approve the platform. Sometimes someone did try to amend the platform. But the usual procedure was for the platform committee to prepare a minority report that was voted upon by the entire convention. Minority reports were not rare in the pre-reform era (see table 2.1).

The 1952 conventions provide typical examples of the procedures used to draft platforms in the pre-reform age. The Republicans, who were out of power, began the process of creating their platform by establishing a subcommittee, selected by the Republican National Committee. The function of this subcommittee would be to gather

TABLE 2.1 *Number of Convention Votes on Minority Reports*

	Democratic		Republican	
Period	Voice	Roll Call	Voice	Roll Call
1864–1892	10	4	6	1
1896–1924	7	7	3	5
1928–1956	14	3	0	2

SOURCE: Reprinted by permission of the publisher from Paul T. David, Ralph M. Goldman, andRichard C. Bain, *The Politics of National Party Conventions* (Washington, D.C.: Brookings Institution, 1960), 408.

drafts and suggestions that would then be turned over to the Resolutions Committee, which would be charged with the actual drafting of the platform. The Resolutions Committee was composed of two members from each state and territory represented at the Republican convention.

The Resolutions Committee convened before the convention began and divided itself into several subcommittees, each with responsibility for a specific policy area. Subcommittees received testimony from individuals and groups concerned with their policy area and, upon completion of the testimony, drafted their planks. They submitted their planks to a small committee that labored under the chairman of the Resolutions Committee, Senator Eugene Millikin of Colorado. This small committee was responsible for blending the many planks into a cohesive whole, editing the work of all the subcommittees, and consulting the candidates about the content of the platform. Once this drafting committee completed its work, it submitted the platform to the full Resolutions Committee, which then accepted it by voice vote.

Problems that arose in the drafting subcommittee were passed on to the full committee. In the case of the 1952 Republican platform the drafting subcommittee could not agree on the civil rights plank. The subcommittee therefore passed minority and majority reports on to the full committee. When the full Resolutions Committee had resolved the problems and completed its debate, it sent the platform to the full convention with a recommendation of approval.

The Democratic Party's procedures were similar. Before the national convention opened, the Executive Committee of the Democratic National Committee selected a subcommittee to receive testimony on the platform. Representative John McCormack of Massachusetts was its chairman. At the end of the public hearings the full subcommittee created a drafting subcommittee of most of the individuals on the first subcommittee.

The drafting subcommittee, also under McCormack's direction, had to consider the positions submitted by President Harry Truman and his White House staff. The drafting subcommittee labored to create a balanced platform that incorporated the various demands of the White House and other interests. The resulting draft was then presented to the full platform committee. The full committee worked through the various planks and voted on all.Then it submitted the platform to the whole convention, which also approved it.

The procedures used by the two parties in the pre-reform era were remarkably similar. They had similar institutions structure the drafting of the platform. However, differences did exist between the two parties because of their differing electoral situation. The party in power normally drafted a platform under the direction of the White House, whereas the party out of power relied on other centers of influence within the party, such as the national chair and other prominent party officials. Furthermore the ideological make-up of the two parties partly determined the procedures emphasized in drafting the platform. The Democrats, with their diverse coalitions, accommodated more interest groups and caucuses than did the Republican Party. According to Martha Weinberg, "Perhaps because of this relative homogeneity, the Republicans have no tradition similar to the Democrats' of using the platform-writing process as an occasion for pork-barrel bargaining over the conflicting demands of diverse groups."[4] Even so, stability and predictability were the noteworthy characteristics of the platform-drafting process in the pre-reform era.

Drafting of the Platform in the Post-Reform Era

The increased role of presidential primaries and caucuses turned the national conventions into a forum for ratifying decisions the primary voters had made during the campaign season. Because the conventions no longer needed to nominate candidates, other functions of the conventions assumed greater prominence, including the drafting of the party platform. In the wake of the reforms the major political parties, which once had stable and established routines for formulating their platforms, faced pressure from political activists and candidates' organizations to restructure the entire process. The reforms have brought two complications.

First, the delegate-selection reforms have attracted people who are increasingly issue oriented and independent of local party leadership.[5] The issue-oriented delegates have taken the place of local and state party officials who, for one reason or another, are unable to gain a delegate slot and are thus excluded in large numbers from post-reform conventions. Unlike the party leaders the "new" delegates are committed to a particular issue, candidate, or caucus. According to Tip O'Neill, these first-time delegates, or "amateurs," "failed to understand that the real purpose of a platform is to express a general philosophy, and to be as inclusive as possible. Instead, they seemed eager to come up with a document that would be taken literally."[6] The result is greater attention to issues and language in the platform, enhancing the possibility of conflict over its content.

Second, the proliferation of caucus groups inside the parties has created additional pressure to include the demands of particular groups in the party platform. The internal caucuses of women, blacks, and Hispanics have generated additional demands on the platforms and pressure to open the process further. These groups have become better organized and more adept at bargaining and have gotten many of their policy objectives incorporated in the platforms.[7]

This evolution is particularly evident in the Democratic Party where "women, blacks, and Hispanic-Americans have all insisted upon a larger voice in platform decision-making."[8] These groups are well organized and highly skilled at having their issues publicized, abilities that their pre-reform counterparts did not necessarily have. Therefore these groups, unlike previous groups, are capable of putting a great deal of pressure on the party to have their objectives inserted into the platform.[9]

Finally, and somewhat paradoxically, delegates to the national conventions are more committed to the candidates. Indeed state electoral laws mandate that delegates be pledged to specific candidates. Furthermore the Democratic Party allows candidates to approve or disapprove of delegates who want to appear on the ballot. This power ensures that the delegates are loyal to their candidates and their concerns rather than to a party leader or a state delegation. Their loyalty provides all candidates, even those who are not victorious, with a tremendous amount of discretionary power to shape the party platform.[10]

The cumulative effect of all these changes on the drafting of the platform is mixed. On the one hand the increase in the number of issue-oriented delegates and caucus groups means greater pressure to include specific demands in the platform, some of which will certainly go against the stated positions of the candidate, a volatile mixture.[11] On the other hand the presidential candidates have used their control over the delegates and the platform-drafting process to tailor the platform to their electoral needs, even if it means suppressing a potentially controversial position advocated by an important group or caucus. Consequently party platforms in the post-reform era are candidate-centered documents rather than party centered.[12]

The 1972 Democratic platform is a good example of how these two tendencies have been handled. Like the platform drafted in 1952, the bulk of the 1972 Democratic platform was written by a fifteen-member drafting subcommittee. The subcommittee relied heavily on drafts of planks that had been prepared by a staff organized by Richard Neustadt, the chairman of the 150-member Platform Committee. The staff had compiled a number of proposals and ideas from a variety of organizations inside and outside the Democratic party, including the Democratic Policy Council, several civil rights organizations, and organized labor.[13]

With all this material compiled by the original staff working under Neustadt, the fifteen-member drafting subcommittee and representatives of the presidential candidates met in executive session to begin the process of creating a platform. Meanwhile the rest of the Platform Committee received testimony from various groups.

But this arrangement fell apart when members of the Platform Committee demanded a greater voice in the actual drafting of the document. To appease their demands Neustadt put them on task forces that corresponded to the policy areas of the platform. The task forces subsequently collaborated with the drafting subcommittee to fashion the planks. The full Platform Committee then substantially revised the final document that was cobbled together from the planks.[14]

This method of drafting the platform contained pitfalls as well. While the full committee was considering the final draft from the subcommittee, delegates introduced several extremely controversial amendments from the floor. Some observers noted that "on abortion and homosexuality, the committee came close to adopting planks that might have cost votes in November. . . . In both cases, the hearts of most McGovern delegates were with the proposals, but McGovern's organization made its opposition clear, and enough of his backers voted against the amendments out of fear of alienating Catholics and other voters."[15]

The Democrats' experience in 1972 amply illustrates the often conflicting tendencies inherent in the drafting of the platform in a post-reform convention and the efforts needed to achieve harmony within the party. Most delegates have specific policy concerns that they want to see the party address. They also make commitments to a candidate they hope will become president. The presidential candidate has a list of policy preferences and most certainly wants to win in November. Presidential candidates face the dilemma of reconciling the policy demands of the delegates and their own policy preferences and electoral goals. Resolving the dilemma means that several groups and the candidate's organization engage in bargaining and may even require the candidate to use some strong-arm tactics.

And no matter how the candidate attempts to deal with the problems, not everyone will be satisfied. Some intraparty strife almost always occurs. The political trick is to minimize the strife and to emerge from the convention with a unified party, lest squabbling damage the image of the candidate and compromise the campaign's ability to raise money. The candidates certainly have the means to control the conventions and the drafting of the platform—the efforts of Democratic Chair Ron Brown at the 1992 Democratic convention stand out here—but the pervasive presence of issue-oriented delegates and caucus groups means that the presidential candidates must exercise these powers cautiously.[16]

Some political observers argue that the platforms continue to be meaningless to party leaders, candidates, and the electorate. They maintain that any agreement between the platforms and the candidates is unimportant because few people know or care whether the candidate stuck to the platform during the campaign or upon assuming office. Political parties possess no formal mechanism by which they can demand that their nominees conform to the platform after the convention.

Several studies have found a link between party platforms and policy, a sign that the ties between disparate electoral and governing coalitions may not be as frayed as popularly assumed.[17] Furthermore, because platforms are used to bring the demands of various organized interests into the mainstream of the political party, they are a way to build coalitions and elect candidates. Normally the party platform symbolizes the unity of the political party. In the age of the prereform or brokered convention the platform was a document usually drafted a number of months before the convention by prominent party leaders. Now, more often than not, the platform is the product of several informal and formal subcommittees and committees, some of which are more susceptible to the control of party leaders than others. In an effort to put together a document that is representative of the various groups comprising the party, the platform committee routinely receives suggestions during platform hearings (which are held around the nation before the convention) and from the various interest groups—proceedings now often televised live on C-SPAN.[18]

Furthermore the various groups that comprise the party coalition have certain issues that they expect the platforms and the candidates to address. Interest groups are involved in party platforms because

> having such planks can help a group achieve its policy objectives in at least two different ways. If the group's presence at the convention, and therefore its ability to win concessions, is based on its campaign activities, those same activities in the fall may result in some administration appointments. If the candidate's reluctance to endorse the group's plank is based on electoral tactics rather than substance, an appointment might settle the issue. If the group fails to gain such power through appointments, however, or if the president remains dubious for substantive reasons, the platform's promises still retain some influence. Virtually every group able to win a plank will have congressional allies. Presidents may choose not to honor a pledge, but doing so will mean alienating somebody in Congress.[19]

Without the attention of the candidates the interest groups might also be tempted to withhold their support, which can take the form of denying endorsements or campaign volunteers. In the worst of cases the group may decide to switch its allegiance altogether. Candidates use platforms as vehicles to demonstrate attentiveness to the policy objectives of interest groups. The amount of time and attention devoted to the crafting of a platform should dispel any doubt about the value of the document.

All these modifications to the party system have substantially altered the political environment in which candidates act; consequently the behavior of the candidates and the conduct of the conventions are dramatically different from what existed during the '50s and '60s. Because of the control exercised by local, state, and national party leaders in the selection of presidential nominees and the relatively closed nature of the nomination process in the brokered convention era, we could reasonably expect a high level of correspondence between the policy positions of the presidential candidates and their respective party platforms. The question that remains is how the changes in the political environment have affected the links between the coalitions that nominate the candidate and the electoral coalitions to which the candidate tries to appeal. Does the combination of candidates who are increasingly independent of the political party and the greater number of issue-oriented delegates foster disagreements between the nominating and electoral coalitions?

Presidential Candidates and Promises: Party Cohesion or Disintegration?

The forty years from 1952 to 1992 saw some of the most notable changes in the electoral landscape. The party reforms implemented in 1972, the subsequent tinkering with party rules, and the change in electoral norms dramatically altered the political environment in which campaigns take place. The changes have provoked some commentators to lament the chaos of the new order and to question whether democracy is well served by a party system in which candidates hold the upper hand.[20]

"Changing the rules of politics changes the incentives for political actors; . . . changing incentives leads to changes in political behavior; and . . . changing behavior changes political institutions and their significance in politics," notes Nelson Polsby.[21] If the transformation of political institutions has significant implications for American democracy, we should be seeing specific changes in the campaigns—particularly in the promises that presidential candidates make and the relationship of the party platforms to those promises, one area in which the nominating and electoral coalitions intersect.

The promises of presidential candidates signal the kind of electoral coalition that a presidential candidate hopes to assemble. For example, a promise to repeal the Taft-Hartley Act, like the one that Adlai Stevenson made in 1952 and 1956, showed that Stevenson wanted the support of organized labor. Political parties traditionally help and support the candidate in making appeals to such groups.

The historically strong ties between the Democratic Party and organized labor certainly facilitate the acceptance of a candidate's positions that are favorable to labor. But as the strength and cohesiveness of political parties wane in a candidate-centered system of politics, presidential candidates must fashion nominating and electoral coalitions with little or no assistance from party organizations. These coalitions can be heterogeneous in their appeal and may vary substantially from traditional stands of the political parties. Consequently we can expect that as the candidate-centered system of presidential politics evolves, the number of positions that candidates take would increase.[22]

And that's exactly what has happened. This hypothesis, that presidential candidates make more campaign promises in the post-reform era than in the pre-reform era, is supported by the actual number of promises made by each presidential candidate between 1952 and 1992 (see table 2.2).[23]

Indeed presidential candidates seem to make ever more promises with each subsequent election. Michael Dukakis achieved a high of 119 positions in 1988. Perhaps significantly, Democrats hold all the records, and Democrats' rates of promises are growing more rapidly than Republicans.'

The difference between Democrats and Republicans is even more obvious when looking at averages for the two party eras. In the pre-reform era Republican candidates averaged only 59 issue positions per election. This number increased only slightly, to 64 in the post-reform

TABLE 2.2 *Number of Issue Positions Held by Candidates in Presidential Campaigns, 1952–1992*

Year	Republican	Democrat
1952	45	39
1956	34	111
1960	82	80
1964	60	37
1968	76	70
1972	22	95
1976	55	77
1980	89	84
1984	31	48
1988	102	119
1992	85	111
Total	681	871
Total mean	62	79
Std. dev.	26.72	28.88
Pre-1972 mean	59	67
Post-1972 mean	64	89

era. The Democratic candidates, however, took an average of 67 positions in the pre-reform elections and averaged a whopping 89 issue stances in the post-reform elections, an increase of 32 positions from the pre-reform average.

Perhaps part of the difference between Republicans and Democrats, and subsequently the large increase from the pre-reform to the post-reform era, can be explained by the number of incumbents that each party fielded. Incumbents tend to take fewer policy positions, choosing instead to emphasize their record as president and their leadership style and qualities. Presidents who have to state their positions on a large number of issues do not appear to be very presidential. Therefore incumbent presidents emphasize their accomplishments and the importance of returning their leadership skills to office.

In the eleven presidential elections since 1952 the Democrats have fielded only two incumbents, one in each era: Johnson in 1964 and Carter in 1976. Meanwhile the Republicans have had five incumbents, four in the post-reform era. Generally a candidate takes about seventy-one policy positions in a presidential contest, but the numbers are quite different for incumbents and nonincumbents. The average nonincumbent stakes out eighty positions. However, the average incumbent takes only fifty positions (see table 2.3). Clearly, with a number of Republican incumbents running in the post-reform era, the average number of positions taken by Republican candidates would be substantially smaller.[24]

Interestingly, particularly vulnerable incumbents seem to take the most policy positions. Jimmy Carter took 84 positions in 1980, and George Bush took 85 in 1992. Compare these numbers with the paltry 31 positions that Ronald Reagan took in 1984 and the 22 positions that Richard Nixon enunciated in 1972. The latter two incumbents were perceived as too strong to unseat. Consequently they had no need to imperil precious electoral resources by staking out positions that could have upset an element of the electoral coalition. The more

TABLE 2.3 *Average Number of Presidential Campaign Issues by Era and Incumbency*

	Incumbents	Nonincumbents
Pre-reform era	36	70
Post-reform era	55	92
Average for both eras	50	80

secure presidential candidates have a strong incentive to avoid policy positions at all costs because they may needlessly alienate some voter. It is better to leave unstated what the president plans to do in a second term, letting the record from the previous term speak to those who may be inquisitive about the president's plans.

On the other hand challengers or weak incumbent presidents must take many positions, which helps to account for the increase in the average number of promises that nonincumbents have made since 1972 (see table 2.3). A weak incumbent must entice groups and interests to continue their support despite any problems that may have occurred in the first term. The incumbent can court their support by enunciating a position that benefits the group in some meaningful way.

Challengers must also enlist the support of groups by taking positions. Groups unsure of a candidate's stand on a particular issue will be reluctant to become part of the nominating or electoral coalition. Unequivocal and public promises from the candidate can help to secure the group's support. Finally, a challenger must appear knowledgeable and credible to the general public, which is achieved by making pronouncements on issues that are important to voters.

For example, the conditions for both candidates to take a large number of positions were clearly present in 1960. Dwight Eisenhower was finishing his second term in office, and voters generally were satisfied with his performance. Indeed at the end of his second term Eisenhower had a public approval rating of 59%, one of the highest ratings for modern presidents.[25] Because it was largely successful, Eisenhower's record was not a focal point of the debate between the two nonincumbent contenders. But Richard Nixon and John F. Kennedy were able to stress issues and themes that addressed which policies were needed to move the country forward and which candidate was more capable of taking the country beyond the Eisenhower years. Both candidates followed this strategy, and both made a large number of promises.[26]

Consequently the rise in the number of issue stances does not seem to be directly connected to the broader trend of party decline but to incumbency and relative vulnerability. The changes that have freed presidential candidates from the scrutiny of party leaders may indirectly contribute to the increase in the number of positions that presidential candidates have taken in recent campaigns because the incumbents were vulnerable. But do the promises that presidential candidates make to gain election remain connected over time to the coalitions that helped them acquire the nomination?

Candidate's Agreement with the Party Platform: Cohesion or Disintegration?

The raw number of issue positions does not reveal the entire story of how the ties between elements of the nominating and electoral coalitions may have changed as a result of transformations in the electoral system. If they are to win the presidency, candidates must assemble coalitions to win the nomination. And then they must strengthen, solidify, and broaden these coalitions into an successful electoral coalition.

For example, the national convention as a political institution has been radically restructured. The convention now only endorses decisions made in primary elections in the months before the convention. With the diminishing of the nominating function of the convention, "latent functions" have assumed greater importance.[27] Indeed the convention provides a unique atmosphere in which the delegates of the various candidates can unite behind a single candidate. Furthermore, through bargaining over the platform and selecting the vice presidential candidate, the candidate and the factions can mold their regional and issue differences into a coalition that anticipates a victory in the general election. But as these latent functions become more important, the risks of disagreement become greater. As platform planks loom larger as prizes to be captured, delegates may be less apt to back a candidate and to work for this person in the general election if no compromise is reached on a platform plank. Thus the candidate may be forced to allow a controversial plank into the platform—even a plank with which the candidate disagrees. This situation further strains the links between a candidate's need to appease the nominating coalition while reaching out to a broad electoral coalition.

However, candidates now exercise more control over their delegates than in pre-reform conventions. Candidates once bargained with the leaders of delegations because the delegates were pledged to a certain slate rather than to a candidate. Today the delegates are pledged to the candidate and are committed to supporting the candidate on the first ballot. Because they normally share the candidate's positions, delegates tend to support decisions their candidate makes during the convention. But today's delegates are also more politically active and issue oriented. Thus, although the candidate can exert tremendous influence over the delegates, the candidate must work to assure that the platform does not anger specific groups. This process can make it that much more difficult to compromise with losing factions at the convention because it constricts the terrain on which the candidate can maneuver.

In this environment political power has been distributed among a larger number of players. The candidates, their staffs, the interest groups and caucuses within the parties, and the news media have a real stake in playing the game and playing it well. This opens up a whole new spectrum of possibilities. Candidates can now disagree with their platforms. Or candidates and their private organizations—with the help of a majority of delegates committed to them—can completely dominate a national convention.

In this new political environment outcomes are less predictable because there are simply too many election-specific variables to control. For example, how many candidates seek the nomination? How do the media treat these different candidates? Are these candidates popular with the voters already, or do they need to build popularity in the primaries? Is an incumbent in the race or not? All these factors can affect how the campaign is conducted, the tone of the national convention, and the presence or absence of disagreements between the nominating and the electoral coalitions. Thus presidential candidates may be less inclined to agree with the party platform.[28]

The rates of agreement between the platforms and the positions of both parties' candidates have fluctuated over time (see figure 2.1).[29]

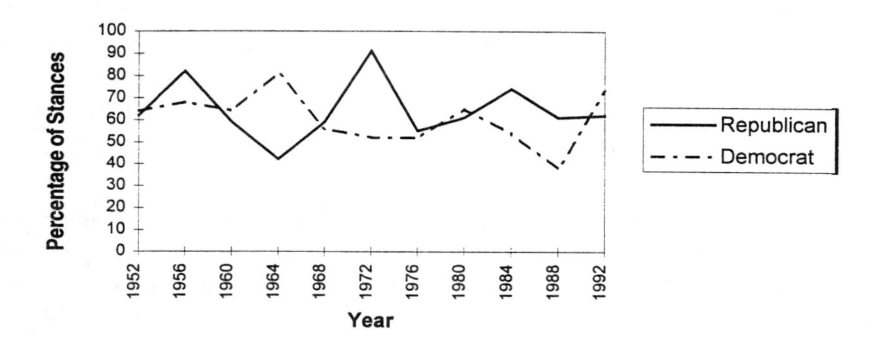

FIGURE 2.1 Candidates' Agreement with Party Platform

The rate of agreement ranges from a high of 91% for Richard Nixon in 1972 to a low of 38% for Michael Dukakis in 1988. At first glance these large swings seem to show that the relationships between the nominating and electoral coalitions are basically unstable in both the pre-reform and post-reform party eras, with no discernible pattern to the fluctuations.

Yet further examination shows that 1952 to 1968 was a time of relative stability for both political parties. The Republican Party saw a slight decrease in the number of presidential policy positions mentioned in the party platform, and the Democrats saw practically no change at all. The agreement between Republican presidential candidates and the party platform averaged 61% from 1952 to 1968. For the Democrats the average rate of agreement during the same period was 66%.

The pre-reform era also was marked by only one disagreement between the presidential candidates and the party platform. This does not mean that no tension existed. The campaign of 1952 provides perhaps the best example of a pre-reform candidate's behavior resulting from devotion of candidates to their parties. Both Eisenhower and Stevenson had opportunities to deviate from the positions staked out by the party platforms. For example, the prominence given to the air force in the Republican platform did not necessarily coincide with the defense and foreign policy of Eisenhower, who wanted to get away from such isolationist strategies. As for Stevenson, his first position on the Taft-Hartley Act called only for amendments. But the platform endorsed repeal of the act, and Stevenson chose to go along. In both cases the costs associated with disagreement outweighed any need to dictate the agenda for the campaign.

Rather than emphasize their disagreements with the platform, the candidates either remained silent or simply made small references to the issue. Eisenhower emphasized his foreign policy of alliances and cooperation and deemphasized weapon programs. But he did adopt the position of repudiating the Yalta Pact, a position important to the Taft wing of the party. Similarly Stevenson highlighted the alliances he would pursue in his foreign policy while gingerly avoiding any statements about the conduct of the Korean War. The bonds between the candidates and the parties seemed to be strong enough to withstand the pressure. Each candidate needed a unified party in order to prevail in the November election, and the candidates deemed that the best way to secure a unified party was to conform to various party stances rather than strike out on their own. Such a strategy normally guaranteed the much needed support of party leaders in the general election.

Adlai Stevenson's 1952 campaign also provides some concrete illustrations of how candidates manage the inevitable strains between nominating and electoral coalitions. Stevenson began his campaign by saying the position that the Taft-Hartley Labor Act needed only to be amended. But the Democratic platform urged repeal of the Taft-Hartley Act, calling it "inadequate, unworkable, and unfair."[30] Labor is an extremely important faction in the Democratic Party, and this was particularly true in 1952. Stevenson certainly needed the support of the major labor unions if he was going to win the presidency; therefore he had a strong electoral incentive to commit to repeal of the act.

His reversal is significant for two reasons. First, it was a noticeable attempt to retain the support of an influential coalition. Second, the reversal occurred on a highly salient issue, which demonstrates the effect that influential members of nominating and electoral coalitions can have on the agenda of a presidential candidate.

Still, such influences are not always determinative. The Taft-Hartley Act was not the only controversial issue in the Democratic ranks. The matter of federal ownership of off-shore oil reserves was also quite consequential. Stevenson endorsed federal ownership of the off-shore oil reserves despite the boisterous opposition of several prominent Democratic Party leaders. Specifically Stevenson's stance cost him the support of Governor Alan Shivers of Texas, who played a conspicuous role in the presidential politics of his state. But the possibility of losing Texas and other tideland states was not enough to make Stevenson change his position.

Stevenson also committed himself early in the campaign to establishing the Fair Employment Practices Commission (FEPC), designed to permit federal enforcement of certain civil rights in the states. The platform also expressed support for establishing FEPC, but only after the drafting committee worked out a compromise between the White House draft and the McCormack draft. The full committee did not alter this plank.[31]

Furthermore Stevenson voiced his support for modifying the Senate cloture rule so that debate and votes on civil rights legislation could occur. The platform agreed with his position because of the work of Senator John Sparkman of Alabama, Stevenson's running mate.[32] These two positions, on FEPC and the antifilibuster rules, were not popular in the Southern states. Indeed, although the two positions most likely cost Stevenson the endorsements and campaign activity of a number of Southern leaders, the candidate remained committed to both policies.

The case of Adlai Stevenson demonstrates quite clearly that presidential candidates in the pre-reform era were exposed to assorted risks as they articulated their policy preferences. Some issues are not salient, and the candidate may simply avoid taking a position on them. Other positions that the candidate may articulate do not arouse passions within the party coalition. Yet the candidate imperils the broader party coalition by advocating a particular stance on still other issues. Certainly this was the case with Stevenson's policies toward the Taft-Hartley Act, civil rights, and the off-shore oil reserves. But only in the case of the Taft-Hartley Act did Stevenson believe that he had to alter his position. On the other two issues Stevenson apparently did not believe that the risks to the party coalition outweighed other considerations, such as simply doing what he believed to be right. During his campaign swings through the South Stevenson stressed that he would say what he believed about civil rights and not what the voters in this region wanted to hear. This strategy was admirable. But in the 1952 election Eisenhower made the first significant Republican gains in the South by carrying Tennessee, Virginia, Florida, and Texas.

A conspicuous feature of the 1952 campaign was that the nominees did not make a large number of promises relative to the other campaigns. Indeed the total number of issue stances was the second lowest for the eleven elections covered in this study. The 1960 election was similar in many respects to the one in 1952, except for the number of promises. Perhaps more campaign promises would mean greater likelihood of conflict with members of the party's coalition about the position the nominee would take. Yet that seems not to be the case. Neither Nixon nor Kennedy adopted a position that disagreed with the party's platform. Moreover, unlike 1952, in 1960 neither candidate publicly switched his stand in order to pacify a specific group within his political party, although both made other types of compromises.

There are good reasons for the agreement between the issue stances of the two 1960 candidates and their respective party platforms, and the reasons are similar to those for the unanimous agreement forged in the 1952 campaign. Like Nixon and Kennedy, most candidates depended upon party regulars to help them win the nomination. That candidates won easy nomination during this period, often on the first ballot, should not be regarded as evidence that the presidential candidates totally dominated the parties.

For example, in 1960 Nixon was nominated on the first ballot only after working out a compromise with Governor Nelson Rockefeller of New York. Rockefeller withdrew from the race shortly after Nixon agreed to a fourteen-point compromise on key platform issues. The intent of the compromise was to create a platform that Rockefeller would be able to support. Seven of the fourteen points concerned foreign policy and national security, whereas the other seven involved domestic issues such as agriculture, civil rights, and economic growth. The compromise guaranteed Nixon a victory on the first ballot of the nomination.

Furthermore the meeting between Rockefeller and Nixon, held in Rockefeller's apartment in New York City, secured the unity of the Republican Party by merging the conservative and liberal wings. Indeed the compromise was significant because it did not resemble traditional Republican platforms and even represented a minor break from the economic and defense policies espoused by Eisenhower. The compromise contained a promise to stimulate the economy in order to achieve a certain rate of growth—a practice that violated the free-market principles that the Republican Party had so adamantly defended to that point. It further contained a pledge to increase the rate of defense spending, a position that Eisenhower regarded as a repudiation of his policies. This conflict with Eisenhower, the result of an attempt to compromise with Rockefeller, placed additional political pressure on Nixon.[33]

Ultimately Nixon found himself trying to appease both Eisenhower and Rockefeller. At one point he tried to assure Eisenhower that the platform would contain no wording that could be interpreted as critical of the administration's defense policies. Nixon said he would have to reject the platform if it contained such wording. His position was complicated because Rockefeller wanted the original compromise between the two men placed in the platform. Only after another compromise on the wording did it become possible to include the Nixon-Rockefeller fourteen-point compromise in the platform.[34]

Senator Charles Percy of Illinois, the chairman of the Resolutions Committee, was aware of the Nixon-Rockefeller compromise. Percy, along with several members from the White House staff who had assembled their own draft, was influential in drafting the platform.[35] The wording about foreign and domestic issues in the final platform was similar to the wording in the Nixon-Rockefeller compromise. But the compromise "expressed a sense of urgency" about the achievement of these goals and the platform did not.[36]

Nixon agreed to the issues presented in the platform, and no floor fight erupted over the platform at the Republican convention. If Nixon had not agreed to these issues, a floor fight could have crippled his chances in the Northeast where most Rockefeller Republicans lived.[37] But the compromise did not please everyone in the Republican Party. Senator Barry Goldwater of Arizona called the compromise a surrender and the "Munich of the Republican Party" and said it would certainly result in a defeat in the general election.[38]

Kennedy's experience with his party coalition was similar to Nixon's. Kennedy assembled support for his nomination by proving his popularity in the primaries, particularly with a key victory in West Virginia over Senator Hubert Humphrey of Minnesota. Kennedy's strong showing in the presidential primaries, especially in Protestant West Virginia and Wisconsin, demonstrated to the leaders of the Democratic Party that he possessed enough popular appeal to win the general election. Even with Kennedy's primary victories, large amounts of money, and his well-organized campaign, the Massachusetts senator won only 53% of the delegates, a mere forty-six more than a majority.[39]

The critical element here is that Kennedy had to demonstrate his popular appeal to the *party leaders* in order to win the nomination. According to Schlesinger, "The religious issue . . . left him no choice but to go into Wisconsin. It would be a gamble, but his only hope of forcing himself on the party leaders was to carry the primaries."[40] Kennedy's victories in the primaries were not sufficient to secure the nomination; unlike the process today they were only the means to an end. Kennedy was still faced with the difficult task of persuading the party leaders that he was both qualified and electable. Even after the primary victories the party leaders, who controlled large blocs of delegates, could have denied him the nomination.

Although the presidential candidates and their respective platforms disagreed in only one instance in the pre-reform era, the highest rates of agreement between the party platforms and presidential decisions are found during both periods in elections in which a party has a strong incumbent. In 1956 Eisenhower had a rate of agreement of 82%; in 1964 Johnson had an agreement rate of 81%. The highest rate of agreement, though, occurs in 1972; Nixon's policy positions agreed with the Republican platform 91% of the time. Only 9%, or two, of his positions were not contained in the platform. Merely 52% of South Dakota senator George McGovern's proposals agreed with the Democratic platform that year, whereas a rather large 46% were not mentioned.

The reasons for the high rate of agreement in 1972 between Nixon and his platform are not difficult to discern. Nixon was an incumbent who acknowledged he was pursuing a strategy that minimized the risks of the campaign. His strategy did not involve running on any new issues but on his record. Nixon was a known quantity because he had established a record that the voters either liked or disliked. To minimize the risks of the campaign Nixon acted presidential and strived to guarantee that the media portrayed him as such.

The office of the presidency already enjoys the benefit of a tremendous amount of news coverage, and as a candidate it was certainly in Nixon's interest to capitalize on the coverage without appearing to be a candidate. To accomplish this Nixon needed to concern himself only with the ordinary business of the White House. This strategy would ensure a steady flow of favorable media coverage. Only a true cynic would maintain that the reason for Nixon's trip to the Soviet Union and China was to secure his reelection. But with a reelection campaign looming the opportunities for favorable press arising from the two historic trips were not lost on the president or his staff.

The differences between Nixon and McGovern in the amount of agreement with the party platform can be attributed in part to what James Davis has labeled the "strategic environment." Davis maintains that the party platform is a product of the strategic environment in which the platform is assembled. The strategic environment is determined by whether the party is in or out of power—and if the party is in power, whether the incumbent is seeking another term. For example, an incumbent running for another term tends to dictate the drafting and assembling the platform. One example cited by Davis of how the strategic environment influences the platform was the Republican platform of 1972. The 1972 "Republican platform, written mostly in the White House and endorsed by the GOP platform committee *pro forma,* was approved on the convention floor after two hours of routine summarizing by seven platform subcommittees."[41]

Richard Nixon was quite unlikely to disagree with any planks in the Republican platform because he was chiefly responsible for the issues it contained in the first place. This drafting process explains the high rate of agreement between the party platform and the electoral campaign. We can expect rates for strong incumbents to be much higher than the average rates because of the influence they exert on the writing of their party's platform.[42] Presumably a strong nominee possesses the resources to win the nomination and the election without having to include in the platform the demands of numerous groups, which might jeopardize the nominee's electoral fortunes.

The lowest rates of agreement between candidates and their platforms seem to occur when the nomination campaigns are particularly intense and divisive. The Goldwater campaign of 1964 had an agreement rate of only 41%, the lowest rate of agreement registered by Republican candidates for the eleven elections studied. The second-lowest rate of agreement was achieved by another vulnerable Republican candidate, Gerald R. Ford in 1976. Ford's troubles are good examples of the problems that can occur in the wake of a divisive primary challenge. Ford gained the Republican nomination only after a long and difficult struggle with Ronald Reagan, the conservative ex-governor of California.

Many analysts point to Ford's difficult battle to show that even incumbents are vulnerable in the new political environment. Whether Ford could be truly considered an incumbent is debatable, however. In the strictest sense of the word he was an incumbent, and he certainly possessed all the perquisites that the presidency places at a candidate's disposal. But Gerald Ford came to the presidency without ever being popularly elected. He was named vice president in 1973 when Spiro Agnew resigned amid charges of tax fraud, and Ford ascended to the presidency when Nixon resigned in 1974 in the wake of the Watergate scandal. Ford never received a popular mandate in the form of a general election, so he really did not possess the same right to another term in office that most incumbent presidents claim.

Furthermore Ford was hampered by his pardon of Richard Nixon. Many people, both inside and outside his party, were outraged by this action; some even suspected that Ford and Nixon had struck a deal. This controversy, coupled with Ford's uncertain status as an incumbent, made him extremely vulnerable to a challenge from within his party and seriously handicapped him in the general election.

But Gerald Ford possessed other characteristics that made his candidacy appealing. He had served for many years in the House of Representatives and was the leader of his party in that chamber. He was certainly well known around Washington by all party officials and was therefore considered an insider. Ford's main rival for the nomination, Ronald Reagan, was not considered an insider, even though he had been involved in the politics of the party for a number of years. Reagan had already tried to gain the Republican nomination and had enjoyed little success. The conditions in 1976, however, made it possible for him to come extremely close to capturing the nomination. With the proliferation of primary campaigns a candidate who raised substantial sums of money and who possessed a loyal following could be successful, especially when challenging a vulnerable incumbent. Reagan possessed both characteristics. Both Reagan and Ford scored a number of impressive primary victories, and the culmination of the primary season was a close vote at the convention.

Despite the highs and the lows associated with the various levels of agreement in divisive and nondivisive primary campaigns, the two party eras show few differences (see table 2.4). The average rate of agreement for the pre-reform era is 64%, whereas the rate for the post-reform era is 62%.

Furthermore the two parties show little difference. The average rate of agreement for Republican candidates was 64%, whereas the average rate for Democratic candidates was 61%. Both parties had a fair share of divisive primary campaigns, a factor that seems to decrease the candidate's rate of agreement with the party platform. The appearance of divisive primary campaigns in both parties certainly helps to explain the narrow differences between the two parties in their rates of agreement.

Another reason for stability over time in the rate of agreement is that the candidates are responding to the same set of issues. One of the

TABLE 2.4 *Presidential Candidates' Rates of Agreement with Party Platform: Pre-Reform Versus Post-Reform Eras*

	1952–1968	1972–1992	All Elections
All candidates	64%	62%	62%
Republicans	61	67	64
Democrats	66	56	61

biggest issues to which candidates responded was the war in Vietnam. Here the 1968 campaign can be instructive. Hubert H. Humphrey pledged to prod the government of South Vietnam to undertake political, economic, and social reforms that would increase popular support for the South Vietnamese government. He also proposed a cease-fire that would be supervised by the United Nations, and he favored free elections for South Vietnam that would include members of the National Liberation Front. However, neither proposal was mentioned in the party platform. Ten percent, or seven, of the positions that Humphrey staked out concerned the Vietnam War. The war dominated his foreign policy agenda—30% of his positions were on foreign policy.

In the area of domestic policy Humphrey addressed the problem of crime by proposing the registration of firearms and federal aid to local law enforcement agencies for better salaries, training, and equipment. He also advanced the ideas of creating a federal school for criminal justice and providing federal aid to state and local correctional institutions. To stem the tide of illegal drugs entering the United States Humphrey wanted to increase surveillance and other intelligence-gathering activities along the borders. He also endorsed more federal funding for drug treatment facilities.[43] Humphrey's program reflected the nation's concern with crime. Nearly one-third (32%) of all the issue positions that Humphrey stressed during the campaign dealt with the problems of crime and drug control.

These pledges agreed with the Democratic platform, but even though the platform took a tough stance, it did not contain as many specific pledges as the Republican platform. In fact the plank in the Democratic platform dealing with crime was entitled "Justice and Law" in order to avoid the more politically sensitive phrase "law and order."[44]

Nixon promised to bring an "honorable" end to the war. To accomplish this task he favored maintaining the military level in Vietnam in order to convince the enemy "that he isn't going to . . . win something militarily at the time we are talking."[45] He also endorsed "the suspension of aid and credit to any country which supplies North Vietnam."[46] Only 7%, or five, of Nixon's positions involved the Vietnam War. Although lower than Humphrey's 10%, Nixon's positions on the Vietnam War involved 38% of his foreign policy positions, larger than Humphrey's 30%.

In the area of domestic policy Nixon, like Humphrey, devoted a large portion of his campaign to the issues of crime and drug control. Here Nixon was well in tune with the tone of the platform. The platform contained strong language and harsh denunciations of Johnson's policies on crime and drug control. In one sentence alone the platform declared, "We will not tolerate violence!"[47]

These issues were considered so important that fifteen of the seventy-six issue positions (20%) in Nixon's campaign dealt with the problems of stemming crime and drug abuse. Nixon advocated the use of nationwide "town hall" conferences on crime prevention and control and the creation of a "National Academy of Law Enforcement" designed to provide local agencies "with training in the most sophisticated, modern methods of law enforcement.' "'[48] He also promised to triple the number of customs agents and to hasten the development of methods for detecting the smuggling of drugs, although the platform mentioned neither position.[49]

Nixon's stress on the issue of law and order was not greater than the Democratic program's, despite his strong language. Only 19% of Nixon's program was devoted to law and order as compared to 32% of Humphrey's. The Republicans, however, enjoyed a position as the party of law and order, even though Humphrey and the Democrats articulated a larger share of promises. The rhetoric of Nixon and Agnew was tougher because of the constituencies to which the Republican Party was appealing. The Democrats, on the other hand, had to moderate their rhetoric because they did not want to alienate support from youth and minorities. Indeed throughout the campaign leaders from these two constituencies often accused politicians of using "law and order" as code for police brutality and repression. Under these conditions the Republicans were able to project an image as the party that stood for law and order without suffering the same electoral consequences as the Democrats, although the Democrats enunciated more promises for dealing with the problem of crime.

Of course the strength of the various party organizations is not the only variable that determines agreement between a candidate and the nominating coalition. A candidate might persuade the party to accept certain positions, and a perfect understanding between candidates and the parties is likely at the outset. However, in the era of the brokered convention the political party possessed the means to ensure a high degree of agreement. So long as those links existed between the nominating and the electoral coalitions, agreement between the candidates and the party could be expected.[50]

To be sure, the change from the pre-reform to the post-reform era allowed candidates more freedom to strike out on their own. But this freedom has not resulted in less agreement; it has actually produced more. Although the 1988 Democratic platform mentioned only 38% of Michael Dukakis's promises, the low rate is partly attributable to the conspicuous attempt of the Dukakis campaign and the Democratic Party to minimize conflict by diluting the positions in the platform and emphasizing principles upon which all Democrats could agree.[51] In this way conflict would not alienate voters, and the party would shed the image of being captive to a plethora of special interest groups, a label that burdened the campaign of Walter Mondale and the Democratic Party in 1984.

Yet the real story behind the increased rates of agreement of the candidates and their party's platform thus far seems to be that more candidates in the post-reform era have not struck out on their own. The rates of agreement are high and have actually increased across the two party eras. Nominating and electoral coalitions appear to agree at a rather impressive rate, despite changes in the party system that would seem to predispose them to disintegration.

Disagreement with the Party Platform: Cohesion or Disintegration?

Although nominees' positions and party platforms often agree, the number of disagreements increases over time (see figure 2.2). Significantly only one instance of disagreement occurs before 1972; all others occur after 1972, the first presidential election following the McGovern-Fraser reforms. By this time both parties had had time to digest the various demands for reform.

In 1972 signs of tension between the nominating and the electoral coalitions begin to show up in the emergence of a disagreement and another decrease in the percentage of agreement between the candidates and the platforms. The participatory nature of the platform-drafting process is perhaps reflected best by the two McGovern positions that disagreed with the party platform: cutting funding for the space program and supporting government-sponsored pensions. These two disagreements are the first multiple instances of disagree-

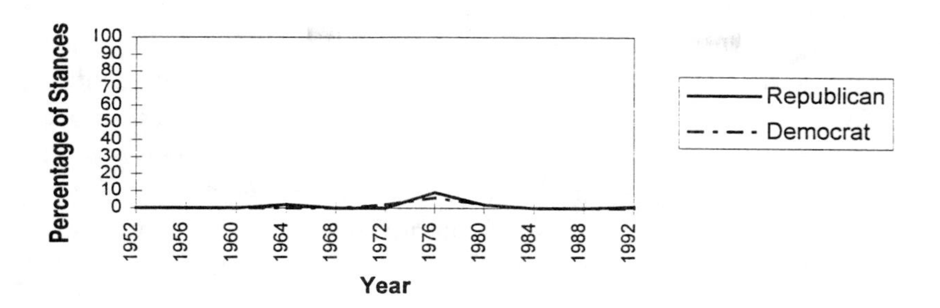

FIGURE 2.2 Candidates' Disagreement with Party Platform

ment between a candidate and the platform reported thus far, and they merit further examination.

The 1972 Democratic Party platform attacked the Nixon administration because it "paid scant attention" to the plight of workers in defense and aerospace industries. The Democratic Party pledged "to increase efforts by the federal government and to stimulate research in private industry."The platform also stated that the "Democratic Party is committed to increasing the overall level of scientific research in the United States . . . and [is] eager to take management methods and techniques devised for the space and defense programs as well as our technical resources, and apply them to the city, the environment, education, energy, transportation, health care and other urgent domestic needs."[52]

Despite these platform positions McGovern proposed to reduce the budget of the space program. These differences certainly constituted a disagreement in principle.

The second disagreement occurred on a much less visible issue: the age at which a person could collect government-sponsored pensions. This was not a disagreement about the direction of public policy but a disagreement over retirement-related issues. McGovern proposed that men should become eligible for Social Security benefits at age sixty-two, the same age at which women would become eligible.[53] The Democratic platform, however, expressed support for "lower[ing] retirement eligibility age to 60 in all government pension programs," presumably including Social Security.[54]

The disagreements between McGovern and the Democratic platform can be explained in a number of ways. First, the disagreements may signify real ideological differences between McGovern's nominating and electoral coalitions. But the issues over which the disagreements occurred were not particularly salient. Furthermore McGovern commanded a majority of delegates at the convention. That the delegates pledged to McGovern had serious ideological differences with the candidate is quite improbable. Therefore any differences that might have existed between the two coalitions were of little political significance.

Second, although the disagreements did not occur on salient issues, the disagreements may indicate that McGovern's program was simply too large for him to keep track of all the issues included in the platform. "Presidential candidates seeking the White House for the first time are usually far more occupied with winning the nomination than in platform-writing," notes James W. Davis.[55]

Unless a presidential contender has a clear road to the nomination before the convention, candidates generally are preoccupied in nailing down the nomination, talking with the various state delegations, holding press conferences, and considering various vice presidential possibilities, not in putting the final touches on the party platform.[56]

Although the disagreements were not over issues that had a high profile in the campaign, their occurrence signals the dissolution of the traditional bonds between the electoral and the nominating coalitions. Presidential candidates and their personal organizations are called upon to accomplish tasks once performed by the political party leaders. These tasks include monitoring the drafting of the platform, helping to screen the vice presidential candidates, and working to keep the party unified. If party leaders do not perform these tasks, issue-oriented delegates are more likely to exercise a measure of control. Thus tension arises between the demands to satisfy the ideological proclivities of the nominating coalition and the need of the candidate to broaden the electoral coalition.

Tip O'Neill's comment about being defeated by "the cast of *Hair*" probably reveals some hazards connected with the tensions between a narrow nominating coalition and a broad electoral coalition. The coalition that McGovern assembled to win the nomination and the stances he assumed to activate that coalition may have created early perceptions, favorable or unfavorable, among voters. Yet early perceptions are difficult to alter. This certainly seems to have been the case with

McGovern. The general electorate had concerns about the coalition that nominated McGovern and the positions he took, and McGovern's attempts to moderate his image were unsuccessful. The more prominent policy choices that he advocated—an immediate end to the Vietnam War and his welfare proposals—appear to have nurtured the perception among some voters that he clearly was outside the mainstream of politics and was too radical to be entrusted with the presidency.

These tensions were also glaringly apparent in 1976 with an increase in the number of disagreements between Jimmy Carter and his platform. The large number of disagreements between the candidates and their respective party platforms is a feature that distinguishes the 1976 election from all the other elections examined in this study. Of the seventy-eight policy positions, 5%, or four, of Carter's positions disagreed with the party platform. Nine percent, or five, of Ford's issue positions disagreed with the Republican platform.

Even so, the 1976 election was in some ways similar to previous elections. The two candidates had similar percentages of agreement with the party platform. Fifty-five percent of Ford's pledges and 52% of Carter's agreed with their respective platforms. These percentages, although slightly lower, are not dramatically different from the percentages reported for other elections. Indeed recent platforms resemble the pre-reform elections from 1952 to 1968, with the exception of the disagreement percentages.

Although their agreement and disagreement rates were similar, the two candidates made different amounts of promises. The differences can be attributed partly to the campaign styles of the two candidates and how Carter fit into the strategic environment. As a challenger, Carter needed to come out early in the campaign, publicizing his positions and attacking Ford. But Ford did not become totally active in the campaign until late in the season.[57]

The disagreements between Carter and the Democratic platform are noteworthy because the Carter forces expended a special effort to assist in the platform's construction. During the platform committee hearings held in June in Washington, D.C., Carter's staff worked closely with Governor Wendell Anderson of Minnesota, the chairman of the Platform Committee, to construct the document. When the platform was completed, it resembled a "Great Society document" or "a throwback to earlier years—a broad statement of party goals rather than a list of legislative programs and controversial stands on issues."[58] However, the platform's insistence on an increase in federal spending did not seem compatible with the anti–Washington sentiments that Carter had continually expressed during the campaign.

A report prepared by members of the Democratic Advisory Council of Elected Officials served as the basis of the 1976 Democratic platform.[59] It is conceivable that Carter accepted a platform embodying a philosophy slightly at odds with his stated campaign goals in an attempt to appease party leaders and to appeal to the mainstream of the Democratic Party.

Jimmy Carter's most significant disagreements with the party platform, at least in terms of his future policy agenda, probably were the specific energy proposals. For example, Carter opposed a general breakup of oil companies into different companies to handle the various operations from the oil field to the gas pump. But the platform stated that "when competition inadequate to insure free markets and maximum benefit to American consumers exists, we support effective restrictions on the right of major companies to own all phases of the oil industry."[60]

Carter's energy program also called for the deregulation of natural gas prices. But here too the Democratic platform expressed the opposite position. Although it spoke of regulating the cost of oil, the platform stated that "this oil-pricing lesson should also be applied to natural gas. Those not pressing to turn natural gas price regulation over to OPEC [the Organization of Petroleum Exporting Countries], while arguing the rhetoric of so-called deregulation, must not prevail." The platform went on to argue that "the pricing of new natural gas is in need of reform. We should narrow the gap between oil and natural gas prices with new natural gas ceiling prices that maximize production and investment while protecting the economy and the consumer."[61]

Such stark differences between various party coalitions and Carter certainly could be viewed as a precursor of the immense problems that he would have with his energy package in Congress.

Another disagreement that could be considered part of the energy package concerned the use of nuclear energy. Carter, who majored in nuclear engineering at the U.S. Naval Academy, promised to expand the uses of atomic energy. In addition, he proposed a number of specific safeguards to make nuclear energy much safer. The Democratic platform, however, declared that "nuclear power should be kept to the minimum necessary to meet our needs."[62] Therefore three out of the four differences between Carter and the platform occurred on the highly visible subject of energy.

The final difference between Carter and the platform concerned amnesty for draft evaders. Carter drew a distinction between the blanket pardon, which he supported, and the blanket amnesty, which the platform supported. These were serious differences.

Although George McGovern in 1972 also had his differences with the party platform, they were not over issues that were as volatile as the draft evaders or as visible as the energy issues. Indeed McGovern's disagreements with the party platform occurred only on funding for the space agency and a proposal to lower the eligibility age for government-sponsored pension programs. A compromise between the nominating coalition and McGovern's electoral coalition would have been easy to forge on those issues. But Carter's 1976 disagreements with the platform were much more critical because they were sharp disagreements on policy regarding pressing issues.

On other issues, perhaps even issues that could be considered highly controversial by the general electorate, Carter agreed with the Democratic platform. For example, on foreign policy and defense issues Carter advocated the withdrawal of atomic weapons from South Korea and the removal of troops over a period of four to five years. He further called for a reduction of the defense budget and for negotiations to settle differences with Panama over the Panama Canal. Also, Carter championed negotiations with the Soviet Union to achieve a comprehensive test ban treaty for nuclear testing. The platform supported all these positions.

In the area of agricultural policy Carter risked disagreeing with one major coalition in his party: farmers. Carter announced his backing for raising crop support prices to a level that at least would cover the costs of production, but he refused to guarantee he would seek to raise the supports to a level that would secure profits for the farmers. The Democratic platform stated, "We must assure parity return to farmers based on costs of production plus a reasonable profit."[63]

Carter further jeopardized his standing in the Democratic Party by stating his opposition to the wording of the plank on abortion. He agreed with the plank in its opposition to a constitutional amendment outlawing abortion, but he believed that people should be allowed to seek a constitutional amendment.[64] The platform stated, "We fully recognize the religious and ethical nature of the concerns which many Americans have on the subject of abortion. We feel, however, that it is undesirable to attempt to amend the U.S. Constitution to overturn the Supreme Court decision in this area."[65]

Whether Carter's disagreement with the plank was real or imagined because of the ambiguous wording of the plank, Carter pledged to "do everything I can as president within the rules set down by the Supreme Court to minimize the need for abortion," and he "opposed all government aid to secure abortions."[66] The Democratic platform made no further mention of abortion.

Carter's campaign of openness and honesty in government found ample support from the party platform. He favored universal voter registration through the mail, "public financing of congressional campaigns, [and] merit selection of Federal judges, diplomats and other appointees."[67] Two of his "honesty" pledges that were not in the platform included a ban on all gifts to public officials and financial disclosure by high-ranking employees of the federal government. According to Carter, these measures would help restore confidence in the federal government that had been eroded by the Watergate scandal. In his memoirs Carter wrote, "As an American, I had been embarrassed by the Watergate scandal and the forced resignation of the President. I realized that my own election had been aided by a deep desire among the people for open government, based on a new and fresh commitment to changing some of the Washington habits which had made it possible for the American people to be misled."[68]

Carter's issue stances are graphic evidence of his moderate ideology, which appealed to both the liberal and conservative elements of the electorate. Carter later recalled that "throughout the 1976 campaign, the most persistent question of the news reporters was, 'Are you a liberal or a conservative?' When forced to answer, I would say that I was a fiscal conservative but quite liberal on such issues as civil rights, environmental quality, and helping people overcome handicaps to lead fruitful lives" (pp. 73–74).

He acknowledged the usefulness of this ideology when in 1985 he urged the Democratic Party to offer a mix of liberal and conservative policies to attract more voters to the party.[69] Indeed during the campaign several jokes circulated about Carter's mixed philosophy, which some analysts thought was a calculated vagueness on the issues. One joke had Carter's father asking him if he was responsible for cutting down the family peach tree. Jimmy's reply: "Well, perhaps."[70] However, this purely utilitarian approach to winning elections is not without its disadvantages, the least of which is risking a conflict with both the conservative and liberal elements of the party's coalition.[71]

Similar forces had buffeted the presidential campaign of Gerald Ford. When the Republican convention convened in August, Ford and Reagan were still battling for the nomination. This protracted struggle profoundly affected the tone of the party platform. The conservative Reagan and moderate Ford forces were reluctant to make the platform a battleground, although both candidates were well represented on the platform committee. Their reluctance was rooted in the electoral position of the two candidates: "Since it was not clear which candidate would be the nominee, neither candidate's organization wanted to go far out on a limb to battle for specific issues in the platform at the risk of alienating the party or the electorate."[72] Furthermore the platform committee held public hearings to collect the thoughts and ideas of party rank-and-file. But the Republicans did not put together a full-time staff until July 1.[73] The uncertain electoral status of the two candidates and the late start in forming a full-time staff resulted in a platform drafted in large measure by members of the platform committee.

Because the platform was largely drafted by the delegates, it often reflected the conservative tendencies of the Republicans. Of course candidates offered some changes that altered the tone or direction of a plank. For example, the Ford forces intervened to ensure that the platform continued its endorsement of the Equal Rights Amendment. But Ford's basic strategy was to "stand still and absorb whatever the delegates decided was appropriate, and not to engage in unnecessary, divisive battles."[74] Both Ford and Reagan said they were pleased with the platform, but neither candidate was able to claim a complete victory.

The platform was restrained in its praise of President Ford. This tone was partly a product of the tough battles endured by the Ford forces on foreign policy. Conservative forces, led by Senator Jesse Helms of North Carolina, were outspoken in their criticism of Henry Kissinger and several of his positions. The conservative forces and Ford's delegates clashed over planks on the Panama Canal, expressions of support for Taiwan, and aid to emerging states in Africa. In the words of one observer, "There was a clear rupture between those who wanted the platform to praise administration foreign policy and those who wanted tougher Cold War language, even at the risk of embarrassing the President."[75]

Although both Reagan and Ford later expressed approval for the platform, the amount of compromise was great, and the final product was bound to contain planks with which Ford disagreed. This ultimately meant that disagreement with the platform was not confined to the Democratic Party. Oddly enough, the explicit disagreements did not occur over issues of foreign policy, where the conservative forces had concentrated their efforts.

Like Carter, Ford differed with his party on a specific energy proposal. Ford proposed the establishment of a $100-billion government corporation to provide various financial incentives to develop new sources of energy. The platform, however, flatly stated that "Democrats have . . . proposed that the federal government compete with industry in energy development by creating a national oil company. We totally oppose this expensive, inefficient and wasteful intrusion into an area which is best handled by private enterprise." The platform also expressed support for "measures to assure adequate capital investment in the development of new energy sources"[76] The Republican Party seemed to agree with Ford's goal but to oppose his methods.

Two clear disagreements occurred on issues that were relatively new to the political scene and seemed to cut across traditional party cleavages: abortion and school busing. Ford expressed a preference for amendments that would permit each state to regulate abortion. The Republican platform acknowledged the various positions on the issue of abortion and then stated that the "Republican Party favors continuance of the public dialogue on abortion and supports the efforts of those who seek enactment of a constitutional amendment to restore protection of the right to life for unborn children."[77] This plank was largely preferred by the Reagan forces, and they won a fight to retain it. Ford denied that his position constituted a disagreement with the party's platform, but he refused to elaborate. Throughout the remainder of the campaign he stressed the rights of states to decide the issue without ever passing judgment on the legality of abortion—which the platform addressed directly.

On the issue of busing Ford asserted his opposition to mandatory busing to achieve school desegregation. However, he also revealed that he opposed constitutional amendments to outlaw busing. The platform, which agreed with Ford's opposition to mandatory busing, stated, "We oppose forced busing to achieve racial balances in our schools." But the platform went on to state, "If Congress continues to fail to act, we would favor consideration of an amendment to the Constitution forbidding the assignment of children to schools on the basis of race."[78]

The final disagreements involved Social Security and catastrophic health insurance. Ford committed himself to a program of catastrophic health insurance, which would insure beneficiaries by raising the fees paid by Medicare recipients for short-term treatment. The platform contained expressions of support for catastrophic health insurance but added, "We should utilize our private health insurance system to assure adequate protection for those who do not have it."[79]

On Social Security Ford proposed raising the Social Security tax rates paid by employers and employees from 5.85% to 6.15%, although he opposed raising the maximum income, $16,500, on which the tax is paid. The platform declared, "The cost to employers for Social Security contributions must not be raised to the point where they will be unable to afford contributions to employees' private pensions programs."[80] The question here is whether an increase from 5.85% to 6.15% constitutes the breaking point for employers to contribute to private pension programs. Given the outspoken behavior of the conservative faction at the 1976 convention, this plank appeared to be an attempt to influence Ford's position.[81]

On issues of foreign policy Ford agreed with the platform on the sensitive issue of a grain embargo. He further pledged his support to Israel, and he promised to seek more immigration of Jews from the Soviet Union. This support included pledges to seek legislation to prevent American corporations from complying with an Arab boycott of Israel and to oppose any U.N. resolution that condemned Zionism as racism.

Other issues of foreign and defense policy where Ford agreed with the platform included his support for the B-1 bomber, his commitment to continue the sale of arms to Iran, and his expression of support for Taiwan as well as for normalization of relations with mainland China.

On domestic policy Ford and the party platform agreed to seek an increase in the personal tax exemption from $750 to $1,000 and greater tax incentives for businesses to move into inner cities and other economically depressed areas. He also expressed his support for balancing the federal budget and restraining federal spending, two positions traditionally popular in the Republican Party.

The 1976 Republican platform was quite conservative. Ford found it difficult to consistently agree with some policies it outlined. During this election Ford and the party were unquestionably under a tremendous amount of pressure. The Republican Party, suffering from the lingering effects of the Watergate crisis and Ford's pardon of Nixon, was exposed to a number of political risks. In this situation Ford did his best to keep the Republican Party unified by compromising on the platform wording and stressing some conservative positions. However, the disagreements in the party were too severe, and to secure a victory in November Ford could not completely surrender to the conservative wing of his party. The result was some disagreement with the platform.

Together the campaigns of George McGovern, Jimmy Carter, and Gerald Ford provide evidence that the new political environment, created by the proliferation of primaries and the pervasive influence of the mass media, is strewn with numerous political pitfalls. Incumbents can be exposed to serious challenges, issue-oriented delegates press their views at the conventions, and candidates are free to articulate stances that they believe will attract voters without concern for the positions of the party. The 1976 election demonstrated that the party coalitions were becoming more difficult to manage and that the potential existed more strongly than before for disputes to occur over even minor policy matters. With the advent of the new party system the formal mechanisms once used to provide a modicum of harmony among the coalitions disappeared, and the new organizations on the political scene (i.e., the candidates' organizations) were ill equipped to replace them.

The period from 1952 to 1992 includes some of the most notable changes in the electoral landscape ever documented by political scientists. The party reforms implemented in 1972 and the subsequent tinkering with the rules have dramatically altered the electoral environment. The changes have been so significant that the conduct of campaigns in 1952 and the conduct of campaigns today bear little or no resemblance to each other. Yet the significant question that arises is how the changes have affected the functioning of institutions headed by elected officials. The restructuring of the parties led to a change of behavior by the candidates and the other prominent players in the presidential contests.

Yet the relative stability of the levels of agreement between candidates and platforms attests to the strength of the links between the nominating coalitions and the party apparatus. Because a stable group of party leaders in the pre-reform era nominated the candidates, helped to develop the issue agenda, and assisted the candidates during the general election, conflicts between the nominating coalitions and party organizations was kept to a minimum. When conflict did occur, the party organization was strong enough to moderate the differences, either by seeking a compromise or by simply overruling the dissident faction. Moreover, although disagreement occurs in the post-reform era, the parties are equally stable in both eras.

But does the unpredictability in the electoral system as a whole seriously hamper the formation of governing coalitions? The next chapter examines the types of policy statements made by the presidential candidates. From the standpoint of governing, some kinds of policies are easier to deliver than others. If presidential candidates are making statements on issues over which they have little control once they begin the task of governing, the changes in the electoral environment may be responsible for the decline in governability.

3

Issue Stances and Issue Types: Governance Without Leaders?

The most enigmatic feature of the current perception of crisis in government is that it spans a wide range of issues. Public opinion polls and scholars alike agree that American policy makers can do little that is right, let alone move complex pieces of legislation through fragmented institutions.[1] A 1995 public opinion poll recorded the extent to which citizens expect American government to fail: 56% of the people said that government programs do more to hinder rather than help in the achievement of the American dream.[2]

But blanket condemnation of the policy-making apparatus neglects the often stark differences in types of policy and the politics associated with each type. Theodore Lowi first introduced the idea of different policy types: distributive, regulatory, and redistributive.[3] He further delineated several types of distinctions that can be made in the three kinds of policies, such as the size and kind of interest groups involved, the relative influence of different institutions within Congress and the executive branch, and the visibility to the public of the decisions being made. These policy types actually "constitute real arenas of power. Each arena tends to develop its own characteristic political structure, political process, elites, and group relations" (pp. 689–90). Therefore a failure to enact a certain kind of policy should not imply a general failure of democratic politics but perhaps only the inability to act or project influence in a particular policy arena.

Distributive policy is pork barrel legislation. Distributive policies are devised in relatively conflict-free environments in which interest groups, executive agencies, and members of Congress on committees and subcommittees cooperate to ensure the delivery of discrete benefits to specific groups or regions. Generally the coalitions that form to enact and implement distributive policies are quite stable. Norms of mutual accommodation and noninterference predominate.[4]

Regulatory policies involve more political conflict and coalitions that are less stable because these policies are more controversial than distributive policies. For example, groups and individuals disagree over the best trade or educational policies to enact. Therefore, when coalitions do form to enact a policy that is regulatory, they are not durable. Successful cooperation on one issue does not ensure continued cooperation on others.

The coalitions arrayed for and against the passage of the General Agreement on Trade and Tariffs (GATT) in 1994 illustrate how temporary these alliances can be. Labor organizations aligned with Ross Perot for defeat of the agreement, whereas business groups and a Democratic president sought passage. The common grounds uniting the groups within these coalitions proved to be unstable, and the coalitions dissolved almost immediately after passage of the agreement. Unlike distributive policy, regulatory decisions are normally made on the floor of the chambers, not in the committees and subcommittees. Consequently the profile of the conflict is much higher. The shared policy interests of groups and legislators create the coalitions in regulatory policy, as opposed to the narrow economic benefits bestowed by government that form the basis of coalitions in distributive policies.

The most visible and stable coalitions are formed around redistributive policies. These policies actually involve the appropriation of resources from one group or segment of society in order to disburse them to another group or segment. Consequently the debate over these policies is ideological and often involves class conflict, even if in muted form. Because of the ideological nature of redistributive policies, the politics are controversial and demand the attention of the president, party leaders, and large coalitions of interest groups that speak for much broader segments of society. In redistributive policy class considerations replace the particularistic interests of distributive policies, making the political issues relevant to broader segments of the electorate. The debate over health care reform in the second half of the 103d Congress, for example, assumed redistributive proportions. Health care taxes and employer mandates dominated the thoughts and concerns of the president, the party leaders who were attempting to cobble together a coalition in Congress, and the various interest groups favoring or opposing changes in the current health care delivery system.

Since Lowi's initial work, the theory of distinct policy types has been refined and used in a number of different ways.[5] For example, regulatory policies can be subdivided into protective and competitive regulatory policies because of the disparate politics that the two kinds of policy engender.[6] Even with such refinements, associating the distinctive policy types with particular kinds of politics and the political arrangements they engender makes it possible to test the argument that democratic governance no longer occurs because it has become too difficult to link nominating, electoral, and governing coalitions in the absence of strong political parties. According to this argument, presidential campaigns place far too much emphasis on activities that do not have a discernible benefit once the candidate begins the task of governing. Indeed the modern means for assembling nominating and electoral coalitions, having excluded party leaders from the bulk of the process, actually inhibits the formulation of governing coalitions.

The theory of public policy developed by Lowi and others can help to test this argument. For example, might candidates benefit from campaigns that rely almost exclusively on distributive policies to attract support for nominating and electoral campaigns? Do candidates emphasize a particular policy type in order to increase the likelihood of a successful campaign? Perhaps with the exception of legislation for which discrete benefits and mutual accommodation are crucial, political candidates have strong incentives to neglect redistributive issues, even if the issues happen to differentiate the candidates. Furthermore the theory of policy argues that presidents have little influence over the passage of distributive policies because the arrangements that facilitate their passage probably remain constant across administrations. Can a president claim credit for governing when the bulk of the positions taken by the president demand little, if any, direct attention from the president?

Finally, if the neglect of redistributive policies occurs at all, can it occur without the candidates' suffering any serious ramifications from the national political parties? The American party system does not have the centralized structure necessary to prevent presidential candidates from using the discrete promises of distributive benefits to lure particular groups to support their campaigns. Therefore candidates may appeal to particular groups without worrying that they may be forced to focus on issues that would have the most effect on governing the nation. The promise of discrete benefits has a political payoff but does nothing to erase the perception that government is unable to solve the intractable problems facing the nation. And is governability merely the ability to enact redistributive policies, or does it also encompass the presumably easier task of passing distributive policies, which have higher thresholds for conflict?[7]

If the involvement and influence of the president and party leaders vary across policy type, as the theory of policy type predicts, any discernible shift in emphasis from one policy type to another over the last forty years should signal a change in the influence on the campaign of a particular member of a governing coalition. For example, a significant increase in the number of distributive promises made from one campaign to the next may indeed reflect the dissolution of presidential governance because presidents are said to have much less influence in this arena. To evaluate the effects of party change on the possibility of constructing governing coalitions, we need to ask two questions: To what extent do presidential candidates address the different types of issues? And has the proportion of issue types changed with the evolution of the party system from the era of the brokered convention to the candidate-centered era?

Trends and Issue Types in Presidential Campaigns

The different arenas of power and the electoral consequences associated with each policy type provide an opportunity to assess whether the campaign promises made by presidential candidates vary by type over time. If a serious disjunction between campaigning and presidential governing capacity exists, it should manifest itself clearly in the proportion of distributive promises made by presidential candidates. After all, presidential candidates would be making promises in policy areas in which they are least likely to have, or desire to have, any influence. Furthermore distributive policy positions are less ideologically divisive. If political parties are becoming less relevant to the calculations and decisions that average voters make, and if the ideological distinctiveness between the two parties has faded over time, presidential candidates would need to make fewer ideological appeals to voters—ideological appeals would be less reliable as means for gaining electoral support.[8] Therefore we expect to find presidential candidates featuring more distributive policies in their campaigns.

The average proportion of a campaign agenda devoted to distributive issues over the last eleven presidential elections is 22%.[9] The average for redistributive issues is slightly higher at 25% (see table 3.1). This means that, on average, presidential candidates devote approximately half their campaign agenda to domestic policies of a distributive or redistributive character.

The 1964 and 1984 campaigns had the lowest percentages of distributive policies, 10%, whereas 1956 had the highest percentage, 46%. This finding is counter to expectations, for if distributive policy positions had increased over time, the highest percentages should have appeared in a post-reform campaign. Although some fluctuation occurs, the overall trend seems downward; that is, presidential candi-

TABLE 3.1 *Percentage of Presidential Campaign Issue Stances by Issue Type*

Year	Distributive	Redistributive
1952	26%	19%
1956	46	18
1960	28	18
1964	10	29
1968	26	23
1972	13	41
1976	20	19
1980	13	31
1984	10	29
1988	21	22
1992	24	23
Average	22%	25%
Std. dev.	10.49	7.14

dates are not taking more distributive issue stances; they are actually taking fewer as a percentage of the overall number of positions in a presidential campaign. Finally, over the last eleven presidential elections the percentage of campaign promises categorized as distributive issues seems to be somewhat unstable (see figure 3.1). The standard deviation for distributive issues is 10.49. Indeed the thirty-six percentage-point difference between the 1956 and 1984 campaigns is almost twice that which occurs between campaigns with redistributive issues.

The opposite is true for redistributive issues. Whereas the percentage of redistributive promises reached a high of nearly 41% in 1972, a post-reform campaign, and fell back to a low of only 19% in 1976, the trend appears to be upward. The campaigns with the lowest proportion of redistributive issues are 1956 and 1960. Furthermore the standard deviation for redistributive issues is one-third smaller than it is for distributive issues. It certainly seems that candidates, although taking positions on more redistributive issues, also tend to rely on them much more consistently. Indeed another way to look at the differences between distributive and redistributive issues is often the difference between low and high salience issues. As the presidential system evolved, candidates began stressing the latter as a way to attract more media attention, particularly in crowded primary fields.[10]

Table 3.2 compares the numbers by party era, namely, pre-reform versus post-reform. The percentage of policy positions on distributive issues actually declines from the pre-reform to the post-reform period.[11] With the loosening of ties between the political parties and the candidates, candidates might be expected to cobble electoral coali-

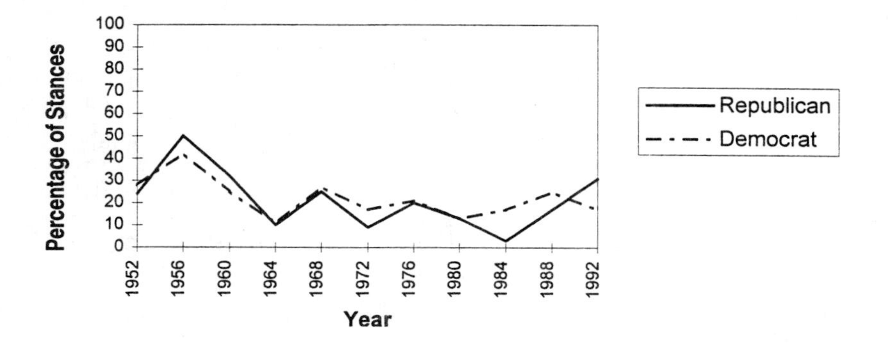

FIGURE 3.1 Distributive Policy

tions together by making large numbers of discrete promises to specific groups, most of which would be distributive in nature. But the opposite has actually transpired. The decline is rather dramatic, from roughly 27% of issue stances to 17%, a difference that is statistically significant.[12]

Furthermore it is also reasonable to expect a decline in the number of redistributive promises that candidates make. After all, as candidates tear themselves away from the influence of political parties, the traditional redistributive basis for differences between the two parties would recede. Candidates would avoid taking redistributive positions because doing so tends to polarize voters. Redistributive promises pit classes and categories of citizens against each other. Thus declaring any position on an issue of a redistributive nature presumably would attract and repel voters at the same time. Distributive promises possess the distinct political advantage of only appealing to voters, not repelling them, making their use an attractive strategy for modern candidates to pursue. But the percentage of promises categorized as redistributive actually increases by seven percentage points from the pre-reform to the post-reform era (table 3.2).[13]

These findings seem to warrant revision of our earlier speculations. As political parties shift to an ancillary role in the selection of candidates and the definition of campaign issues, presidential candidates succumb to the temptation to take more attention-grabbing redistributive stances rather than fewer. That's why the modern campaign arena prompts candidates to take redistributive positions. And although redistributive issues are more likely to attract the attention and influence of presidents as they govern, the stakes are much higher and the likelihood of success is lower, given the enlarged scope of conflict.[14] Yet presidents need to act on these redistributive issues or face retribution from their supporters at the ballot box. The occasional failure to deliver on a redistributive promise may fuel both elite and popular perceptions that the American system is indeed ungovernable.

TABLE 3.2 *Percentage of Presidential Campaign Issue Stances by Issue Type and Party Era*

	Distributive	Redistributive
Pre-reform era (1952–1968)	27%	21%
Post-reform era (1972–1992)	17	28

Apparently this generalization holds for both political parties, although the proportion of each candidate's campaign agenda devoted to distributive issues differs by political party (figure 3.1). Republican candidates from 1956 to 1964 committed a larger proportion of their promises to distributive issues than did Democratic candidates. Then in 1968 Democratic candidates began to consign larger proportions of the campaign agenda to distributive issues, a pattern that was interrupted only in 1992. As a group Democratic candidates gave a larger proportion of their agenda to distributive issues in six of the presidential elections since 1952 than the Republicans did. This finding is somewhat at odds with the prevailing wisdom that the Democratic Party is a conglomerate of disparate interests held together by the promise of the discrete benefits that an active federal government can bestow. A casual observer would expect Democrats to have the higher proportion in all the elections.

Furthermore the trends for the two parties are roughly similar (figure 3.1). Over time both parties have assigned smaller proportions of their campaigns to distributive issues. Whereas Democrats devote, on average, more attention to distributive issues, over time both parties have paid less attention to that type of issue. The similarity of the trends is not surprising, given the competitive nature of the two-party system in presidential elections. Candidates must anticipate and respond to the positions of competitors. Therefore the type and number of issues addressed by both nominees during a campaign cannot differ too drastically.

Republicans and Democrats also have strikingly similar patterns

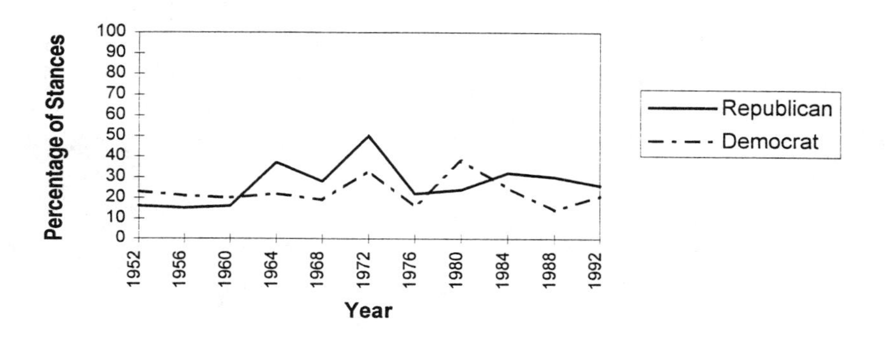

FIGURE 3.2 Redistributive Policy

for redistributive issues (see figure 3.2). Republican devotion to redistributive issues remains relatively constant across the two party eras, with the exception of 1972, at 16%. Democratic candidates are also relatively predictable in the proportion of their campaigns given to redistributive issues. Although the numbers appear to fluctuate more after 1972, the percentage of the campaign agenda devoted to redistributive issues declines slightly from the pre-reform era to the post-reform. The Republican candidates have a smaller proportion of redistributive issues in only four of the eleven elections (figure 3.2). The biggest difference between Republicans and Democrats occurs in 1972, with a 20% difference between Nixon and McGovern. Probably not too much should be made of this. Following the practice of most incumbent presidents, Nixon took comparatively few issue stances. Consequently any response he made to the redistributive proposals of McGovern would tend to skew the percentage.

Excluding 1972 as an anomaly, the largest percentage of redistributive issues appears in Carter's 1980 reelection campaign. This may have been the result of the challenge posed by Ronald Reagan and his agenda, which emphasized tax cuts and other redistributive measures. Of the eighty-four policy positions that Carter took in 1980, more than thirty were redistributive. In one debate Carter pronounced his commitment "to move toward national health insurance" and to create youth employment and training programs.[15] He also said he supported an increase in the minimum wage, a guaranteed minimum income, and an expansion of Social Security benefits.

Carter successfully used redistributive issues to attract electoral resources, such as endorsements, to create his electoral coalition. In reference to equal rights for women Carter proclaimed that the "ERA is not just a question of laws . . . it is a clarion call to end an historic injustice."[16] New York leaders of the National Organization for Women endorsed Carter's bid for reelection. They explained that Carter had committed to make the Equal Rights Amendment a "top priority," committing the "full resources of the White House and the entire Carter Administration" toward that goal.[17]

Perhaps significantly the two largest percentages of redistributive issues emphasized by Republican candidates, once again excluding Nixon in 1972, were the conservative campaigns of Barry Goldwater in 1964 and Ronald Reagan in 1984. The core of the conservative appeals in both campaigns was the promise of lower taxes and reduced spending for social programs of a redistributive nature. Goldwater opposed proposals for Medicare and favored "a regular program of automatic annual cuts in income taxes"—a program that would reduce taxes over a five-year period while holding government expenditures to their current level.[18] Finally, like many Republicans who would capture control of the House and Senate thirty years later, Goldwater also called for a "critical re-examination of federal grant and aid programs with a view to eliminating those no longer necessary and channeling the remaining ones through the states." The federal government, moreover, should "think very seriously of turning [federal] lands back to the states so they can be used profitably for taxes" at the state level of government.[19]

In his reelection campaign in 1984 President Reagan spoke firmly against any possibility of a tax increase under his administration. Not only would he not propose an increase in the personal income tax, he would "veto any tax bill that would raise personal income tax rates for working Americans or that would fail to make our tax system simpler or more fair."[20] The whole income tax system needed to be reformed, according to Reagan, and he committed to "simplify[ing] the entire tax system; to make taxes more fair, easier to understand, [and] most important, to bring [the] tax rates of every American further down, not up." Reagan also promised to continue his fight for a constitutional amendment mandating "that government spend no more than government takes in." As a second source of spending control Reagan promised to continue seeking the line-item veto. "There is no better way than the line-item veto," he said, "now used by governors in 43 states, to cut waste in government."[21] He proudly extolled his frequent use of that power during his time as governor of California. Perhaps moderating his conservative themes slightly, Reagan also favored a youth unemployment wage that would help unemployed teenagers land their first jobs.[22] Additionally he promised to seek a cost-of-living increase for Social Security benefits, even if inflation fell below the 3% that would have mandated an automatic increase.[23]

Although all candidates respond to the campaign environment, replete with demands from groups and challenges from the opponent, subtle differences between the political parties emerge when the numbers are broken down by party era and by political party (see table 3.3). An interesting finding in the pre-reform era is the larger amount of attention that Republican candidates on average devote to distributive issues as compared to Democrats. Traditionally the Democratic Party has been characterized as the party of special interests, a perception that normally would have led Democratic candidates to be more solicitous to special interest groups and the types of distributive demands that they normally make. But the one-point advantage of the Republican Party over the Democrats in the pre-reform era suggests that such a characterization may not be entirely accurate. The Democrats in the post-reform era do devote more attention to distributive issues than the Republicans, but the difference is only 2%. Indeed in 1992, the year in which Democratic presidential candidate Bill Clinton was disparaged for his public mindfulness of Democratic constituencies, he devoted only 17% of his campaign promises to distributive issues, whereas George Bush devoted 26%, a difference of nine percentage points.

Both Republican and Democratic candidates have devoted smaller proportions of their campaign agendas to distributive issues in the post-reform era. The decline is nine percentage points for the Democrats and twelve points for the Republicans (see table 3.3).[24] Conversely the nominees from the two parties in the post-reform era also consign a larger share of the campaign agenda to redistributive issues. The increase is not particularly large for Democratic candidates, only a little more than three percentage points. But the increase is nine percentage points for Republican candidates.[25]

This pattern is perhaps relevant to the prevailing perception of ungovernability. Republican candidates have won the presidency a great deal more in the post-reform era than have the Democrats. Partly because of their incumbent status and partly because of the

TABLE 3.3 *Percentage of Presidential Campaign Issue Stances by Issue Type, Party Era, and Political Party*

	Republican Candidates	
	Distributive	Redistributive
Pre-reform era (1952–1968)	28%	22%
Post-reform era (1972–1992)	16	31
	Democratic Candidates	
	Distributive	Redistributive
Pre-reform era (1952–1968)	27%	21%
Post-reform era (1972–1992)	18	24

nature of their appeals, Republicans have devoted a greater proportion of their post-reform campaign promises to redistributive issues. One consequence of this may be the creation of the perception of ungovernability because this redistributive agenda runs smack into a Congress that was, until the elections of 1994, overwhelmingly Democratic. The naturally ensuing political brouhaha between Republican presidents and Democratic Congresses is enough to convince most people that the institutions are completely and totally incapable of working together. The perception may be even worse for a Republican Congress and a Democratic president when they clash over redistributive issues. The 104th Congress, led by Speaker Newt Gingrich, was not afraid of confrontation. The subsequent shutdowns of the federal government only confirmed for voters their strong belief that the political system doesn't work.

Thus the trends in distributive and redistributive policies do not conform to expectations. The proportion of a campaign agenda devoted to distributive issues actually decreased from the pre-reform era to the post-reform era, whereas the share given to redistributive issues increased. Furthermore the two parties differ significantly in the changes they have experienced over time. The portion of the campaign agenda given to distributive issues by Republican candidates has dropped markedly, whereas the decline for Democratic candidates has been smaller. Republican candidates have also increased the share of the agenda allotted to redistributive issues. The increase is nine percentage points. The share of the agenda devoted to redistributive issues by Democratic candidates has also increased, by three percentage points. Although this rise is not as large as the Republicans', it is noteworthy.

The increase in redistributive issues is puzzling indeed. Ideology and class conflict characterize the politics of redistributive issues, features that produce unmistakable contrasts between the two parties. But political parties are said to be weaker organizationally and ideologically less cohesive than they were just thirty years ago. Consequently it seemed reasonable to expect that candidates would downplay redistributive benefits, using instead promises of discrete benefits. The irony of such a strategy is that presidents have less influence on distributive issues because of the congressional subcommittees, interest groups, and executive bureaus that dominate policy making in these issue arenas.

Although the trends in the proportion of distributive and redistributive issues are relatively similar for the two parties, this does not imply that they are saying the same thing. Candidates from the two major parties do differ in what they plan to do in these policy areas. For example, Republicans are much more likely to emphasize a decrease or a reduction in spending or benefits when discussing redistributive policies (see table 3.4).[26] Democratic candidates, on the other hand, are much more likely to say that they will increase spending on benefits of a redistributive nature. Neither party is particularly prone to maintain the policies at their current level.[27]

The differences between the two parties' candidates on increasing or decreasing support for policies do not carry over into distributive issues (see table 3.5). Candidates from both parties are much more likely to want to increase their support for a distributive issue. Democrats and Republicans show slight or insignificant differences, with Democratic candidates more likely to want to increase their support for a distributive policy.[28] Consequently both parties tend to erect electoral coalitions on the promises of support for distributive issues, which helps to explain reliance on distributive promises across the two eras for both parties.

But although presidents may have more influence in redistributive

TABLE 3.4 *Presidential Nominees' Positions on Redistributive Issues*

	Decreased Support	Status Quo	Increased Support
Republicans			
Count	68.0	4.0	101.0
Row pct.	39.3	2.3	58.4
Col. pct.	78.2	66.7	36.6
Total pct.	18.4	1.1	27.4
Democrats			
Count	19.0	2.0	175.0
Row pct.	9.7	1.0	89.3
Col. pct.	21.8	33.3	63.4
Total pct.	5.1	0.5	47.4
Pearson chi-square	46.85337		
Degress of freedom	2		
Significance	.00000		

TABLE 3.5 *Presidential Nominees' Positions on Distributive Issues*

	Decreased Support	Status Quo	Increased Support
Republicans			
Count	11.0	9.0	127.0
Row pct.	7.5	6.2	86.4
Col. pct.	52.4	69.2	40.4
Total pct.	3.2	2.6	36.5
Democrats			
Count	10.0	4.0	187.0
Row pct.	5.0	2.0	93.0
Col. pct.	47.6	30.8	59.6
Total pct.	2.9	1.1	53.7
Pearson chi-square	5.18111		
Degrees of freedom	2		
Significance	.07498		

issues, and although these issues better reflect the differences between the two parties over time, it is not clear that the candidates would do well to readjust the amount of support that they promise. The relationship between influence and success is uneven at best. Presidents may be able to take advantage of opportunities to enact redistributive measures, but many of the reasons for their success remain outside presidential control.[29] Nonetheless the candidates from both parties do appear to be making more promises of a redistributive bent, and those promises differ by political party. This increase could mean that the candidates, even though they have been freed from the control of the political parties, still rely upon their parties' traditional coalitions. Coalitions that support Democratic candidates expect support for various government programs to increase, whereas Republican candidates are telling their supporters that they will reduce or eliminate these programs. Historically and contemporaneously presidential candidates need the support of such coalitions and for the most part do not appear to be reluctant to articulate the issues, even of a redistributive sort, that can attract this support. Therefore, despite the evolution of the electoral system from party centered to candidate centered, presidential candidates cannot completely neglect the traditional coalitions that form around domestic issues.

Issue Types and Foreign Policy

Presidents are said to have the most influence and greatest chance for long-term success in foreign policy.[30] The different politics that surround domestic issues are also evident in foreign and defense policies. Three different policy types are identifiable in the areas of foreign affairs and defense: structural, strategic, and crisis.[31]

The differences in the three policies mirror differences in domestic policy. For example, structural policy is similar to distributive policy because specific constituencies dominate the most important decisions. The main participants in structural policy are legislators, defense contractors, and Pentagon officials, all of whom are highly motivated to service the needs of their clients.[32] The decisions they make are decidedly low profile, and the dominant relationships are between subcommittees and bureaus in the executive branch. Once again these relationships recall the manner of decision making in distributive issues, in which the president has little influence in the management of day-to-day affairs.

Strategic policy differs from structural policy by the amount of influence exercised by the entire Congress, the profile of the decision being made, and the influence of the executive branch. Indeed the decisions made in this issue arena are particularly prone to solution by the executive branch.[33] Consequently presidential awareness and involvement are higher than in the structural arena.

If the presidential campaigns are promoting positions on policies over which presidents have little control, the incongruity between campaigning and governing may indeed be real. But given the importance of national security and defense to the conduct of presidential campaigns and governance, we would expect that the proportion of campaign promises that presidential candidates consign to foreign policy would increase over time. Also, as campaigns have evolved toward more direct appeals over time, presidential candidates probably feature a higher percentage of structural policies in their campaigns. So what proportions of their agendas do the candidates allocate to foreign policy generally and to issues of a structural and strategic nature specifically?[34]

Of the eleven presidential campaigns 1964 had the largest proportion of foreign policy issues. Forty-eight percent of the issues were either strategic or structural. This finding is inconsistent with the idea

TABLE 3.6 *Percentage of Presidential Campaign Issue Stances by Issue Type*

Year	Structural	Strategic	Total
1952	6%	20%	26%
1956	8	18	26
1960	9	28	38
1964	8	40	48
1968	3	26	30
1972	7	14	22
1976	3	27	30
1980	7	31	38
1984	13	33	46
1988	9	25	34
1992	9	13	22
Average	7%	25%	33%
Std. dev.	2.41	8.07	8.91

that presidential candidates would be relying more upon foreign policy issues in their campaigns. Table 3.6 bears this out, even though three of the five highest proportions occur since 1972. The average for all eleven elections is 33%.

The proportion of issues that can be classified as structural or strategic has remained relatively stable over time (see table 3.6). The low for structural issues is 3% in 1968 and 1976, whereas the high is 13% in 1984. Most campaigns are between 6% and 9%. The average amount of structural issues for the last eleven presidential elections is 7% with a standard deviation of 2.41.

Strategic policy displays a little more variation, but even this issue area shows some stability. The low is 14% in 1972 and the high 40% in 1964, but most campaigns fall between 18% and 28%. The average for strategic policies over the eleven presidential elections is 25% with a standard deviation of 8.07.

The larger proportion devoted to strategic policy bodes well for the issue of presidential control of the policy-making process. Presidents potentially wield a tremendous amount of influence in strategic policy. Thus, if large amounts of the campaign agenda are pledged to strategic policies, president do indeed have the opportunity to fulfill these pledges if they can assemble the necessary governing coalitions.

TABLE 3.7 *Percentage of Presidential Campaign Issue Stances by Issue Type and Party Era*

	Structural	Strategic	Total
Pre-reform era (1952–1968)	7%	27%	33%
Post-reform era (1972–1992)	8	24	32

But of particular importance here is that presidents in fact have some control over these policies areas. The implication is that, because of electoral exigencies, presidential candidates are not making promises that they have little or no hope of actually fulfilling while in office.

The stability of the numbers is further confirmed by the averages from the two party eras (see table 3.7). The averages for the pre- and post-reform eras are almost identical, at 33% and 32%, respectively. The percentage of structural issues shows a small increase from the pre-reform to the post-reform era. If modern presidential candidates are convening electoral coalitions by promising discrete benefits to groups, they are not doing this more than they were forty years ago. Indeed the last eleven presidential elections demonstrate little variation in this area for either of the two political parties (see figure 3.3).

Strategic issues are a smaller proportion of the candidates' agendas in the post-reform era, although the decrease is only three percentage points. Almost 27% of a candidate's campaign agenda involves strategic policies in the pre-reform era; this number decreases slightly to 24% in the post-reform era.

The differences between Republicans and Democrats on structural policy never exceed 8%. But large differences between the parties

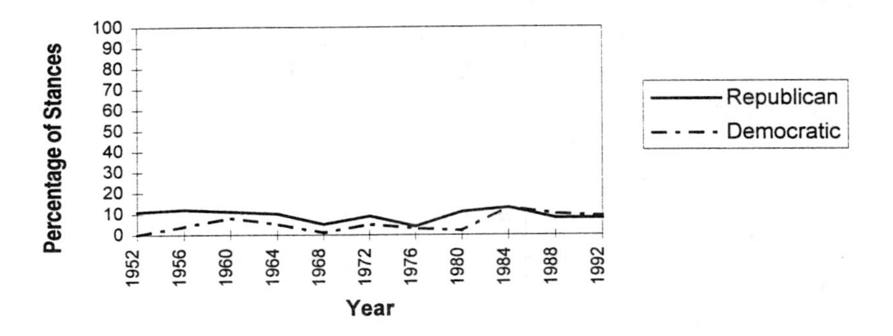

FIGURE 3.3 Structural Policy

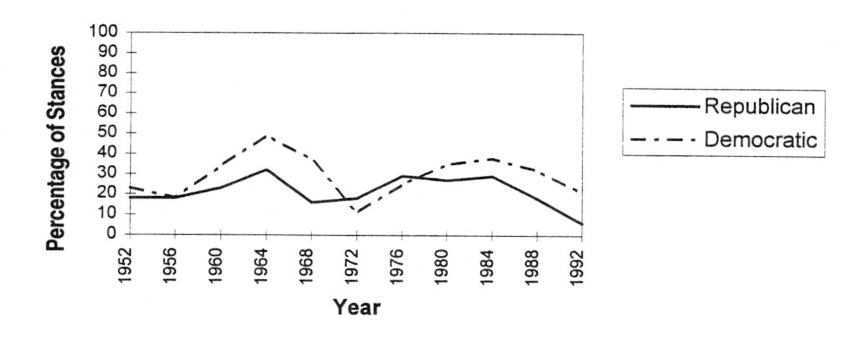

FIGURE 3.4 Strategic Policy

often emerge on the proportion of strategic policies featured in a campaign. For example, in 1988 Bush devoted 18% of his campaign agenda to strategic policies, whereas Dukakis assigned 38%. For all campaigns the average difference between the two parties on strategic policy is 10% (figure 3.4). Republican candidates do consign a larger portion of their agenda to structural issues than do the Democrats. Republican candidates devoted a larger percentage of the campaign agenda to structural issues in five out of the eleven elections. In two elections the proportions are identical. The situation is somewhat surprisingly reversed for strategic policy; in ten of the eleven elections Democratic candidates had a greater proportion of strategic issues. Finally, the two parties tend, somewhat imperfectly, to mirror each other. An increase from one election to the next in the proportion assigned by one party's nominee to one kind of issue area is usually emulated by the other party.[35] In eight presidential elections the two parties' candidates moved in the same direction on structural policy. The same is true in the area of strategic policy. Generally the trends in both issue areas tend to coincide.

However, important differences are worth mentioning (see table 3.8). The difference between the two parties on structural policy is largest in the pre-reform era but still relatively small at 6%. The difference for the post-reform period is smaller still, two percentage points.

Democratic candidates make strategic issues a larger part of their campaign agendas than do Republicans, a feature of both the pre-reform and post-reform eras (see figure 3.4). Indeed the difference between the two parties in the pre-reform era was 11%. But the gap

TABLE 3.8 *Percentage of Presidential Campaign Issue Stances by Issue Type, Party Era, and Political Party*

	Republican Candidates	
	Structural	Strategic
Pre-reform era (1952–1968)	10%	21%
Post-reform era (1972–1992)	9	21
	Democratic Candidates	
	Structural	Strategic
Pre-reform era (1952–1968)	4%	32%
Post-reform era (1972–1992)	7	27

between the two parties actually narrows in the post-reform era, although Republican campaigns did not increase their proportion of strategic policies. The difference between the two parties in the post-reform era is six percentage points.

The greater emphasis by Republicans on structural issues helps to account for, or is created by, the perceived advantage that Republican candidates enjoy in the handling of defense policy. Perhaps because Republican candidates possess a distinct advantage with voters in the area of defense policy, they tend to feature these issues more frequently than Democrats do.[36] The greater attention given to structural defense issues leaves voters and citizens alike with the impression that Republican candidates are simply more concerned about military preparedness.

But the larger proportion of strategic issues featured by Democrats is somewhat puzzling. In the post-reform era Democratic candidates have decreased the share of the campaign program given to strategic issues by 5% but still average 27%. Yet, as in defense policy, the voters do not give the same kind of faith and confidence to the Democrats that the Republicans enjoy. Democrats' comparatively larger percentage of issue stances in the strategic area may be a conscientious attempt to compensate for their weak showing in the public opinion polls.

Still, the differences between the two parties in the amount of space granted to strategic policies are not great. Perhaps the similarity can be explained by the relatively stringent environment in which campaigns take place. Candidates know that voters are interested in only a particular kind and number of issues. Consequently, when a candidate takes one position, the candidate from the opposing party has to respond, if even halfheartedly.[37] The closeness of the numbers may represent nothing more than Democrats and Republicans simply responding to each other's issue appeals. The similarity could also result from the bipartisan nature of U.S. foreign policy. But this explanation does not account for party differences in the substance of the policy.

The differences between the two parties emerge even more clearly in particular elections. The election of 1964 had the largest proportion of strategic issues for both Republicans and Democrats. However, a close examination of the issues reveals that Goldwater took aggressive military positions, whereas Johnson's stances were less aggressive and more economic. For example, Goldwater pledged to bring back the doctrine of brinkmanship and the use of limited nuclear weapons to support anti–Soviet uprisings. These policies were supported by plans to give the North Atlantic Treaty Organization (NATO) a stockpile of small conventional nuclear weapons while denying individual NATO nations control over the nuclear weapons.

Johnson, on the other hand, argued that the U.S. government is not a "government of ultimatum."[38] He also stressed the need to find peaceful settlements so that atomic power would not have to be used. He wanted to strengthen the United Nations to create a forum in which to find these peaceful settlements and sought further safeguards by supporting a test ban treaty and efforts to end all nuclear testing. Johnson also urged expansion of the Food for Peace program, called for immigration reform, and proposed a new multinational foreign aid program. To curb the influence of the Soviet Union Johnson sought economic cooperation to bring Eastern Europe closer to the West. Thus Johnson did make quite a few more strategic promises than did Goldwater, but Johnson's were not nearly as inflammatory or aggressive.

The same pattern is evident in 1984, the year with the second-highest proportion of foreign policy issues. Walter Mondale took almost twice as many strategic positions as Reagan, but Mondale's do not sound nearly as aggressive, mainly because of Reagan's tough anti-communist rhetoric. For example, Reagan called for economic and military aid to El Salvador and military aid to assist the Nicaraguan rebels. Reagan said he would send economic, social, and military aid to Central America, three-fourths of which would be military. Mondale opposed the war in Nicaragua and promised to stop it during the first one hundred days of his administration. He stressed the need for land reform in El Salvador and pledged to press for human rights in Central America. Mondale did plan to continue military aid to Honduras and El Salvador, but he wanted all foreign forces removed from Central America.

Republicans and Democrats do have identifiable differences that persist across the two party eras. These differences, like the differences in the domestic arena, demonstrate that the parties have distinctive appeals that the candidates adopt as they assemble their electoral coalitions. The distinctiveness emerges even more clearly when the structural and strategic issues are classified by direction of the promise. The Republican emphasis on defense spending is borne out by the overwhelming propensity of Republican candidates to favor increasing support for structural policies (table 3.9). Although Democratic candidates also favor spending for defense-related issues, a much larger proportion of their promises calls for decreasing defense spending. The two political parties have discernible differences in the levels of support they are willing to commit to structural policies.

The differences between the two parties do not carry over into the strategic area. Although Democratic candidates average a larger number of strategic positions, they are no more likely than Republicans to want to increase support for these strategic policies (table 3.10).

TABLE 3.9 *Presidential Nominees' Positions on Structural Issues*

	Decreased Support	Status Quo	Increased Support
Republicans			
Count	7.0	6.0	48.0
Row pct.	11.5	9.8	78.7
Col. pct.	24.1	100	63.2
Total pct.	6.3	5.4	43.2
Democrats			
Count	22.0		28.0
Row pct.	44.0		56.0
Col. pct.	75.9		36.8
Total pct.	19.8		25.2
Pearson chi-square	18.10954		
Degrees of freedom	2		
Significance	.00012		

Republicans and Democrats alike tend to support policies that have strategic implications. Indeed the order in foreign policy is a reversal of what occurs in domestic policy. Democratic candidates overwhelmingly want to increase support in the redistributive area, whereas Republicans want to reduce that support. In the distributive area the candidates from both parties tend to favor increasing support. However, the less visible arena of structural policy shows major differences in the kind of support offered by the two parties, although the more visible arena of strategic policy shows no significant differences. Republican candidates have long based their appeals to the electorate on promises of reduced domestic spending and increased defense spending. Democrats have countered this message with promises of support for domestic programs and pledges of reductions in various foreign and military programs.

As campaigns have evolved from a party-centered to a candidate-centered system, presidential candidates have resisted the temptation to load their campaigns with the appeal of distributive benefits. Several factors may explain the apparent stability in the amount of distributive appeals made in the last eleven presidential elections. First, political parties have particular constituencies to which they are beholden. These constituencies do not change dramatically over time but evolve

TABLE 3.10 *Presidential Nominees' Positions on Strategic Issues*

	Decreased Support	Status Quo	Increased Support
Republicans			
Count	20.0	7.0	113.0
Row pct.	14.3	5.0	80.7
Col. pct.	33.9	43.8	37.4
Total pct.	5.3	1.9	30.0
Democrats			
Count	39.0	9.0	189.0
Row pct.	16.5	3.8	79.7
Col. pct.	66.1	56.2	62.6
Total pct.	10.3	2.4	50.1
Pearson chi-square	.57498		
Degrees of freedom	2		
Significance	.75015		

slowly and consistently.[39] Furthermore the presidential candidates depend on a loyal core of supporters to advance their career objectives.[40] In either case the candidates cannot take the claims of the party members or the core supporters lightly. Consequently, when they do articulate promises to provide distributive benefits, presidential candidates must be ever vigilant to avoid offending traditional supporters.

Another explanation for the apparent stability in the proportion of distributive benefits mentioned in presidential campaigns has to do with the potential return of a campaign strategy that uses distributive benefits. Broad electoral coalitions are difficult to form if the only appeals are distributive, which should be true in both the pre-reform and post-reform eras. Because general election campaigns involve rallying large numbers of people to a candidacy, such a feat would be much easier to accomplish with broader appeals that create electoral coalitions whose members share more than the promise of specific gains. Without campaign issues that revive and assemble broad electoral coalitions, candidates would be hard-pressed to give their campaign the necessary national dimension. If distributive stances dominated the appeals, energizing voters in the electorally disparate states of Illinois and California would be difficult, for example. Redistributive issues are national in character and can therefore be placed in the service of the one truly national campaign in the United States.

The increase in the number of redistributive issues perhaps means that political parties are not as weak as they were thought to be or at least their ideological base is not as nondescript as the decline-in-party literature would make it out to be. Republican and Democratic candidates alike feature larger proportions of redistributive issues in their campaigns than they once did. The increase is three percentage points for Democrats and nine for Republicans (see table 3.3). Indeed the occurrence of more than distributive issues in a campaign reveals why certain practices are necessary in modern presidential campaigns. If a larger number of voters can be attracted through the broader appeals that may revive class antagonisms or ideological discord, it may be reasonable for candidates to engage in this behavior. The utility of such a strategy helps to explain the increase in the proportion of both redistributive and strategic issues across party eras. Candidates in the post-reform era might be expected to take advantage of the merits of redistributive and strategic issues; the increase in strategic issues and the stability in redistributive issues confirm this observation.

If the theory of public policy is taken seriously, the implication for presidential campaigns and governance should be clear: even in a candidate-centered electoral system candidates must contest for nomination and election under a particular party banner. Each banner has a history and an ideological foundation. This being the case, party activists and other groups have certain expectations as the candidates labor for the nomination and the presidency. Candidates cannot easily reshape these expectations in their quest for successful campaigns. Consequently they cannot entirely avoid redistributive and strategic issues, even in an effort to avoid controversial and polarizing issues. Indeed the irony of the evolution of political parties may be that candidates need to rely more on redistributive and strategic issues than they would have, had political parties maintained the organizational upper hand in the conduct of the presidential campaigns.

4

Party Leaders and Presidential Candidates: An Old Remedy for a New Problem

Perhaps more than at any other time since the institutionalization of political parties, the presidential nominating process today is most clearly defined by its openness. Presidential hopefuls organize their campaigns and press their appeals to the people relatively free of the scrutiny of party functionaries. The large number of eager Republican candidates vying for the 1996 presidential nomination attests amply to the diminished gatekeeping function of the political party. During the prelude to this election at least ten individuals were elbowing each other for the opportunity to challenge President Bill Clinton.

The consequences of this openness are manifested in the behavior of the presidential candidates and the kinds of coalitions constructed to nominate them; more specifically the changes have made it possible for the presidential candidates to disagree with the party platforms. The candidates also devote a larger proportion of their agenda to redistributive and strategic issues. Nevertheless the magnitude of these changes from the pre-reform era to the post-reform era has not been large. Candidates and their platforms still have substantial agreement, and the issues championed during presidential campaigns still reflect the ideological distinctiveness of the two major parties.

However, the possibility that the nominating and the electoral coalitions will disagree and the greater reliance on redistributive issues do reveal an instability or unpredictability in the electoral system that did not exist in either the 1950s or the 1960s. Some observers believe that this instability and unpredictability reinforce the propensity in American politics to fragment and disperse political power. The disparity between nominating and electoral coalitions, they argue, results in diminished opportunities for governing in a system in which such precious opportunities are already rare. Consequently the openness in the presidential nominating process directly or indirectly contributes to the difficulty of forming governing coalitions.

Various studies have shown that coalition building continues in this new party system despite the loss of control by party elites.[1] Certainly changes have occurred in the manner in which candidates construct coalitions and recruit support; nevertheless the activity of building coalitions, even in a somewhat altered form, seems to persist. Although candidates now control the bulk of the resources needed to build nominating and electoral coalitions, they still are subject to constraints. Candidates must still take positions on issues, which is how they retain some control over the political agenda. The decisions to discuss some issues and to neglect others identify the kind and breadth of the coalitions that the candidates hope to assemble in order to achieve electoral and finally legislative support.[2]

This chapter explores the links between a presidential candidate's electoral coalition and a key component of the governing coalition: the party leaders in Congress. Because the issues and alternatives discussed during the general election play an integral part in the formation of the political agenda, the extent to which candidates and congressional leaders hold the same policy positions provides an indicator of the prospects of forging a successful governing coalition once the presidential candidate takes office.[3] In other words, can the candidates who win the presidency under the conditions of relative openness and freedom still govern?

Party Leaders in Congress

The success of presidential initiatives depends in part on the willingness of congressional party leaders to commit their resources to the legislation. In the Introduction I defined a party leader in Congress as one of the following: president pro tempore of the Senate, Speaker of the House of Representatives, Senate majority leader, Senate minority leader, Senate majority whip, Senate minority whip, House majority leader, House minority leader, House majority whip, or House minority whip.[4] These are the leaders who are critically important to the passage of a president's legislative program. For example, party leaders in general and the Speaker in particular can use House rules to promote the agenda of the president of the United States, especially if the leader and president are members of the same party. Conversely they can use these rules to thwart the wishes of the minority party or the president.

As the chief officer of the House the Speaker "rules on parliamentary questions, decides which members will be recognized to speak or offer amendments, determines voice and division votes, and refers bills to committees."[5] According to former Speaker Tip O'Neill, "The most important power [of the Speaker] is to set the agenda, and if he doesn't want a certain bill to come up, it usually doesn't."[6] Control of the House agenda often involves the manipulation of House rules and procedures. The Speaker often controls the legislative process by scheduling bills as favors to members or by postponing a vote if a member will be out of town when the bill is to be considered.[7] Conversely the Speaker can make the legislative process difficult for the minority party. Speaker Newt Gingrich lost a vote on an environmental issue and then brought the issue to a vote when a number of Democrats were out of town and the GOP had enough votes to prevail. As the person who stands astride the legislation that moves through the House, the Speaker thus controls a valuable resource that all other members need.

Congressional leaders can use more subtle forms of control to achieve a semblance of party discipline. These forms include appointing members to special committees or task forces, intervening with the White House or the bureaucracy on behalf of a member, and helping to organize campaign contributions for the reelection efforts of a member.[8] Often the Speaker will create a special task force or committee to investigate a special issue or to get a bill through Congress. By appointing members to these task forces the Speaker gives the members a chance to gain some prestige and publicity both inside and outside the House, while the Speaker gains the representative's support for the bill.[9]

The Speaker also can gain the attention of the White House or heads of agencies in ways that a regular member cannot. If the member needs the help of an agency within the executive branch to perform a service for a constituent back home, the Speaker, by intervening on behalf of the representative, can create a reservoir of goodwill. The Speaker may later tap this reservoir to obtain support for a key party proposal. Finally, the Speaker can help a representative with the unpleasant task of raising campaign money. An appearance at a fundraising dinner in the member's district can go a long way to boost contributions and to create in the district the idea that the member is important and powerful in the daily business of the House of Representatives.[10] For these kinds of services the Speaker will certainly expect future support. Such favors do not usually go unrecognized by members of Congress. Consequently bills that have the backing of the party leadership and to which the leadership has committed its "scarce resources" are much more likely to clear the numerous obstacles in the legislative process.[11]

It is important to recognize that each Speaker uses these resources in highly individualized ways. Ultimately a leader's greatest resources are personal characteristics. The essence of a party leader's power lies in the ability to create compromises, draft quality legislation, and efficiently organize the business of the House. These qualities attract in return the admiration, respect, and loyalty of party colleagues.[12]

In performing all these duties the Speaker of the House relies on the assistance of the majority leader. The primary task of the majority leader is maintaining the House party organization to ensure the passage of legislation deemed critical to the party. This task is accomplished by coordinating with committee chairs and members, by helping to forge compromises between factions, and by publicly articulating and defending the party's positions.[13]

Both the Speaker and the majority leader depend on the work of whips to organize the support necessary to keep legislation moving through the House. Whips of both parties have essentially two critical tasks: to converse with representatives about party views and to gather information about the representatives' views on legislation so that the political leaders can best determine how to get legislation enacted.[14] Whips act as arms of the political party to persuade party members of the need to support the party leadership or in some cases to inform party members how to vote. In this sense the party leadership acts as a valuable determinate of congressional action.[15] The leaders also perform services useful to the representatives because most have neither the time nor the inclination to stay current on all matters before the House.

The Constitution mentions two leaders in the Senate: the president pro tempore and the vice president of the United States. Both are designated as the formal leaders of the Senate. The majority party in the Senate selects the majority leader and the president pro tem of the Senate. Of these two positions the majority leader wields considerably more influence. The president pro tem has traditionally been the most senior member of the majority party. Little power is associated with the office of the president pro tem, and the duties are largely ceremonial. Any power held by the president pro tem emanates largely from other posts, such as chair of a key committee.[16]

The Senate majority leader must often speak and plan for the interests of all one hundred members of the Senate and is responsible for leading the majority party in the formulation of policy.[17] Yet the leader also has the formal duty of scheduling the business of the Senate. This is no simple task because the majority leader is expected to accommodate the schedules and demands of *all* senators, not just those senators from the majority party. Furthermore the majority leader is in charge of overseeing the business on the floor. This charge demands that the floor leader seek "unanimous consent agreements," which regulate the amount of time that senators can spend on debates and votes. In addition to performing these procedural duties the majority leader acts as the main link to the Senate, White House, and House of Representatives.[18] In addition, any media coverage of the Senate is likely to be about its leaders.[19] Today's majority leaders are expected to be articulate in front of television cameras as well as capable builders of legislative coalitions.

To discharge all these functions the Senate majority leader is assisted by the majority whip. The majority whip in the Senate performs essentially the same tasks as the majority whip in the House. However, the Senate position differs qualitatively from the position in the House because the Senate is not as large as the House. With only one hundred members a more collegial atmosphere pervades the Senate. The majority whip can be more familiar with the personalities and needs of the members, an element that helps to prevent surprises from occurring on the floor.

Minority leaders are included in this study because of the influence that they can have on legislation. A minority leader is responsible for the president's program if the president's party does not have a majority in that chamber. Although the minority leader does not have the resources of the Speaker or the majority leaders, a minority leader is a potentially important asset in the president's efforts to get the legislative program enacted. Without the support of these leaders the president's program would have less chance of success.[20]

Despite the resources available to party leaders and the pervasiveness of parties in Congress, strict and consistent party government seems to be beyond the capabilities of the U.S. system.[21] Party leadership can be strong, but the overall ability of parties to lead is inconsistent because of will and circumstance. The powers that even the most assertive party leaders in Congress claim for themselves are not sufficient to enforce conformity in an institution that is increasingly characterized by the individual styles of its members and by diffused authority.[22]

Members of Congress are subject to several competing pressures. Constituents in the district and state, interest groups, party leaders in Congress, and the member's interests and ideology create an environment with many variables.[23] If the party were the most important influence, the representative would be less inclined to vote against a position articulated by the party. Yet this is clearly not the case. Although levels of party voting remain relatively high, they remain far below the levels achieved in other nations.[24] Because senators and representatives owe little to the party in terms of their election, their allegiances always rest with those forces that are chiefly responsible for their election to Congress.[25] This situation reflects the differences in the goals of the representatives and the political parties. In the words of Gary Jacobson, "The collective interests of a party do not coincide with the individual interests of each of its candidates."[26] In other words, most representatives will be slow to vote for or against legislation that the party leaders want if a majority of voters in the representative's district could find the measure controversial.

Party leaders have sought to soften the effects of countervailing pressures by restructuring the rules that govern consideration of legislation in the chamber, but no iron-clad mechanisms exist to prevent the representative from voting against the party if the vote could jeopardize a reelection bid.[27]

Moreover, despite efforts to centralize legislative activity, the organization of the modern Congress still offers numerous opportunities and even encourages individual members to pursue individual goals.[28] Power in the House, even in the wake of Republican reforms, devolves toward committees, subcommittees, and their chairs. Even highly publicized cuts in staff belie committees and subcommittees with full-time staffs, rules that guarantee that important legislation will be sent to them, and sources of funding. With the proliferation of committees and subcommittees legislators in both chambers of Congress have a real opportunity to influence legislation and to leave their mark on public policy. Thus legislators in the U.S. Congress do not always find it in their best interest to follow a collective strategy when electoral security, more power, or prestige may result from individual pursuits.

All signs seem to indicate that the role played by political parties in Congress will remain significant. But so long as representatives and senators are responsible for their own elections, so long as the House and Senate remain organized in a way that maximizes each member's participation in public policy, and so long as the electorate seems more concerned with the personal characteristics of congressional candidates than with party identification, political parties can have little hope of increasing the influence they wield in both houses of Congress. The only hope for a party that is effective in government is to continue to elect strong active leaders who are committed to the parties' proposals and who are from the mainstream of their political party. Otherwise the centrifugal pressures in Congress will prevail, and what little resources the political parties and the president possess to construct governing coalitions will disappear altogether.

During the period from 1952 to 1968 congressional leaders from both political parties participated actively in the nomination of their respective presidential candidates. Indeed the support of key congressional leaders was considered crucial in securing the party's presidential nomination. These congressional leaders usually controlled large delegate slates that had to be courted to obtain the nomination. Furthermore an endorsement or a commitment from a congressional leader demonstrated that the political skills and beliefs of the presidential candidate were held in reasonably high esteem.

The support of congressional leaders was indispensable once the candidate took office. If the candidate and the congressional leaders enjoyed a good working relationship and respected each other, the chances for executive-congressional cooperation certainly improved when the task of governing began. Presidential candidates actively courted the support of congressional leaders and other members of Congress during the general election period.

The election period has always provided the opportunity for congressional leaders and presidential candidates alike to state their positions on issues. The presidential candidates, moreover, are constrained by a number of factors when choosing to state a certain position, one of which is the effect that it will have on congressional leaders. The candidate who is concerned about upsetting congressional leaders might try to avoid taking positions that are contrary to the stated positions of the leaders. Sometimes the leaders stake out positions in the hope of influencing the presidential candidate on a certain issue. But more often than not the candidate has incentive to fudge on various issues so as to provoke neither the electorate nor the party leaders in Congress.[29]

With such factors in mind the general election should be viewed as an attempt by the presidential contenders to balance the interests of their electoral coalition and their governing coalition. Sometimes the two coalitions are clearly at odds, and the candidate faces the difficult choice of taking a position that is against the wishes of either the general electorate or a congressional leader. For example, Bill Clinton criticized Congress quite heavily during the primary and general election campaigns for becoming embroiled in several scandals. The criticisms were not popular on the Hill, especially among the Democratic leadership, and some said the criticism could cost the candidate important support were he to win the presidency.[30] But because of the unpopularity of Congress in the general population, Clinton may have found it difficult, for electoral reasons, to resist the urge to chide the institution for its practices and scandals.

The question confronting American democracy in the wake of such significant electoral changes is whether the current electoral system increases the frequency of conflict with party leaders. Are presidential candidates and congressional leaders less likely to agree because congressional leaders are not as active in general campaigns as they once were? Are presidential candidates sufficiently liberated from the constraints of party to articulate positions that will appeal to a majority of voters, or do ideology and concern for the party program still provide some link between the leaders and the candidates? Answers to such questions are not easy to find, and little research has examined where the positions of presidential candidates and party leaders in Congress might intersect during the election cycle.

Presidential Candidates and Party Leaders: The Development of Separate Coalitions?

The changes in the party system since the mid-1950s have certainly transformed the way that presidential candidates are nominated for and elected to office. Consequently we might reasonably expect some loosening of the ties that bind congressional candidates to presidential hopefuls. To determine how loose those ties have become we must evaluate the issue stances of congressional leaders and systematically compare their stances to the positions articulated by presidential candidates. If the comparison shows wide areas of agreement, we can conclude that some ideological bases for governance persist in the face of perpetual change in the party system generally and the nominating system specifically. In other words, the fragmentation in the nomination process means that we can expect a congressional leader's rate of agreement with the presidential candidates to decrease over time.[31]

I first compared the policy positions of Democratic and Republican congressional leaders to those espoused by their respective presidential candidates. The data from 1952 to 1992 show that agreement between the Democratic leaders in Congress and their presidential candidates ranges from a low of 2% in 1964 to a high of 19% in 1976 and 1992 (see table 4.1). These findings are at odds with our initial expectations. The highest rates of agreement between Democratic leaders and their presidential candidates should show up in the pre-reform era. (The average rate of agreement for the eleven elections is 12%. The rate of agreement between Democratic leaders in Congress and the Democratic presidential candidates fluctuates moderately over time because the standard deviation is 5.58 [see table 4.1].)

The story is quite different for Republican leaders. Their level of agreement achieves its highest points in 1952 and 1972 at 15%. Then their agreement rate remains relatively stable for the next ten elections, never going above 13%. Indeed most elections never exceed 11%. The parties' average rate of agreement also differs; the Republican average is 9%, which is three percentage points lower than the Democratic average. Although Democratic leaders and their presidential candidates have a higher average rate of agreement, the Republican rate tends not to fluctuate nearly as much, with a standard deviation of 4.23.

At first glance the relatively low rates of agreement for both Dem-

TABLE 4.1 *Rates of Agreement Between Congressional Leaders and Presidential Candidates from the Same Party**

Year	Democrats	Republicans
1952	13%	15%
1956	4	8
1960	18	11
1964	2	11
1968	11	8
1972	5	15
1976	19	1
1980	14	3
1984	13	13
1988	13	6
1992	19	8
Average	12%	9%
Std. dev.	5.58	4.23

*Percentages are rounded. Data are from the *New York Times* and *Congressional Quarterly Weekly Report.* The issue positions of Republican and Democratic congressional leaders are compared to the issue positions of candidates from their respective parties.

ocrats and Republicans appear to support the theory that the decline of the political parties has resulted in a corresponding decline of governability, that is, in a decline in the links between the electoral coalition and one segment of the governing coalition. But the percentage of agreement between the Democratic candidates and the Democratic congressional leaders actually is greater and more consistent from 1972 to 1992 than in the earlier era. The percentages of agreement in 1976 (19%), 1980 (14%), and 1992 (19%) are three of the four largest rates of agreement documented and are comparable to the largest percentage from the pre-reform era, which was 18% in 1960 (see table 4.1). If the electoral and governing coalitions were actually splitting as a result of reforms in the party system since 1972, the results for 1976, 1980, and 1992 are counter to what we would expect.

Republicans did indeed show a decline from the high rate of agreement they achieved in 1952. A rather large decline occurred in the next election, followed by some recovery and then a rather large dropoff in 1976. In 1984 the percentage of agreement increased and then declined once again in 1988. A modest increase in the rate of agreement marked the 1992 campaign, but that rate is still below the 15% attained in 1952.

The differences between Democrats and Republicans may be partly the result of status. The Democratic Party controlled the House for all but two years from 1952 to 1992 and the Senate for all but six years. A minority party in Congress may have little incentive or opportunity to stake out national issues, especially when some leaders see conciliation or accommodation as a means for gaining the favor of the party that controls the chamber.[32] Another explanation for the differences may rest in the kind of media coverage given to a party prone to minority status during this forty-year period. Congress receives little coverage compared to the presidency; precious air time and print space are not lavished on what some regard as minor players in a subordinate institution.[33]

Rates of agreement do not tell the entire story. Disagreements may occur more frequently because of the dissolution of bonds between party leaders and presidential candidates. Repercussions for staking out positions that are critical of Congress or disagree entirely with positions articulated by its leaders are much less dire for modern presidential candidates; they do not rely on congressional leaders for delegate slates or campaign funds. Consequently the fragmentation in the nomination process may mean that a congressional leader's rate of disagreement with the presidential candidates may have increased over time.

Even with the involvement of party leaders, disagreement certainly has never been out of the question. But it occurs much less frequently than we might expect, particularly in light of the major changes in the party system. Furthermore the overall level of disagreement between the congressional leaders and the Democratic candidates has remained relatively stable and indeed even shows a slight decline from 1952 to 1992. The same trends hold true for Republican presidential candidates: low rates of disagreement that do not vary much from election to election. In fact the standard deviations for both parties are similar (see table 4.2).

The highest rate of disagreement between Democrats, 9%, occurs in 1972, the year the party nominated what was arguably its most liberal candidate. The second-highest rate appears in 1952, an election in which the party struggled with its conservative heritage in the South. Republicans disagreed the most in both 1960 and 1968 when Richard Nixon was the candidate. The high rates occurring in these elections

TABLE 4.2 *Rates of Disagreement Between Congressional Leaders and Presidential Candidates from the Same Party**

Year	Democrats	Republicans
1952	8%	2%
1956	1	2
1960	1	5
1964	0	3
1968	3	5
1972	9	1
1976	1	0
1980	2	2
1984	3	2
1988	3	1
1992	2	1
Average	3%	2%
Std. dev.	2.76	1.57

*Percentages are rounded. Data are from the *New York Times* and *Congressional Quarterly Weekly Report*. The issue positions of Republican and Democratic congressional leaders are compared to the issue positions of candidates from their respective parties.

lend credence to the idea that Nixon was indeed more liberal, at least on some social policies, than large segments of his party.

As the last of the premodern campaigns or the first of the modern campaigns, the 1952 campaign tested the relationships between party leaders and presidential candidates in an era in which party leaders and presidential candidates closely collaborated. General Dwight Eisenhower's primary competition for the Republican nomination was Senator Robert A. Taft of Ohio, already the spokesman for the conservative wing of his party and the man who would become the Senate majority leader when the Republicans captured the Senate. This contest between Eisenhower and Taft could have produced problems for the Republican Party and Eisenhower. But in a highly publicized meeting between the two shortly after Eisenhower won the nomination, they came to an agreement on basic issues, which allowed Taft to campaign on Eisenhower's behalf in the general election. After this meeting Taft issued a statement that said,

> I am convinced that he [Eisenhower] will carry out the pledges of the Republican platform, which expresses that philosophy,

adopted unanimously by Republican representatives from all parts of the country under the leadership of Senator Millikin. I recognize, of course, that the platform is not specific in every regard and that the candidate must have the right to develop the details of the program within the general spirit of the platform.[34]

Taft went on, commenting that "I cannot say that I agree with all of General Eisenhower's views on the foreign policy to be pursued in Europe and the rest of the world, but I think it is fair to say that our differences are differences of degree."[35] Taft then emphasized the areas in which he and Eisenhower found broad agreement. These areas included the need to hold government spending in check, halt the spread of communism, and restrain the growth of federal power. For these reasons Taft strongly endorsed the candidacy of Eisenhower and pledged to undertake a busy schedule of campaigning, mostly in the Midwest, to ensure the nominee's election.

Other Republican Party leaders were active as well. Senator Leverett Saltonstall of Massachusetts, the Senate minority whip in the 82d Congress and the Senate majority whip in the 83d, was actively involved in the campaign and publicized his opinion on issues. Senator Styles Bridges of New Hampshire, the Senate minority leader and later the president pro tempore, also worked in Eisenhower's campaign. Eisenhower also had the support of a number of key Republican representatives and senators early in the campaign season. On February 22, 1952, several members of Congress sent a letter to Eisenhower urging him to seek the nomination of the Republican Party. They stated that the people of the United States wanted him as their leader and that numerous critical issues demanded Eisenhower's unique brand of statesmanship and leadership. They concluded the letter by writing, "We are practical and not hysterical and venture the thought that perhaps you do not fully appreciate the serious state of our country's domestic affairs. We pledge ourselves to your leadership without thought of any kind of reward—what we want to do is to save America and promote peace."[36]

The involvement of Taft and other Republican leaders did not mean perfect harmony between them and General Eisenhower. Taft and Eisenhower differed on policies ranging from farm price supports to the constitutionality of the Korean War. Taft believed that the parity program, if it was to exist at all, should be flexible, with no specific percentage of support. Eisenhower favored price support of at least 90% of parity and wanted to achieve 100% parity. All these policies are evidence of Eisenhower's moderate course and his attempts to balance the needs of his nominating coalition with the need to broaden his electoral coalition.

In foreign policy Taft stated that communist-controlled countries must be liberated by infiltrating at certain weak points. Eisenhower took a more conciliatory stance and promised liberation for these countries through "peaceful means." Taft was also much less committed to foreign aid for the defense and economic rebuilding of Europe than Eisenhower; both Democrats and Republicans often called Taft an isolationist. But the two men did not let disagreement on foreign policy poison the general campaign. Instead Taft tended to emphasize the similarities between him and Eisenhower. Thus Taft stressed his commitment to a reduction of the federal budget and taxes, both of which are traditional Republican issues.

These efforts at reconciliation apparently paid dividends during the governing phase as well as during the election. As President Eisenhower later wrote in 1954, "Of all the legislative leaders with whom I thought in advance, that I would have constant trouble, there was none with whom incessant difficulty seemed more probable than with Senator Taft. While Senator Taft was, as I saw him, far more personal in his attitude toward politics than I could ever be, yet in his case the exact reverse came about."[37]

President Eisenhower went on to say that he considered Taft to be his "ablest associate on the Hill, and indeed one of the stalwarts of the Administration." Moreover Eisenhower wrote, "In actual practice, whenever differences developed between the White House and some of our Republican Senators on matters of importance, we could count on Senator Taft to assert his great influence to bring them into line" (p. 6).

During the general campaign and throughout his time in office Taft seemed to moderate some of his earlier stances, and President Eisenhower wrote that "I found him extraordinarily 'leftish'" (p. 6). But the disagreements that persisted between Eisenhower and other members of his party would later push Eisenhower toward coalitions outside the Republican Party.[38]

An interesting disagreement with a party leader occurred in regard to civil rights. In 1952 Republican senator Leverett Saltonstall favored a fair employment practices law, which Eisenhower opposed. This disagreement highlights the precarious position that Eisenhower occupied between the liberal and conservative wings of his party.

Eisenhower's campaign and subsequent governing experience were not unique for the pre-reform era of the American party system. The presidential candidate needed support from party leaders in the nominating, electoral, and governing phases. The interaction between the candidates and the congressional leaders in the first two phases proved eminently useful in the third, or governing, phase. This interaction is one resource said to have disappeared in the post-reform era and is thought to be at least partly responsible for the gridlock gripping the nation's institutions. However, the lack of interaction does not seem to have undermined the capacity of party leaders and congressional leaders to agree on issues.

The campaign of 1960 between Kennedy and Nixon also tested the relationships between congressional leaders and candidates, although perhaps not as rigorously as the 1952 campaign. And unlike 1952 there was significant agreement between the Democratic candidate and his party and little agreement between the Republican and his party. Kennedy enjoyed the benefits of substantial agreement with the congressional leaders. But this high rate of agreement did not magically appear. Kennedy worked hard to make himself acceptable to the liberal wing of the Democratic Party, which was not easy because of Kennedy's earlier reluctance to condemn McCarthyism publicly. Contrary to the rumors circulated during the 1960 campaign, Kennedy never did display even the smallest support for Joseph McCarthy. But he did not condemn McCarthy as ardently as some people would have liked because of Joseph Kennedy Sr.'s relationship with the senator.[39]

Kennedy acknowledged that he had arrived at his liberalism through a rather circuitous route. Schlesinger writes that Kennedy had explained to James MacGregor Burns, "Some people have their liberalism 'made' by the time they reach their late twenties. I didn't. I was caught in cross currents and eddies. It was only later that I got into the stream of things."[40] But by the time Kennedy captured the nomination, his liberalism was sufficiently established to attract the support of senators like Hubert Humphrey of Minnesota.

Throughout the campaign season Humphrey took a number of policy positions. In fact Humphrey had the most positions of any party leader in 1960, and the bulk of these concerned foreign policy.

Humphrey and Kennedy promoted the development of a Marshall plan for Latin American countries and articulated the need for new mechanisms to distribute the money. Furthermore Humphrey advocated, like Kennedy, the creation of a national peace agency. They agreed that this agency would not be responsible for policy but would research new methods for dealing with nuclear arms and their regulation. Humphrey also called for the establishment of an international space peace agency, but Kennedy did not mention this proposal during the campaign.

Humphrey also articulated a liberal agenda for domestic policy. He called for "the establishment of a broad system of health insurance for retired workers" and for an increase in federal aid for areas in the country that continually suffered high levels of unemployment.[41] Kennedy articulated both positions during his campaign.

Humphrey was not the only Democratic congressional leader with whom Kennedy agreed. The House majority leader, John McCormack of Massachusetts, and Kennedy called for federal aid for the construction of schools. This issue was particularly divisive because it involved the problem of local versus federal control of schools. Conservatives feared that federal aid for school construction was simply a pretext for the federal government to assert control over the content and management of local school programs. For this reason Everett Dirksen of Illinois, the Senate minority leader, was adamantly opposed to any kind of federal aid for classroom construction and renovation.

Another important element of Kennedy's liberal agenda included an increase in the federal minimum wage from $1 to $1.25. Both McCormack and Speaker Sam Rayburn heartily supported this proposal. These agreements on policy provided Kennedy with the critical support he would later need in Congress to ensure passage of his far-reaching domestic agenda.

But as in the 1952 campaign the Democratic nominee and members of the Democratic leadership in Congress disagreed on some points. The first disagreement was with Rayburn. Kennedy stated during the campaign that he would reassess all the depletion allowances, and if he found any inequities in oil or in any other commodity, he would seek to eliminate that allowance. Rayburn, who represented the oil-rich state of Texas, favored the continuation of the oil depletion allowance. In 1952 Rayburn had similarly disagreed with Stevenson over the ownership of offshore oil lands.

These are clear examples of how disagreements can occur in presidential campaigns. Rayburn obviously acted out of concern for the interests of his constituents in Texas, which led him to oppose measures he believed would harm the oil industry in his state. Kennedy courted a national constituency and advocated policies he deemed would best serve the national interest. But this disagreement did not prevent Rayburn from working for Kennedy's election, just as the disagreement with Stevenson in 1952 did not keep him from trying to deliver Texas for the Stevenson campaign.

Another disagreement with a Democratic congressional leader arose over nuclear testing. Kennedy stated during the campaign that he opposed any immediate resumption of nuclear testing. Humphrey, on the other hand, called for a "resumption of underground nuclear testing by June of 1961 if no agreement to ban such tests had been reached with the Soviet Union."[42] This disagreement did not seem to cause any serious problems within the Democratic coalition.

In two cases Kennedy agreed with the positions of a Republican leader. Thomas Kuchel of California, the Senate minority whip, believed that the United States should bear the ever increasing cost of foreign aid. This position was not insignificant because the Republican Party was still attempting to shed the remnants of its isolationist past. Kennedy too wanted more money for foreign aid.

The second case involved a civil rights issue. Senators Kuchel and Humphrey favored changing Senate Rule 22—the rule that essentially permitted filibuster by requiring a two-thirds majority to stop debate in the Senate and allow voting on an issue. Dixiecrats had used the filibuster to prevent passage of civil rights legislation. Kennedy expressed his complete commitment to the Democratic platform plank on civil rights, which included the "duty of Congress to enact the laws necessary and proper to protect and promote these constitutional rights."[43] Earlier the Democratic platform called on Congress "to improve Congressional procedures so that majority rule prevails and decisions can be made after reasonable debate without being blocked by a minority in either House."[44] These two examples demonstrate bipartisan support for issues that were extremely important to Kennedy as president. Such support can do much to ensure the success of a legislative agenda.

Nixon's relationship with his party's leaders was not as clear. Many of the issue stances of the congressional leaders found no mention in the positions of Nixon, and those positions that Nixon did mention were most frequently those of Democratic leaders, which suggests that Nixon was not inclined to take the Republican Party back to the days of the hard-line conservatives. Like Eisenhower, Nixon realized that many programs of the New Deal were important and that these benefits should be preserved. A disagreement between Nixon and Dirksen underscored this last point. Nixon believed in giving some kind of federal aid to needy school districts for classroom construction. Dirksen was opposed, and their disagreement highlights the tensions that still existed between the members of the conservative and moderate factions of the Republican Party.

Like Kennedy, Nixon agreed with Humphrey on the creation of a system of national health insurance for retired workers. Furthermore Nixon believed, as did Humphrey and Kuchel, that the Senate rules should be modified to allow easier passage of civil rights legislation. On these issues Nixon's domestic concerns paralleled the agenda of many Democrats.

Unlike Kennedy, Nixon agreed with Rayburn about retaining the oil depletion allowance. This issue represented the traditional affinity of the Republican Party for large companies, particularly the oil companies, and the states in which they were headquartered.This agreement also recalls the agreement of Eisenhower and Rayburn on the issue of state ownership of offshore oil lands.

Overall the issue stances of congressional leaders received a mixed review from Richard Nixon. He agreed with some positions of Democratic leaders, but he also did not have a position on many of the issues stressed by congressional leaders. This fact underscores the trouble that Nixon had with the two major coalitions within the Republican Party. The Rockefeller wing demanded moderate but progressive policies from Nixon in order to guarantee its support during the general election. Nixon agreed with a number of its positions, but Nixon clearly was trapped between the moderate wing and the more conservative wing. This dilemma probably accounted for the many positions of the congressional leaders that Nixon did not mention. Indeed if Nixon had been elected, he might have had serious difficulties with his party in Congress.

When the numbers are separated by party era, the two political parties show some remarkable differences. The average rate of agreement for Democratic candidates has actually increased from 10% to 14%, a rise that runs counter to what the decline-in-party literature suggests (see table 4.3). The decline in the Republican rate of agreement is certainly more compatible with the notion of decline, but the decrease is slight, only three percentage points. Furthermore the average rate of disagreement for both Republicans and Democrats is stable across the two party eras and actually decreases for Republicans. Perhaps the most interesting finding is the large differences between Republicans and Democrats in the two eras (see table 4.3). Only one percentage point separates their rate of agreement in the pre-reform era, but the gap widens to 6% in the post-reform era.

The differences between the Democratic and Republican candidates in their agreement with congressional leaders suggest the need to treat the two parties differently in assessing the possibilities for governing. Each party possesses a distinct history, ideology, and unique organizational mechanisms for achieving its electoral and program goals. Furthermore the strengths of their respective coalitions are different. The Republicans have always possessed a close-knit nominating coalition, which makes it easier for them to put forth the candidate who has a reasonable chance of winning. On the other hand the Democrats have recently had trouble nominating candidates who appeal to the broader electorate, even though the candidates may agree substantially with the positions of the party leaders. Finally, the minority status of Republicans during most of the last forty years may have taken its toll. Republican presidential candidates may not

TABLE 4.3 *Average Rates of Agreement and Disagreement Between Congressional Leaders and Presidential Candidates from the Same Party and by Party Era*[*]

	Agreement	
	Democratic	Republican
Pre-reform era (1952–1968)	10%	11%
Post-reform era (1972–1992)	14	8
	Disagreement	
	Democratic	Republican
Pre-reform era (1952–1968)	3%	3%
Post-reform era (1972–1992)	3	1

[*]Percentages are rounded. Data are from the *New York Times* and *Congressional Quarterly Weekly Report*. The issue positions of Republican and Democratic congressional leaders are compared to the issue positions of candidates from their respective parties.

have viewed the congressional leaders as elements important to consult in the nominating and electoral phases because they were likely to be in the minority for the governing phase. A Republican candidate who keeps one eye on the Democrats in Congress and believes that Republicans in Congress would do the president's bidding anyway would have little need to collaborate.[45]

The persistence of agreement between presidential candidates and their party's congressional leaders is only part of the picture. Shifting party coalitions mean that presidential candidates and congressional leaders from the opposition party may be in agreement. Such agreement may be further proof that the dire consequences that seem to flow from the decline-in-party thesis are not being realized. If congressional leaders and presidential candidates agree on various issues, does it matter that they come from different parties? At times party leaders certainly do find it in their best interest to oppose a president even if their policy stances are congruent. However, congressional leaders from the opposition also have often have gone out of their way to forge alliances with presidents. The question that concerns us here is whether the increasingly candidate-centered party system means that the opportunity to forge governing coalitions, whether those coalitions are party or cross-party based, endure over time. Therefore we need to evaluate the extent to which presidential candidates agree with the issue positions of congressional leaders from both parties.

The relatively high levels of agreement between the congressional leaders from both parties and the presidential candidates undermine the contention that the advent of a candidate-centered electoral system produces frayed governing coalitions. The average rate of agreement is 19% for Democrats and 15% for Republicans. The highest combined rate (the rate at which a candidate agrees with congressional leaders from both parties) occurs in 1952 with Adlai Stevenson, a candidate who articulated a moderate political philosophy. The rate of agreement has fluctuated for both parties, but like other measures the standard deviation for Republicans is smaller (see table 4.4).

The rate of agreement has been relatively high since the 1984 election. Democratic nominees average a 21% rate of agreement since 1984, whereas the Republican nominees average 15% during the same period (see table 4.4). If the candidate-centered tendencies had indeed produced residual effects in the governing arena, we would expect the rates of agreement to have declined, especially over the last several elections.

Interestingly enough the Republican nominees enjoy the highest rate of agreement with congressional leaders from both parties in 1972, the year Nixon sought and won reelection. During the election campaign of 1972 the congressional leaders were confronted with two candidates who were quite different ideologically. The strategic as well as ideological differences between the two candidates are evident in the different rates of agreement (see table 4.4). Whereas Nixon may have had problems forming governing coalitions with members of his own party, he avoided the perils to some extent because of the agreement he had with Democratic leaders. Indeed many issues addressed by the congressional leaders were considered controversial. Taking positions on several of these issues would have been risky for the president. It is always better to let the electorate guess at your position or at least to be presidential enough to transcend issue differences.

Nixon did have support among some Republican congressional leaders for his policies regarding the Vietnam War. Gerald Ford of Michigan, the House minority leader, and Robert P. Griffin of

TABLE 4.4 *Rates of Agreement Between Congressional Leaders from Both Parties and Presidential Candidates**

Year	Democrats	Republicans
1952	33%	21%
1956	10	8
1960	29	20
1964	4	13
1968	22	15
1972	10	23
1976	25	12
1980	16	8
1984	21	16
1988	19	13
1992	23	17
Average	19%	15%
Std. dev.	8.3	4.72

*Percentages are rounded. Data are from both the *Congressional Quarterly Weekly Report* and *New York Times*. The issue positions of Republican and Democratic congressional leaders are compared to the issue positions of candidates from both political parties.

Michigan, the Senate minority whip, agreed with Nixon's policy of mining the harbors of North Vietnam. Furthermore Hugh Doggett Scott Jr. of Pennsylvania, the Senate majority leader, called for an increase in defense spending, a policy also advocated by Nixon. And although Nixon did not comment on this policy, Ford and Scott voiced their opposition to the Democratic candidate's promise to stop the flow of arms to South Vietnam and to retrieve other forms of military equipment. Thus Nixon received strong support from the Republican leaders in Congress, at least for his policies toward the Vietnam War.

Mining the harbors of North Vietnam and increasing defense spending were positions that Democratic candidate George McGovern opposed. And of course McGovern disagreed with Scott and Ford over whether to continue the flow of arms to South Vietnam and to reclaim all the military equipment in South Vietnam.

Some Democratic leaders did not publicly support McGovern's positions. Mike Mansfield, the Senate majority leader, did call for the withdrawal of all American military forces from Cambodia and for the restoration of Prince Norodom Sihanouk to power. And both Mansfield and Speaker Tip O'Neill endorsed legislation that would stop funding for the Vietnam War after the return of all prisoners of war. But none of the Democratic leaders mentioned McGovern's proposals to withdraw all American troops within ninety days of his inauguration and to end all political and military support for South Vietnam's government on January 20, Inauguration Day.

Mandatory busing was also a prominent issue in the 1972 election. Griffin, the Senate minority whip, stated his opposition to mandatory busing and encouraged the passage of legislation that would ban courts and federal departments from ordering crosstown busing. In the event that this legislation failed, Griffin advocated a constitutional amendment to ban busing. Nixon agreed with both positions, both of which disagreed with the views of McGovern, who declared his support for the Court's decision on busing to desegregate schools. One other education issue discussed during the campaign concerned support for private and parochial schools. Ford favored some form of federal aid to these schools, and both McGovern and Nixon agreed with that position.

McGovern found substantial support among Democratic leaders for his domestic agenda and even some support among Republican leaders. O'Neill wanted an increase in Social Security benefits, and

Mansfield endorsed raising the amount of money that Social Security pensioners could earn from $1,680 to $3,000 with no effect on their benefits. McGovern favored both positions during his campaign.

Scott called for welfare reform that would create a guaranteed income of at least $2,400 for a family of four. McGovern endorsed the idea of a guaranteed income but called for a $4,000 minimum for a family of four. Although McGovern and Scott disagreed over the amount, they agreed on the direction of the policy. That a Republican leader could favor a minimum guaranteed income was remarkable, given the negative rhetoric surrounding guaranteed incomes during the 1972 campaign.

The 1972 campaign offered stark differences not only in the positions of the presidential candidates but in the positions of the congressional leaders of the two parties. Republican leaders sided with Nixon on his war policies either because they agreed with the policies or because they sought to protect their incumbent during an election year, probably a combination of the two. But agreeing with Nixon meant no compromise with McGovern, whose positions on the war were firm and radically different from Nixon's.

These differences resulted in a hardening of party lines. Nixon had no recorded disagreements with Republican leaders, but he did have disagreements with Democratic leaders. McGovern did not disagree publicly with any Democratic leaders, but he disagreed with Republican leaders on several issues.

But the vastly different positions of McGovern and Nixon on the war did not mean that some form of consensus could not be reached on other issues. McGovern and some Republican leaders agreed in some areas, which suggests that the ideologies encompassed by the presidential candidates and the congressional leaders are sufficiently broad to prevent the kind of disagreements over issues that would result in a total polarization of the two parties.

The number that most clearly stands out in table 4.5 is the 25% rate of disagreement. The disagreements between McGovern and Republican leaders were quite real and account for most of the inflation. Otherwise the rates of disagreement between presidential candidates and the congressional leaders from both parties do not show a significant upward rise over the last eight presidential elections. Furthermore the average rate of disagreement for Democratic and Republican presidential candidates is almost identical. Democratic candidates on average have a disagreement rate with party leaders from both parties of 8%. The number is 9% for Republicans. But the Democratic rate of disagreement has a standard deviation that is more than double the deviation for the Republican rate. But the 1972 election accounts for most of the larger standard deviation for Democrats. Otherwise the disagreement rate for both parties is fairly stable over time.

The average rates of agreement and disagreement, when compared by party era, show that possibilities for governance have not been seriously compromised, at least judging by these measures. Combined rates of agreement for both Republicans and Democrats remain relatively high across party eras. The Democratic average declines by one percentage point, whereas the Republican rate is the same in both the pre- and post-reform eras. The combined rate of disagreement increases by three percentage points for Democrats, whereas the Republican rate of disagreement actually declines by two percentage points (see table 4.6).

In contrast the contest between President Ford and Governor Jimmy Carter had the lowest combined rate of disagreement, only 11%. Instead of the distinct differences between the two candidates

TABLE 4.5 *Rates of Disagreement Between Congressional Leaders from Both Parties and Presidential Candidates**

Year	Democrats	Republicans
1952	13%	10%
1956	4	9
1960	4	13
1964	4	9
1968	6	10
1972	25	6
1976	4	7
1980	3	11
1984	6	10
1988	8	4
1992	7	11
Average	8%	9%
Std. dev.	5.96	2.43

*Percentages are rounded. Data are from the *Congressional Quarterly Weekly Report* and *New York Times*. The issue positions of Republican and Democratic congressional leaders are compared to the issue positions of candidates from both political parties. *Percentages are rounded.

that distinguished 1972, the election of 1976 demonstrated how a number of similarities could exist between the two candidates of the major parties and how presidential candidates that actively move toward the middle can forge agreements across party lines. These similarities and strategies increased the percentage of agreement between the presidential candidates and the congressional leaders and helped to minimize disagreement.

Carter and the Democratic leaders had a remarkably high degree of consensus in 1976 (see table 4.1), although the election featured a small number of issues compared to the other elections. Indeed even Ford and the Democratic leaders had a relatively high level of agreement.But Ford and the Republican leaders agreed on little.

Most of the agreement between Jimmy Carter and the Democratic leaders is a result of Carter's agreement with the issue stances of Speaker Tip O'Neill (see table 4.1). O'Neill spoke out in favor of establishing a national health insurance system, the need to place more significance on the conservation of energy, and the necessity to provide more federal aid to higher education. Furthermore O'Neill argued for a balanced transportation system that provided more aid to railroads and to urban mass transit and for a revision of the tax laws that would place a greater share of the tax burden on the wealthy. Carter agreed with all these proposals in his campaign pledges.

The agreement between O'Neill and Carter is not surprising. Carter characterized himself as "quite liberal on such issues as civil

TABLE 4.6 *Average Rates of Agreement and Disagreement Between Congressional Leaders of Both Parties and Presidential Candidates by Party and Party Era**

	Agreement	
	Democratic	Republican
Pre-reform era (1952–1968)	20%	15%
Post-reform era (1972–1992)	19	15
	Disagreement	
	Democratic	Republican
Pre-reform (1952–1968)	6%	10%
Post-reform (1972–1992)	9	8

*Percentages are rounded. Data are from the *New York Times* and *Congressional Quarterly Weekly Report*. The issue positions of Republican and Democratic congressional leaders are compared to the issue positions of candidates from both political parties.

rights, environmental quality, and helping people overcome handicaps to lead fruitful lives."[46] But Carter's middle-of-the-road philosophy did present some problems. In his memoirs O'Neill wrote that Carter was "progressive on foreign affairs and human rights, but on economic issues he was still a lot more conservative than I was. It was Reagan who promised to get government off our backs, but it was actually the Carter administration that initiated deregulation in banking, railroads, trucking, airlines, and oil."[47]

Carter also backed a proposal by Alan Cranston of California, the Senate majority whip, to assist migrant workers. This California ballot proposal, known as Proposition 14, guaranteed free union elections in the field and granted union organizers access to growers' land before and after work and during lunch hours in order to speak with the workers. Carter may well have endorsed this proposition to attract the support of Cranston and the Hispanic community. In that case it would be a good example of coalition building, both electoral and governing coalitions. But this was certainly not a national issue, and Carter seemed to risk little electorally by endorsing the proposition.

President Ford took a number of positions that agreed with the stances of some Democratic leaders, in particular Speaker O'Neill's. Like O'Neill, Ford believed that the federal government should make a greater effort to encourage the conservation of energy and that part of this program should be to give more money to railroads and urban mass transit systems. Furthermore O'Neill and Ford agreed that more federal money should be spent to revitalize the cities of the nation and that additional money should be appropriated for higher education.

However, Ford disagreed with O'Neill over the establishment of a national health insurance system and the need for tax reforms to place more of the tax burden on the wealthy. On these two matters Ford accentuated the traditional Republican concerns of opposing a nationalization of the health system and depriving the wealthy of their wealth.

This study includes only one foreign policy issue discussed by a congressional leader in 1976. John J. Rhodes of Arizona, the House minority leader, voiced his opposition to yielding the right to operate and defend the Panama Canal in any negotiations with Panama. Ford and Carter agreed with these purposes as stated by Rhodes. A few years later Carter would realize them when he successfully negotiated a treaty with Panama despite the vehement opposition of some conservative groups and members of Congress.

The agreement between the presidential candidates and the congressional leaders seemed to result because they all held relatively moderate views. Jimmy Carter acknowledged that he pursued a centrist strategy during the campaign. Thus his views would be more or less compatible with the ideology of O'Neill. Ford had always been known as a moderate Republican, an ideology that would also ensure him a fair amount of support from Republicans and Democrats alike. But both the candidates and the congressional leaders had limits to their moderation. Because of their electoral concerns they were all sooner or later obligated to take positions that conflicted with some proposals of the opposing party.

The presence of a popular and ideological incumbent does not seem to affect the rate of disagreement dramatically. The election of 1984 produced a combined rate of disagreement of 16% (see table 4.5), not remarkably higher or lower than most of the other elections. Such a finding is somewhat puzzling. President Reagan was conservative and seemed to inspire strong reactions from Democratic leaders. And Walter Mondale proudly boasted of his liberal and Democratic credentials. This mixture of candidates could have been expected to produce large amounts of disagreement. To be sure, the congressional leaders articulated numerous issue stances with which the two candidates agreed. What is notable about this election is the contrast between the two candidates and the inability of this contrast to stimulate large numbers of disagreements.

Reagan was seeking his second term and enjoyed the advantage of a relatively healthy economy. But in addition to running on his record Reagan emphasized his conservative agenda. Mondale attempted to capitalize on the unpopularity of a number of these conservative issues. In doing so Mondale underscored his commitment to the traditional principles of the Democratic Party. Thus the campaign strategies of Reagan and Mondale resulted in several significant agreements and disagreements with the congressional leaders.

Of the issues on which Mondale and the congressional leaders agreed, two concerned foreign policy toward Latin America. Throughout the campaign Mondale stressed his opposition to aid for the Contras battling the Sandinista government in Nicaragua. O'Neill also opposed aid to the Contras. Furthermore Jim Wright, the House majority leader, voiced his support for continued military aid to El Salvador and for providing the president with the discretion to spend that aid, a position Mondale also supported during the campaign. However, O'Neill disagreed with the increase in military aid to El Salvador. Reagan favored both aid to the Nicaraguan rebels and the increased military aid to the government in El Salvador.

O'Neill and Mondale agreed that funding should not be provided to build the MX missile. Reagan, however, believed that the MX missile should be built, and he made this proposal one of the principal components of his defense program.

Reagan disagreed with O'Neill over a measure that would have allowed students to hold religious meetings in public high schools before or after regular school hours. This issue was important to the conservative wing of the Republican Party.

But Reagan's policies were not opposed by only the Democratic leadership. Reagan had a disagreement over domestic policy with a congressional leader from his own party. One major issue during the campaign was how to handle the soaring federal budget deficits. Reagan flatly opposed any increase in taxes to bring the growing deficits under control. However, Robert Dole of Kansas, who would become the Senate majority leader, stated that he favored a tax increase as one means of lowering the budget deficit. Walter Mondale largely based his campaign on his promise to increase taxes in order to trim the size of the federal budget deficit.

Furthermore Reagan and Mondale agreed with Dole's policy of creating "enterprise zones" in rural and urban areas that were economically depressed. This policy involved the provision of tax breaks and other incentives to employers who located their businesses in these economically depressed areas.

Mondale attracted support for his policies because they represented the traditional concerns of the House leadership. His campaign reflected the established concern in the Democratic Party for a number of social programs. This solicitude toward certain Democratic constituencies ensured a degree of conformity between the Democratic congressional leaders and Mondale. For example, O'Neill publicly supported more money for the guaranteed student loan program for college students, and Mondale agreed with him. This was not a major issue and did not risk alienating large amounts of voters, but it did represent a concern of the Democratic Party. Thus this agreement highlighted the extent to which Mondale and O'Neill shared those concerns.

Do the low levels of disagreement between presidential candidates and the congressional leaders simply reflect placid political times? The campaign seasons of 1952, 1972, 1976, and 1984 were not nearly as tumultuous as 1968. Opposition to the Vietnam War was mounting among congressional leaders and the general public. The assassinations of Robert F. Kennedy and Martin Luther King Jr. and the riots in cities and on the campuses of many universities contributed to the widespread feeling that lawlessness was rampant in America. All these concerns were reflected in the types of issues addressed by congressional leaders during the summer and fall of 1968.

Undoubtedly the major issue in 1968 was the Vietnam War. Edward Kennedy, the Senate majority whip, declared his support for an unconditional halt to the bombing of North Vietnam and called for measures to reduce the amount of military activity and personnel in South Vietnam. These measures included a call for a mutual withdrawal from South Vietnam of all foreign forces and a promise to provide economic and political aid to South Vietnam to sustain the South Vietnamese government once American forces left the country.

For the most part these positions were in agreement with the stated positions of Vice President Hubert Humphrey during his campaign for the presidency. But early in the campaign Humphrey opposed an unconditional halt to the bombing of North Vietnam, mostly because President Lyndon Johnson did not favor one. Tip O'Neill recalled "plenty of speculation that Humphrey had private doubts about Johnson's policy, but I knew it for a fact, because Humphrey and I had talked. He was far closer to my position than to the president's, but the job of the vice president is to be loyal to his boss and not to risk irritating him."[48]

But in a campaign speech from Salt Lake City Humphrey did voice his support for an end to the bombing of North Vietnam. Yet Humphrey also agreed with the elements of Kennedy's position that called for aid to the government of South Vietnam after the withdrawal of American forces.

But this study regards Kennedy's position on the bombing as a disagreement with Humphrey. Even though later in the campaign Humphrey supported an end to the bombing, they continued to disagree over whether such a halt should be unconditional. Most Republicans and some Democrats believed that an unconditional halt in the bombing would place the lives of American troops in jeopardy.

Kennedy's differences with Humphrey over specific Vietnam policies did not mean that Humphrey received no support at all. Hale Boggs, the House majority whip and a Democrat from Louisiana, went on record as opposing a halt in the bombing. But Boggs's support was not as important as Kennedy's support could have been. Kennedy represented the more progressive wing of the Democratic Party, and his support would have gone a long way to heal the rift in the party between those who supported Eugene McCarthy of Minnesota and his antiwar policies and the more conservative wing of the party, which sided with Johnson and his policies. An agreement with a leader like Boggs and a disagreement with Kennedy symbolized the serious ideological rift created in the Democratic Party by the Vietnam war. Certainly Humphrey might have fared better in the general election if he had agreed with the other wing of his party and received the support of the followers of senators Eugene McCarthy and Robert Kennedy.

Some congressional leaders agreed with Humphrey on other foreign policy issues. Republican leaders Hugh Scott and Everett Dirksen called for military aid to Israel, which Humphrey advocated. Furthermore Mansfield declared that the bulk of the responsibility for defending Western Europe should be gradually shifted to other NATO countries. Mansfield and Humphrey also believed that the United States should consider removing one of its military divisions each year in order to assure a transfer of responsibility to other NATO countries.

Mansfield and Dirksen also backed Humphrey in his support for ratification of the nuclear nonproliferation treaty. Their backing was not insignificant. The support of the majority and minority leaders in the Senate can be of tremendous use in the ratification of a controversial treaty.

The Republican candidate, Richard Nixon, addressed many of the foreign policy issues discussed by congressional leaders. Although Nixon kept discussion of the Vietnam War to a minimum because he claimed he did not want to compromise the Paris peace talks, Nixon disagreed with Ted Kennedy's call for an unconditional halt to the bombing of North Vietnam. Nixon instead advocated a halt in the bombing only if North Vietnamese visibly changed its position and only if a halt did not jeopardize American lives. Nixon also disagreed with Kennedy over military strength in Vietnam. Nixon wanted to retain all military forces in Vietnam in order to negotiate with Hanoi from a position of strength. Kennedy wanted military strength to be significantly decreased in order to demonstrate the sincerity of U.S. peace proposals to Saigon and Hanoi. Nixon did not discuss the other proposals by Kennedy dealing with the Vietnam War.

The disagreements between Nixon and Kennedy reveal that Nixon's position on the war was essentially no different than Humphrey's. But Nixon did not have the handicap of defending an incumbent president's record, as he did in 1960, so less attention was focused on Nixon's stances. On the other hand the media seemed to be preoccupied with the conflict between Johnson and Humphrey over the war and the speculation over whether Humphrey would break with Johnson. Media commentators realized that Humphrey would have to do something dramatic on the war issue in order to unify his party and to attract the support of disaffected groups. The result was that Nixon's policies on the war did not receive the same kind of scrutiny. Furthermore Nixon was appealing to a different group of voters, and his policies did not prevent him from courting these voters. In other words, Nixon's policies did not create the same kind of disruption in his electoral coalition as Humphrey's policies caused in his.

In another area of foreign policy Nixon supported ratification of the nuclear nonproliferation treaty, a matter that received the backing of both Mansfield and Dirksen. Humphrey also supported ratification of the treaty. Nixon wanted to delay ratification in the Senate for a short time in order to study Soviet intentions. However, Nixon's agreement with the congressional leaders on this issue demonstrated that Nixon was appealing not only to a conservative coalition but to a moderate coalition.

In the area of domestic policy one major issue addressed by the congressional leaders was gun control. The assassinations of Robert Kennedy and Martin Luther King had prompted most congressional leaders to seek some form of gun-control legislation. Senators Kennedy and Mansfield stated their support for gun-control legislation, including a ban on the interstate sales of rifles and shotguns, new controls over the sales of handguns, and the registering and licensing of firearms. Hubert Humphrey agreed with all these positions.

Richard Nixon also agreed with the need for gun-control legislation. His views coincided with the proposals of Kennedy and Mansfield, which would require registering and licensing firearms and a ban on the sale of guns through mail-order houses. Nixon's position calling for controls over the interstate sale of rifles and shotguns brought him once more into conflict with Dirksen, the Senate minority leader. Dirksen supported some licensing and registering of firearms but opposed any effort to regulate the interstate sale of rifles and shotguns. This was Nixon's only disagreement with a Republican leader during the 1968 campaign season.

The volatile campaign environment produced a number of agreements and disagreements over some significant policies. The overall level of agreement between candidates and the congressional leaders was the lowest of any election reported in this study. But the low level of agreement between the candidates and the congressional leaders was not the result of an increase in disagreements but in the number of issues not mentioned by the candidates.

The reasons for this phenomenon—low levels of agreement but a high percentage of issues that were not mentioned—might be found in the unique circumstances surrounding the 1968 campaign. First, the explosion in the number of issues forced congressional leaders to confront a vast array of new political problems. In addition, the issues were extremely divisive. Most congressional leaders had opinions on gun control, the Vietnam War, crime control, and other issues. But because the issues were so volatile, many leaders were in effect forced to take stands even if they preferred to remain silent.

Second, with the end of the sixties came a growing restlessness among members of Congress to assert the power of the legislative branch. As Lyndon Johnson became increasingly alienated from his own party because of the Vietnam War, many members believed they needed to regain a measure of control over the policy-making machinery in the United States and provide leadership on the newly emerging social issues of the day.[49]

Finally, Johnson's decision not to seek reelection created a power vacuum within the Democratic Party. Without a real party leader and with Humphrey subjected to a bitter struggle at the convention, several party leaders were not constrained from speaking out on the burgeoning number of issues on the political agenda.

The question explored here is whether changes in the broader electoral and party system have disrupted the links between the various coalitions that make governing possible. The answer has not been easy to discern, but the data offer some patterns that may reveal some responses. Taking Republicans and Democrats together, one critical component of the governing process has not vanished despite the substantial changes that have occurred in the party system as a whole. The type of candidates who are nominated by the modern nominating coalitions and who are elected by today's electoral coalitions still possess a crucial resource for creating governing coalitions. Thus today's presidential candidates have some of the same resources as the candidates who labored within a party system in which the links between the coalitions were more apparent.

A second lesson concerns the differences between Democrats and Republicans. Each party appears to exhibit certain strengths and weaknesses in regard to the various coalitions. Democrats have higher overall rates of agreement, but the rates are more volatile. These differences may be an indication that the two parties are not totally equal to the task of governing in Congress and the White House, and that simply restoring unified party control, with some finely tuned mechanisms to create party unity within Congress, will not make America's policy-making problems evaporate. When evaluating the possibilities for governing, we must be sensitive to the differences in the kinds of coalitions mobilized by the two parties.

When presidents disagree with the party leaders, they have the option of going over their heads to the electorate in hopes of bringing public opinion to bear on the attitudes and behavior of those who lead Congress.[50] But Republican presidents may need to pursue this strategy more often than Democratic presidents, because Democrats seem to enjoy the benefits of greater agreement with the congressional leaders. The next chapter further addresses all these issues by examining current conceptions of governability and whether they adequately reflect the state of American political parties and account for the many extant possibilities for governing.

5

Rethinking Governability and the Study of Political Parties

The ballyhooed crisis of government accompanying the decline of political parties in the United States seems not to have occurred. The evidence shows that rates of agreement between the nominating and the electoral coalitions have remained stable since the 1950s. Presidential candidates and members of the nominating coalition continue to agree on a large number and wide variety of issues. Furthermore the agreement seems to have carried over into the governing sphere: congressional party leaders, who are pivotal actors in any presidential calculation for policy success, advocate many of the same policy positions as the presidential candidates. Barring some irreconcilable differences in personality between the president and congressional leaders or extreme political conditions in the leader's district, the president apparently enters the White House with important congressional players predisposed to support a segment of the policy agenda articulated in the campaign.

Several factors may explain the frequency—what David Mayhew termed the "constancy" in significant legislation and investigation across the divided party eras—with which members of the nominating, electoral, and governing coalitions agree.[1] First, the Constitution creates a number of different constituencies by distributing power among several offices. But not all these constituencies are mutually exclusive, and some inevitably share values and goals. The incidence of agreement between congressional leaders and presidential candidates may be the result of representatives who come from districts ideologically close to the views expounded by presidential candidates.[2] Thus, although the multitude of constituencies may create problems, it also creates opportunities.

Second, politicians often have strong incentives for bipartisan cooperation. Gridlock can be anticipated by members of both parties, some of whom do not see the benefit of it. The need to claim credit for policy actions is an incentive in both party eras that would impel representatives, their leaders, and party candidates to press for passage of programs, even if the congressional leaders are no longer pivotal players in the presidential electoral system.[3] Note that this incentive helps to explain the enduring agreement between presidential candidates and congressional leaders from different parties, not just between the leaders and candidates from the same party.[4]

Furthermore even those party activists involved in the presidential nominating and electoral system may desire a successful candidate more than an ideologically pure candidate. Consequently recent presidential candidates have not, for the most part, been ideologically outside the mainstream of their party, thus ensuring wide areas of agreement between the party members and the candidates.[5]

Finally, significant shifts in public opinion affect all leaders equally or at least alter the political climate in which all political leaders must act. These shifts in public moods or opinions are superimposed on the party system and are events to which presidential candidates, congressional leaders, and party activists react.[6] Consequently shifts in public opinion may serve to bring candidates, leaders, and activists together, even when the party system no longer has the formal means and structure to do so routinely.

Rethinking Governability?

The constancy and stability in agreement of components of the nominating, electoral, and governing coalitions are strong indicators of the need to rethink the connection between political parties and democratic governance. My conclusions here are dramatically at odds with the prevailing view that democracy in America is undergoing a crisis induced by the decline of the political parties. The discrepancy has two plausible explanations: one is that the evidence used here to appraise governability is inadequate; the other is that the theoretical paradigm used to predict the crisis is defective and incapable of properly assessing the current situation in American politics.

My data could be inadequate, but the evidence challenging the existence of a crisis is ample and indeed demonstrates quite convincingly that the American version of democracy is humming right along. Furthermore, even other measures of governance, such as the overall rates of presidential fulfillment of promises, the behavior of representatives, and the operation of investigative committees in Congress all have remained virtually unchanged over the last forty years.[7]

All this consistent and highly pertinent evidence underscores the need to rethink the notion of governability and the theory of democracy upon which it rests. Nonetheless many still argue for the creation of disciplined parties to cure what ails America.[8] The calls for reform—some trivial, some significant—would streamline the electoral or legislative process, for example, by rationalizing the operation of the parties and rendering them more businesslike.[9]

Although the characterization of democratic problems as dire has some merit, the heavy reliance on a viewpoint that stresses a particular aspect of governability to the exclusion of other equally important considerations disguises a number of serious shortcomings with the conclusion that democracy in the United States is faltering and that political parties are the primary means for restoring its strength.

The tasks of adequately defining governability and understanding the implications of such a definition have been mostly overlooked for several reasons. First, the concept of governability is multifaceted, which requires defining and discussing each of its conceptual components. The two main conceptual components of governability, effectiveness and legitimacy, are linked theoretically but for reasons that have never fully been examined. This would be an arduous, normative endeavor leading away from empirical political studies to the field of political philosophy. Second, the concept of governability is critical for judging the functioning of political systems.[10] Judgments about the performance of party systems are inevitably linked to expectations about how the entire political system should perform. These standards of performance need to be made clear, which is difficult to do. Third, this link raises several questions about the nature of political participation in a democracy and the process by which the individual relates to government.[11] These normative concerns are often lost among the myriad practical considerations associated with observing how parties actually behave.[12]

Thus we must turn to the many aspects of governability, especially government's effectiveness and legitimacy, the two primary dimensions of political regimes, although political parties in a particular era may not be well equipped to fulfill both requirements.[13]

Can the United States Be Governed?

Most definitions of *governing* focus on the effectiveness and accountability of U.S. institutions. The Committee on the Constitutional System has asked, "Has the governmental system been able to meet the challenges of modern times? Has it been able to agree on a definition of the problems that beset our nation? Can it fashion adequate responses to these challenges and see to their timely implementation? Have the people been able to hold elected officials accountable for the performance of the government?"[14]

This formulation of the problem encompasses all the ills popularly associated with the performance of American government. Accordingly, governability involves at least four aspects. First, governability is not simply the ability to enact legislation but entails the added ability to enact legislation that addresses and remedies the most serious problems. Second, governability further presupposes the ability to form a national consensus on the problems that beset the nation and how to solve them.

Third, once the nation has deliberated about the problems, agreed on what those problems are, and settled on the policies that will solve them, it must be able to implement the policies effectively. This third dimension primarily involves the science of public administration. Finally, the electorate must be able to hold government officials accountable for these activities.

How parties relate to these several dimensions and can contribute to their actualization is complex. Too often we simply assume that governability could be achieved by tinkering with the structure of the parties and the rules for participating in them. However, governability is a concept that extends beyond the narrow confines of the party system. Multiple levels of a political system are involved in its realization. These levels are public, organization, party, and state. "The public" refers to the undifferentiated mass of individuals residing within the boundaries of the state. This sphere is most often the subject of studies of public opinion and voting behavior. The organization level of society involves the numerous organizations to which individuals belong. These organizations take the form of voluntary groups or overtly political organizations such as interest groups.[15]

Political parties constitute the next level. They are "the prime vehicles for converting public and organization preferences into institutionalized mechanisms for filling state positions and influencing state policies."[16] Parties are the crucial link between the public and organization levels and the state. As such they deserve much of the attention accorded to them, but parties often are blamed for the performance of tasks that are the responsibility of another level of the political system.

The final level of politics is the state. Like political parties, the state is not a static unidimensional entity but involves different branches of government and their interactions. States possess a number of characteristics, most of which deal with the ability of agencies and political actors to regulate specific territories and activities and to impose sanctions on those who may violate edicts issued by the state.[17]

The broader political system is the level at which many goals associated with governance can be realized, but because the political system consists of many levels, political parties cannot be expected to achieve governance on their own. To be sure, political parties can be the critical means for achieving some governing ideals. Yet it is important to acknowledge up front that multiple organizations are involved in attaining governability and that reaching that goal requires being sensitive to the many levels of a political system and allowing for the realistic scrutiny of the contributions of political parties.

Assessing the performance of political parties with regard to governance is further complicated by the ability of a political system to pursue several goals simultaneously. Because the system has multiple goals, determining how the system is performing may be difficult. Political systems are asked to ensure economic progress and provide various services, including protection from domestic and international harm. Political parties often have little to do with achieving some of these goals. Critics nonetheless often insist that the activities of the parties are the most important. But to judge fairly they need to justify, not simply assume, the extent to which one goal should be given priority over another.[18]

Political parties directly and indirectly touch on many issues related to governance, and they will be more effective and relevant to some than to others, depending on the goal and the level of the political system at which it can realistically be achieved. For example, of the four conditions cited by the committee, American political parties seem best suited to effecting the fourth: responsible parties educate and inform voters of the activities of elected officials; in a competitive party situation the party seeks to call attention to the successes of its officials and to the blunders of the other party's. All these activities should help voters to make choices based on meaningful distinctions and establish a link between the public and the government.

However, it is difficult to argue that political parties can be the primary means to achieve a national consensus—the second condition of governance. When parties are responsible for educating voters and assigning praise or blame, we have no guarantee that a national consensus will emerge from the debate. A party benefits by electing its candidates to office. In a two-party, single-member-district system elections are a zero-sum game, and the intense competition between two parties produces substantial disagreement—not only about what the solutions are but what the problems are.[19] Thus as each party seeks to educate voters and to publicize its activities and those of its rival—essentially seeking to recruit, educate, and inform voters—that very process may damage prospects for policy consensus. In America such a task may need to be performed by institutions capable of transcending political differences.

The third condition of governability, effective administration, actually has little to do with the party system per se and much more to do with the network of federal and state agencies that administers the policies enacted by democratic national institutions. Indeed much evidence suggests that the effective and efficient implementation of public policy can occur only in the absence of interference by political parties and the interests they inject into the process.[20]

Finally, political parties play a significant role in enacting legislation that addresses serious national problems, which is the fourth condition. The party organizations in Congress are active players in the business of the chambers and are becoming even more so.[21] But political scientists and other critics must be careful when assessing exactly what the parties can and should do in this area, because this is where the party system converges most conspicuously with the constitutional system. Most reforms designed to effect a more efficient and responsible party system fuss with the operation of the constitutional order by seeking to dramatically remake relations between the executive and legislative branches. Indeed most recommendations for remaking the policy-making function of our national institutions rely upon the party to be the governing caucus.[22]

Because the political system is complex and pursues multiple goals, we should not ask political parties to shoulder most of the burden for achieving governability, yet that is precisely what happens in much of the academic and journalistic debate on democratic governance. Rather party theorists need to understand the component parts of parties and the party's relation to the whole.[23] Scholars of political parties must specify which component of the political system and which dimension of governability they are using when they are assessing whether the parties are contributing positively to the governing process. This is especially important for those who argue that the weakened state of parties threatens governability. These critics must specify which task they think is most important for parties to perform, whether that task is solving the nation's problems, creating consensus, managing the public administration apparatus, or holding elected officials accountable. Holding elected officials accountable seems to be more important for the maintenance of democracy than does managing the public administration in a particular manner, and it is an activity that parties can actually perform.

Ultimately we can reduce the four facets of governability identified by the Committee on the Constitutional System to two values to democracy: effectiveness and legitimacy.[24] Both values are clearly present in the four dimensions. Effectiveness is clearly the focus of the concern that surrounds the enacting of legislation and managing the public administration, whereas legitimacy refers to the forging of consensus and achieving accountability. But the committee does not make an explicit link between these two values or establish the primacy of one kind of activities over the others.

A definition developed by Ralf Dahrendorf goes beyond the committee's analysis because it recognizes how the achievement of effectiveness and legitimacy are connected. Dahrendorf contends that "governments have to be able to do things which they claim they can do, as well as those which they are expected to do; they have to work."[25] First, governments have to produce results, suggesting the need for effectiveness. They have to identify problems and implement policies designed to eradicate those problems.[26] Because the solution of problems depends upon the identification of problems, we could argue that identifying problems is the primary function of government and that we should explore and understand the means for identifying before we emphasize how the problems are solved. Party scholars are correct in pointing out the deficiencies in the policy-making aspects of American government, but these concerns are secondary to how problems are identified and worked out in the legislative process.

The policy process must also meet certain expectations, a concern that introduces the value of legitimacy. Legitimacy implies that the actions of government are appropriate in two senses: first, the procedures used to make policy decisions must conform to the prevailing democratic standards; second, the policy adopted cannot violate certain cultural values.[27] The inclusion of legitimacy in the broader concept of governability moves it beyond the ideas of effective policy formation and implementation. Thus governability necessitates the creation of policies that recognize the cultural boundaries surrounding the issue and respect the nation's standards of democratic conduct. Policies cannot be illegal or violate recognized standards and mores. These concerns necessarily constrict the range of policy options that can be considered proper and workable. For example, constitutional decisions and cultural norms circumscribe the realm of policy options that would be considered politically practical to deal with the problem of violent crime. But these constitutional decisions and cultural norms are not static. They evolve as perceptions of the problem, and debates over how to best solve the problem interact in the course of political activities.

Sorting out the relationship between effectiveness and legitimacy is not a simple task (see figure 5.1). And it bears repeating that the main concern of the Committee on the Constitutional System, and most modern scholars of political parties, is the question of effectiveness, with its emphasis on policy making and delivery. That this dimension is strongly connected to other concerns about the performance and maintenance of democracy or that contradictions with other values are possible goes largely unrecognized. The interconnections between the various dimensions of governability and their connection to the question of which type of democracy is preferable strongly suggest caution when considering improvements to government performance. Dilemmas about how to proceed with improvements soon arise when it becomes apparent that reforms intended for one sphere produce significant effects in other spheres or that efforts to attain governability may in reality be addressed to the wrong area. For example, campaign finance reforms intended to hold public officials accountable, a concern of proper procedure under legitimacy, helped to spawn political action committees, which complicate the legislative process, a concern of effectiveness (see figure 5.1).

These dilemmas are also apparent in Dahrendorf's discussion of various conditions that hamper the complete achievement of governability in modern democracies. The demand to identify and solve problems facing the public makes modern democracies prone to "overloading," a condition that occurs because "modern governments have taken on more than they can cope with."[28] The voracious appetite for problem solving, explained in large part by political ambition, creates public expectations that governments find difficult to satisfy.[29]

A second dilemma "has to do with the space in which it [modern government] operates." Here the question is decentralization versus centralization and national versus multinational.[30] Modern governments find themselves caught between the competing levels: do they act, provide services, or solve problems? Vacillation over the different spheres in which governments might take action sometimes leaves them unable to act decisively and effectively. Should Medicare be returned to the states or retained at the national level? Should individual states be allowed to negotiate trade deals with foreign countries? The level at which government attempts to solve problems has implications for the kinds of solutions the government seeks and the role played by the public. Some levels of the political system are better able to deal with such issues, but their handling may be viewed

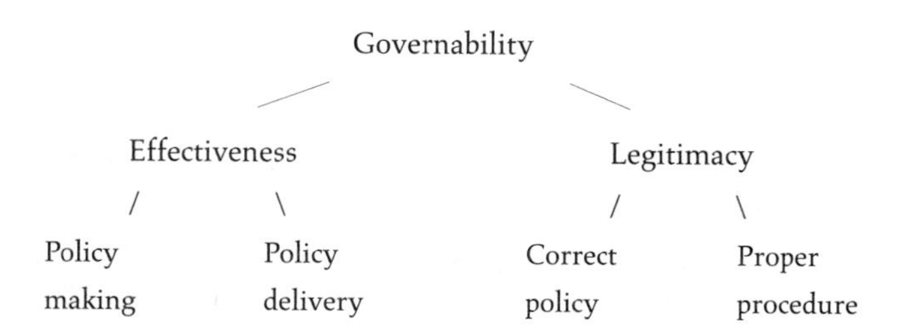

FIGURE 5.1 Components of Governability

suspiciously by the public. Consequently effectiveness and legitimacy are intertwined.

The extent to which the public becomes involved has implications for the final situational constraint that impedes the effective operation of government, or what Dahrendorf refers to as "corporatism, group politics . . . collectivism," or "the great consensus" (p. 402). These phrases describe a politics of conciliation in which private organizations and the state collaborate to solve problems. Consequently competitive party politics are replaced by a corporate system that minimizes conflict and competition.[31] Corporatism thwarts parties in their quest to promote a competitive political system even though the governing arrangements may be effective in the delivery of policy.

The rise of corporatism, in conjunction with the other situational constraints, seriously jeopardizes the attainment of governability. That a reform of political parties can do little for two of these three situational constraints escapes most analysts. Indeed calls for streamlining party relationships between the executive and legislative branches by banishing institutional and partisan gridlock are actually invitations to engage in the kind of overloading that contributes to a state of "ungovernability."

These dilemmas confront those who contend that a reformation of political parties, and the constitutional system in which they operate, is needed in order to achieve governability. Resolving these dilemmas requires going beyond the simple description of gridlock, policy failure, or even the identification of intransigent problems. If scholars of political parties are going to argue that political parties have to be reformed to solve the crisis of governability, they have to expand their normative positions to justify the increased demands made on political parties and to explain why another level of the political system is not more instrumental in achieving that aim.

Party Theory and Governability

The history of political parties in the United States can be divided into distinct periods based on the functions that political parties performed in each period. Parties have always existed to wield some kind of influence over government, but the manner in which they organize and the ancillary benefits of such tactics have varied through the years.

In the early period of American history political parties were little more than policy factions that organized to exert influence on the newly created Congress. The cleavages among the representatives mirrored differences among the leaders of the nation. Although these early parties may have been effective at passing particular pieces of legislation, their scope was not sufficiently large to bring inactive citizens into the process.[32] Parties helped to make policy making easier, but their influence rarely reached beyond Congress to the nation as a whole. Parties were of little help in fulfilling the requirements of legitimacy because their organizations and methods of operation had no way to convince the nation that their efforts somehow conformed to democratic norms, whatever they may have been.

The development of truly national parties occurred during the Jacksonian age. Political parties developed organizations in almost all states to nominate and elect candidates for a variety of offices, including the presidency. Participation was certainly broad based when compared to the first party system, and the political parties began to assume the mass identity that characterizes parties today.[33] During this era political parties acted as agents for including new voters in the electoral process. But the growth of the parties brought about decentralization and autonomy among the various party organizations operating in the various states. Consequently "party mechanisms were better designed for achieving agreement on nominations than for formulating policies."[34]

How the first and second party systems compare is relevant to the discussion of governability. Parties in the first age did a much better job at organizing to enact public policy, a concern associated with effectiveness. Parties in the second age did a much better job of subscribing to democratic norms and procedures, a concern associated with legitimacy. As the parties evolved from the first system to the second, their ability to satisfy the demands of effectiveness and legitimacy evolved.

The evolution of the parties and their functions continues even today. Parties no longer socialize immigrants in American politics or provide economic opportunities the way they once did. Nor do party leaders in Congress control representatives the way they did under the reign of Speaker Joseph Cannon (1903–1911). But political parties do contribute to the governance of the country. Presidential candidates do not neglect the coalitions at the base of the party that nominates them; policy agreements between the president and party leaders endure even though the shift from a brokered system to a candidate-centered system has relieved congressional leaders of their gatekeeping function. The ability to meet the exigencies of governance in one era does not necessarily fade as another period evolves. The attention given to one or all the components of governability may shift. Today's candidate-centered party system seems far removed from the days of machines and policy factions, but modern parties still seem to retain the ability to perform activities that serve the needs of governance.

When we analyze the shifts in party functions in the context of governability, we must remember what functions and activities are important to the question of democracy today. This means that party theorists need to acknowledge the two dimensions of governability and their connection to each other. The inability of parties to satisfy one aspect of governability, such as efficient policy making, does not imply that parties fail at all aspects. Indeed the parties may actually increase their ability to perform activities that are also central to the question of governance. Just as the first party system performed better with regard to effectiveness, the second party system sacrificed effectiveness to create legitimacy. Today's party system sacrifices control by political leaders to foster openness, especially in the primary stages of presidential campaigns.

Party theorists most often evaluate these changes from the perspective of effectiveness, but they also need to emphasize how institutions, and especially reformed parties, correspond to the cultural values of the society. Effective methods of making policy must conform to the prevailing attitudes about democracy and personal liberty. Furthermore a discussion of governability should include not only a discussion of effectiveness and a regard for personal liberties but should incorporate a concern for the development of the individual in society and the relationship of the individual to the state. These several components need to be balanced in order to arrive at a realistic understanding of governability and how parties aid in its achievement. Today's political parties have little in common with the parties of either the first or second party system. But modern parties continue to perform vital functions related to the issue of governability. That parties are less obtrusive in the governing process does not mean that they are not performing other vital functions, such as nominating candidates, structuring the debate, and setting the agenda.

Recognizing the multifaceted nature of governability also helps to focus attention on which factors the study of political parties *and* their connections to governability should analyze. Certainly we can subdivide parties into a number of smaller components for systematic analysis, a practice that has produced numerous books and articles about how political parties are structured and operate. We know a great deal about the patterns of local party organizations, the practices of congressional and national party organizations and their recent resurgence, and the mechanisms that socialize individuals into political parties. But the limited scope of these studies obscures the connection between the specific studies and the broader questions of democratic governance. Of course attempts at making the connections remain popular preoccupations of concluding chapters and paragraphs in these studies, but the conceptual framework for linking a particular form of the political party to the question of democracy is simply not in place, largely because political scientists and other analysts are just as confused about the nature of democracy as the general public is.[35] Therefore most arguments tend to be unconvincing when they deal with the unfortunate effects of a particular change in party structure on achieving governability.

This discussion of governability suggests that the appropriate level for studying the effects of party change on governability is the juncture of the party system and the state. *System*, as used here, is defined by two characteristics: "(i) the system displays properties that do not belong to a separate consideration of its component elements and (ii) the system results from, and consists of, the patterned interactions of its component parts, thereby implying that such interactions provide the boundaries, or at least the boundedness, of the system."[36]

We cannot adequately study the question of governability by isolating the assorted elements of political parties. As the definition of system specifies, a party system does not entail a simple listing of its constituent parts. Nor does it include the expansion of its interactions to subsume the broader polity. Conclusions about the positive or negative effects of political parties should not be unnecessarily broadened to encompass various state activities that, although perhaps vital to the survival of the polity, are nonetheless outside the realm of the party dimension.[37] Therefore to the degree that research questions are attentive to the problem of governability, they need to address the suspected linkages between the components that comprise the party system and the larger political system.[38] Asking these questions can be daunting, for the party system touches so many aspects of political life. But if we take governability seriously as an objective, and if our theories specify that political parties are one of the few institutions that can contribute significantly to its achievement, our theorizing about political parties and governability must specify what functions are critical and which ones are superfluous.

Specifying the connection of political parties to the relevant political phenomena surrounding governability demands a clarification of governability's constituent terms. Such terms as *effectiveness* and *efficiency* are frequently used in the literature on political parties, but they are rarely defined clearly. These terms often are used to refer to the resources parties provide to the president, who uses them to guide legislation through the two chambers of Congress. But without an understanding of how these terms relate to the notion of governability, inconsistencies with an explanation of other facets of the party system are bound to occur. For example, the conceptual definition and understanding affixed to a term such as efficiency is critical. The emphasis on efficiency in the literature on political parties connotes an almost industrial and hence economic usage: the maximization of benefits and accomplishments with a minimal expenditure of resources. However, such a definition may mean that efficiency conflicts with the realization of other democratic values.[39]

Finally, a full elucidation of governability makes it easier to assess the relative strengths and weaknesses of various proposals for party reform. Because of the frustrations suffered by modern presidents in formulating and implementing their agendas, scholars have advanced several proposals to improve the party system and therefore the government's performance. These proposals range from a simple change in the campaign finance laws for House and Senate races to complex constitutional amendments that alter the basic structure of U.S. political institutions. Some proposals use the British parliamentary system as their model.[40] For instance, one proposal involves electing the president and representatives to terms that run simultaneously. The proposal further suggests that the presidential candidate would head the ticket and have some control over who runs on it. The presumption is that the shared electoral fates of the president and the representatives would increase cooperation between the branches and enhance the voters' opportunity to hold the officials accountable. If their performance in office satisfies voters (or does not displease them), they will be returned to office.

For the most part the democratic assumption at the heart of most proposed reforms stresses the effective translation of public opinion into public policy. The reformers further argue that the mechanism used to effect the translation should not complicate the consideration and passage of legislation. Because political parties are both the means to aggregate public opinion and manage the affairs of Congress, restructuring parties to create more efficient management of Congress could impede the expression of public opinion.[41]

Yet these reforms, with their emphasis on the effective conversion of public opinion into policy making, ignore other values that are just as crucial for the long-term health of democracy. We have already discussed one of these other criteria, namely, that governability involves a combination of effectiveness and legitimacy. Perhaps because legitimacy appears to be a normative term and does not possess the economic connotations of effectiveness, its attainment is given short shrift in the party reform literature. Certainly the measures that would substantiate its presence or absence in a particular democracy are not as easy to construct and agree upon as measures associated with a term such as effectiveness.

Legitimacy, Dahrendorf contends, implies that the institutions and procedures of policy making must subscribe to certain cultural norms. Leon Epstein argues that party reform "requires breaking the institutional mold in which our major parties are now set."[42] Part of the institutional mold is the candidate-centered nature of the American electoral process today. Any reform that meddles with this feature of the party system elevates the value of effectiveness over the value of legitimacy. The process of devising a reform must explain the placement of the one value over the other, not just assume that everyone knows why the choice was made. The means for producing public policy must be sensitive to the democratic concerns and values of the society. When reforms challenge these values, at the very least they should explain why there is a dire need to abrogate them. With these thoughts in mind we must look with suspicion on any reform that neglects the dimension of legitimacy, especially if the reform could drastically alter a particular feature of the constitutional system on which the party system rests.[43]

The United States has a complex society, and its constitutional structure institutionalizes several different values.[44] In the arguments offered by some individuals it is not altogether certain that achieving efficiency, an important component of the governability issue, will not encroach on some other value that is also strongly embraced by the bulk of society. This is especially true when the evidence presented here and elsewhere seriously challenges the notion that the party system is not performing adequately in the context of the constitutional system. Data from several different studies show that rates at which presidents fulfill promises and succeed in office, and the rates at which parties achieve cohesiveness, are either increasing or remain relatively stable over long periods of time. This is hardly what we would expect, given the frightful descriptions and dire predictions provided by those who want to reform the party system, constitutional system, or both.

Without an overwhelming cry from the public demanding wholesale change in the form of government, and without any clear understanding of how to reasonably balance concerns of legitimacy with the demands of efficiency and effectiveness, we should avoid any major modifications to the constitutional or party system. If the public is comfortable with the balance between a majority-controlled government capable of exercising its will on occasion and the safeguards placed on that government to protect individual and minority rights, it should view with suspicion any major effort to rearrange the constitutional balance.[45]

Various observers have concluded that policy making today is indeed so difficult that American institutions cannot solve the pressing problems of the nation. They almost uniformly contend that stronger political parties are needed to sustain the efforts of an increasingly embattled executive branch and Congress. However, such judgments must await a clarification of democracy, which in turn clarifies governability and the way that parties can guarantee its fulfillment. We cannot characterize parties as strong or weak unless we are explicit about what democratic value parties are supposed to optimize. Therefore parties can have no real "halcyon" days, only a time when the particular manifestation of the parties unambiguously actualized a particular democratic value, one that the scholar consciously or unconsciously sees as desirable.These values often are made explicit. More often than not, however, these values are not made explicit, and a veil of objectivity masks the argument. But the values nonetheless remain, lurking just beneath the surface.

The challenge of party theorists is to create and use a concept of governability that is sensitive to and relies upon democratic theory. At the very least theorists should specify the most important functions that political parties perform, an exercise that would make their understanding of democracy explicit. Gerald Pomper began this exercise in his book *Passions and Interests,* in which he stresses that different conceptions of the party rely upon different notions of democracy. But this is only the first step. A buffet of different conceptions of parties does not tell us which one we should select and emphasize for the maintenance of American democracy. These concepts are not all theoretically equal. Some are much more advantageous for the realization of the two dimensions of governability. Just because democracy is a multidimensional term does not mean that each of its components can be somehow equally achieved. Structural impediments limit participation and would bias the structure toward a particular mix of the values, with more emphasis given to some than to others. Furthermore the political culture more readily embraces one mixture of values than another. Party theorists need not shy away from the task of exploring the normative dimensions of these functions. At this point students of political parties could go about the task of establishing the empirical links between the dimensions specified by the theory. Such a strategy enables scholars to place the findings in a framework that is more relevant to the real political challenges facing democracy in the United States and around the world.

Appendix 1: Identification of Issue Stances

The texts of speeches and comments of candidates as reported in the *New York Times* are the sources of the policy positions of the presidential candidates. These reports include transcripts of speeches, transcripts of news conferences, reports of speeches by candidates, transcripts of presidential debates, reports of comments made by candidates, summaries of press releases from campaigns, and interviews of candidates by reporters.

I analyzed all stories in the *New York Times* related to the campaign activities and pronouncements of the candidates. The recording unit is the sentence, and the context unit is the paragraph. I read all sentences in the stories and transcripts for issue pronouncements made by the candidates and for the statements released by the campaign. Several issue statements often appear in one paragraph. I did not include all information in a paragraph but only those sentences regarding policy content.

I used four categories developed by Gerald Pomper and Susan S. Lederman to determine an issue stance: "Expressions of Goals and Concerns," "Pledges of Continuity," "Pledges of Action," and "Detailed Pledges." I excluded Pomper and Lederman's two less specific categories.[1] I used the four categories to extract the issue positions of both the presidential candidates and the party leaders.

My goal was to identify all issue stances taken by presidential candidates and recorded in the *New York Times*. Issue stances are those statements that contain a policy content and imply future action or the continuation of an action. These statements may even support or oppose the action of another player. Some statements have more policy content than others. I separated the issue positions from rhetoric and factual pronouncements by the increased reference to specific policies and by the level of specific commitment to some policy.

When I compared the platforms and the positions of the party leaders, I dropped the distinctions between the various types of issue stances. The result was a compilation of issue stances for each candidate during each campaign that made no distinctions according to the specificity of the issue stance.

I took the issue positions of the presidential candidates from stories that appeared in the *New York Times* between the day that the candidate received the nomination and election day. I included the period after the convention because the candidates use it as a time in which to define issues. Had I used only the period after Labor Day, the traditional starting date of presidential campaigns, the study would have excluded many issue stances.

I used the *New York Times* as a source for the policy positions of the presidential candidates because of the extremely important role that electoral coalitions play in the establishment of the governing coalition. As Seligman notes, "The principal link between presidential selection and governance is the president's core electoral coalition that crystallizes as a result of the nominating and election campaign. It is this core coalition that provides the political base for the president's governing coalition."[2] Any appeal to an electoral coalition assumes some publicity of the issue stances of the candidates because a candidate reveals the critical elements of the electoral coalition by declaring positions and ideology.[3] Reports in the *New York Times* contain the issues most visible to the general electorate because they receive the most publicity. Issue stances that do not make the *New York Times* are probably not visible to the electorate and hence do not have the same importance in the building of electoral coalitions. The *New York Times* is the paper to which other media outlets look when determining which campaign stories to cover and how to cover them. It is sensitive to the campaign environment and covers it extensively from beginning to end. Its role as a national newpaper makes it a logical conduit between campaigns and voters. Thus the reports and stories in the *New York Times* identify the links between the electoral and governing coalitions by spotlighting the issue stances that the presidential candidates use to appeal to the general electorate and that constitute the issues at the core of their governing coalition.

Assignment of Issue Stances to Issue Categories

Putting issue stances in policy categories is a relatively straightforward task. I use the definitions of policy types and the ensuing categories outlined in chapters four through seven of Randall B. Ripley and Grace R. Franklin's *Congress, the Bureaucracy, and Public Policy*.[4] I put each policy position in one of six categories: redistributive, distributive, competitive regulatory, protective regulatory, strategic, and structural. I omitted crisis policies from the analysis because they are not a feature of presidential campaigns.

Distributive policy involves the dispersal of various benefits by the federal government to a wide range of recipients. According to Ripley and Franklin, the benefits can take any number of forms, including "a price-support payment; a contract for procurement, construction, or service; a tax loophole; or a special indemnity award" and may accrue to "individuals, groups, and corporations." Thus distributive policy generally has low visibility and fosters cooperative and mutually rewarding relationships (p. 76). Examples of distributive issue stances include proposals for federal programs for soil conservation, urban renewal, rural electrification, training for local law enforcement officers, low income housing, and aid to private schools.

Redistributive policy also involves the allocation of governmental largess to beneficiaries. However, this policy type is distinct in its controversial character. Redistributive policy almost always involves fierce ideological battles and results in clear winners and losers. Ripley and Franklin explain that this is because "such policies seek to reallocate valuable goods and symbols among different economic classes and racial groupings." Thus the benefits that accrue to one party through redistributive policy are provided at the expense of another social group (pp. 121–22). Examples of redistributive stances include proposals for socialized medicine, publicly funded abortions, school prayer, and affirmative action programs.

According to Ripley and Franklin, protective regulatory policies are those policies "designed to protect the public by setting the conditions under which various private activities can be undertaken." These policies tend to be wide reaching in their effort to thwart harmful practices and extend to a large variety of topics, from fair business and labor practices to consumer safety and environmental issues (p. 21). Examples of protective regulatory issues include outlawing the movement of persons between jobs in federal regulatory agencies and the industries they regulate, creating federal regulatory agencies, opposing compulsory arbitration in labor disputes, and extending the Water Pollution Control Act to all navigable rivers.

Competitive regulatory policies, which impose limits or regulations that influence the number of competitors in an industry, were scarce. I found only ten stances on competitive regulatory issues during the forty-year period. Examples of positions on issues concerning the regulation of competition include the lessening of federal control over the radio and television industry, opposition to the breakup of oil companies, and state ownership of offshore oil reserves.

The last two categories relate to foreign affairs and defense. Structural policy involves the procurement and management of military resources. Policy decisions in this area commonly involve "specific defense procurement decisions for individual weapon systems; the placement, expansion, contraction, and closing of military bases and other facilities in the United States; the retention, expansion, or contraction of reserve military forces; and the creation and retention of programs that send surplus farm commodities overseas" (p. 23). Examples of structural issue stances include proposals for creating a post to assist the president with national security and international affairs, establishing an airborne alert for the Strategic Air Command, creating a jet airlift for conventional forces, halting of the deployment of American nuclear missiles, and modernizing military weapons systems.

Strategic policy involves the relation of the United States to other nations and generally involves the assertion of military, economic, or diplomatic influence (p. 23). Examples of strategic issue statements include proposals for a Soviet-American treaty banning intermediate-range nuclear weapons, action against terrorist base camps, the recognition of Jerusalem as the capitol of Israel, a strengthened Peace Corps, and the normalization of relations with mainland China.

Coding Stances for Directionality

The categories of public policy do not allow for the differentiation of how candidates stand in relation to the types of policies upon which they take stances. Thus trying to determine a party's general inclinations toward a policy type can be difficult. For example, from 1952 to 1992 Republican candidates devoted 27% of their issue statements to redistributive policies, whereas Democratic candidates devoted 23% of their issue statements to redistributive policies. This observation may lead to a conclusion that Republican candidates favor redistributive policies slightly more than do Democratic candidates, which simply is not the case.

To refine the analysis I further evaluated the issue statements involving distributive, redistributive, structural, and strategic policies to determine whether they called for an increase, decrease, or a maintenance of the status quo on a particular issue. These distinctions make it possible to examine whether Republican candidates are likely to oppose increases in support for redistributive policies. I identified statements as favoring an increase in a policy type if the statement contained words such as *increase, develop, expand, propose, extend, raise, strengthen, improve, promote, endorse, initiate,* or *call for*. On the other hand statements that use words such as *reduce, cut, oppose, slow,* or *eliminate* usually seek a decrease in a particular policy type. Similarly statements that use words such as *continue, keep, not reduce,* or *oppose the repeal* usually seek to maintain the status quo. Of course I also had to examine the context and tone of the issue statement to determine its directionality.

Distributive issue stances were fairly straightforward. If a candidate says, "I support the Social Security system and want to see it strengthened," the candidate is in favor of increasing a distributive policy. A statement such as, "A critical reexamination is also needed of federal grant-in-aid programs with a view to eliminating those no longer necessary and channeling the remaining ones through the states," is easily identified as favoring a decrease in distributive policy. Similarly a candidate who wants to maintain public control of national forest ranges is in favor of the status quo on the issue. Some issues are less explicit but these can still be coded based on the tone of the stance. For example, a candidate who says, "We should explore at once the appointment of a task force to put the Democratic farm program in shape for swift action at the opening of Congress," is being less than explicit ("explore") but does express a positive position and can thus be coded as a seeking an increase in distributive policy.

The coding of redistributive policy proceeds similarly but is somewhat more complex. Some issues are relatively straightforward, such as a stance opposed to socialized medicine, which would be coded as seeking a decrease in redistributive policy. On the other hand many redistributive issues involve ambiguity. School prayer is a good example. An issue statement in favor of school prayer could be interpreted variously as seeking an increase in civil rights or a decrease in civil rights. This analysis compared issues against what would be a status quo stance. Because the Supreme Court today interprets the Constitution as protecting civil liberties by banning prayer in schools, stances that favor allowing prayer in schools call for an end to a redistributive policy. Thus such a stance would be coded as a seeking a decrease in redistributive policy. This rule tends to understate the differences between Republicans and Democrats on the direction of their redistributive issue stances.

The coding of structural and strategic policies follows the same rules with a few additions. If a candidate called for an end to or limitation on nuclear testing, research on chemical or biological warfare, or any other military resource by means of a treaty or international agreement, I coded the statement as seeking an increase in strategic policy. However, if a candidate called for a unilateral end to or limits on any such activity as a unilateral measure, I coded the statement as seeking a decrease in structural policy. If a candidate proposed a nonspecific revision in foreign policy, such as a revision of immigration laws, I coded the statement as seeking an increase in strategic policy. If an issue statement called for the removal of the United States from the United Nations or an end to funding to the United Nations as a means to another end, such as protecting Israel from negative U.N. resolutions, I coded the stance as seeking an increase in strategic policy. If a candidate called for removal of the United States from the United Nations as an end in itself, I coded the statement as seeking a decrease in strategic policy. The last situation deserving mention is the demand that another nation or group meet a U.N. resolution. If the position called for compliance before talks or recognition, I coded the stance as a status quo. If the position called for compliance to avert military action against a nation or group, I coded the statement as seeking an increase in strategic policy.

Appendix 2: Rules for Selecting Party Leaders

I defined as *party leaders* those individuals holding prominent party leadership posts or constitutional offices in Congress. These were party leaders elected or reelected to their leadership posts after the November presidential elections. This general rule guarantees that agreement between presidential candidates and party leaders considers the views of the actual party leaders serving during the first term of the newly elected president. The rule, however, had to be modified in two ways.

First, the 1972 data use the Democratic Party leaders, Hale Boggs and Thomas "Tip" O'Neill, who served during the second session of the 92d Congress in 1972 rather than those who began their service in the 93d Congress in 1972. The justification for this change is that Majority Leader Boggs was killed in a plane crash over Alaska on October 10, 1972. The accident occurred near the end of the second session of the 92d Congress. Tip O'Neill was elected to fill Boggs's post. O'Neill then appointed Representative John J. McFall of California as majority whip without the benefit of an election. This research uses Boggs and O'Neill as Democratic leaders, rather than O'Neill and McFall, because the change in leadership was neither anticipated nor intended.

Second, the 1988 research requires a note of explanation because of the unique circumstances surrounding changes in House party leadership. I used Representative Thomas Foley of Washington as House majority leader rather than Representative Richard Gephardt, and I categorized Representative Tony Coehlo of California, not Representative William Gray of Pennsylvania,as the House majority whip. Gephardt and Gray became leaders on June 14, 1989, to fill the vacancies created by the resignations of Speaker Jim Wright and Majority Whip Coehlo. I used Representative Richard Cheney of Wyoming as the House minority whip even though he resigned in March 1989 to become secretary of defense after John Tower's nomination was rejected.

Names, Party Affiliations, and Positions of Party Leaders Used in Research, 1952–1992

1952—83RD CONGRESS

Henry Styles Bridges	R-N.H.	President pro tempore
Robert A. Taft	R-Ohio	Senate majority leader
Leverett Saltonstall	R-Mass.	Senate majority whip
Lyndon B. Johnson	D-Texas	Senate minority leader
Earle Clements	D-Ky.	Senate minority whip
Joseph W. Martin Jr.	R-Mass.	Speaker of the House
Charles A. Halleck	R-Ind.	House majority leader
Leslie Arends	R-Ill.	House majority whip
Sam Rayburn	D-Tex.	House minority leader
John McCormack	D-Mass.	House minority whip

1956—85TH CONGRESS

Carl Trumbull Hayden	D-Ariz.	President pro tempore
Lyndon B. Johnson	D-Tex.	Senate majority leader
Mike Mansfield	D-Mont.	Senate majority whip
William F. Knowland	R-Calif.	Senate minority leader
Everett M. Dirksen	R-Ill.	Senate minority whip
Samuel Rayburn	D-Tex.	Speaker of the House
John McCormack	D-Mass.	House majority leader
Carl Albert	D-Okla.	House majority whip
Joseph W. Martin Jr.	R-Mass.	House minority leader
Leslie Arends	R-Ill.	House minority whip

1960—87TH CONGRESS

Carl Hayden	D-Ariz.	President pro tempore

Mike Mansfield	D-Mont.	Senate majority leader
Hubert Humphrey	D-Minn.	Senate majority whip
Everett Dirksen	R-Ill.	Senate minority leader
Thomas Kuchel	R-Calif.	Senate minority whip
Samuel Rayburn	D-Tex.	Speaker of the House
John McCormack	D-Mass.	House majority leader
Carl Albert	D-Okla.	House majority whip
Charles Halleck	R-Ind.	House minority leader
Leslie C. Arends	R-Ill.	House minority whip

1964—89TH CONGRESS

Carl Hayden	D-Ariz.	President pro tempore
Mike Mansfield	D-Mont.	Senate majority leader
Russell Long	D-La.	Senate majority whip
Everett M. Dirksen	R-Ill.	Senate minority leader
Thomas Kuchel	R-Calif.	Senate minority whip
John McCormack	D-Mass.	Speaker of the House
Carl Albert	D-Okla.	House majority leader
Hale Boggs	D-La.	House majority whip
Gerald R. Ford	R-Mich.	House minority leader
Leslie C. Arends	R-Ill.	House minority whip

1968—91ST CONGRESS

Richard B. Russell Jr.	D-Ga.	President pro tempore
Mike Mansfield	D-Mont.	Senate majority leader
Edward M. Kennedy	D-Mass.	Senate majority whip
Everett Dirksen	R-Ill.	Senate minority leader
Hugh Scott	R-Pa.	Senate minority whip
John McCormack	D-Mass.	Speaker of the House
Carl Albert	D-Okla.	House majority leader
Hale Boggs	D-La.	House majority whip
Gerald R. Ford	R-Mich.	House minority leader
Leslie Arends	R-Ill.	House minority whip

1972—93D CONGRESS*

James Eastland	D-Miss.	President pro tempore
Mike Mansfield	D-Mont.	Senate majority leader

* See explanation at beginning of Appendix 2.

Robert C. Byrd	D-W. Va.	Senate majority whip
Hugh Scott	R-Pa.	Senate minority leader
Robert Griffin	R-Mich.	Senate minority whip
Carl Albert	D-Okla.	Speaker of the House
Hale Boggs	D-La.	House majority leader
Thomas P. O'Neill Jr.	D-Mass.	House majority whip
Gerald R. Ford	R-Mich.	House minority leader
Leslie Arends	R-Ill.	House minority whip

1976—95TH CONGRESS

James Eastland	D-Miss.	President pro tempore
Robert C. Byrd	D-W. Va.	Senate majority leader
Alan Cranston	D-Calif.	Senate majority whip
Howard H. Baker	R-Tenn.	Senate minority leader
Ted Stevens	R-Alaska	Senate minority whip
Thomas P. O'Neill Jr.	D-Mass.	Speaker of the House
Jim Wright	D-Tex.	House majority leader
John Brademas	D-Ind.	House majority whip
John J. Rhodes	R-Ariz.	House minority leader
Robert H. Michel	R-Ill.	House minority whip

1980—97TH CONGRESS

James S. Thurmond	R-S.C.	President pro tempore
Howard H. Baker	R-Tenn.	Senate majority leader
Ted Stevens	R-Alaska	Senate majority whip
Robert C. Byrd	D-W. Va.	Senate minority leader
Alan Cranston	D-Calif.	Senate minority whip
Thomas P. O'Neill Jr.	D-Mass.	Speaker of the House
Jim Wright	D-Texas	House majority leader
Thomas S. Foley	D-Wash.	House majority whip
Robert H. Michel	R-Ill.	House minority leader
Trent Lott	R-Miss.	House minority whip

1984—99TH CONGRESS

James S. Thurmond	R-S.C.	President pro tempore
Robert Dole	R-Kans.	Senate majority leader
Alan K. Simpson	R-Wy.	Senate majority whip
Robert C. Byrd	D-W. Va.	Senate minority leader
Alan Cranston	D-Calif.	Senate minority whip

Thomas P. O'Neill Jr.	D-Mass.	Speaker of the House
Jim Wright	D-Texas	House majority leader
Thomas S. Foley	D-Wash.	House majority whip
Robert H. Michel	R-Ill.	House minority leader
Trent Lott	R-Miss.	House minority whip

1988—101ST CONGRESS

Robert C. Byrd	D-W. Va.	President pro tempore
George J. Mitchell	D-Maine	Senate majority leader
Alan Cranston	D-Calif.	Senate majority whip
Robert Dole	R-Kans.	Senate minority leader
Alan K. Simpson	R-Wy.	Senate minority whip
Jim Wright	D-Tex.	Speaker of the House
Thomas S. Foley	D-Wash.	House majority leader
Tony Coehlo	D-Calif.	House majority whip
Robert H. Michel	R-Ill.	House minority leader
Richard Cheney	R-Wy.	House minority whip

1992—103D CONGRESS

Robert Byrd	D-W. Va.	President pro tempore
George J. Mitchell	D-Maine	Senate majority leader
Wendell H. Ford	D-Ky.	Senate majority whip
Robert Dole	R-Kans.	Senate minority leader
Alan K. Simpson	R-Wy.	Senate minority whip
Thomas S. Foley	D-Wash.	Speaker of the House
Richard A. Gephardt	D-Mo.	House majority leader
David E. Bonior	D-Mich.	House majority whip
Robert H. Michel	R-Ill.	House minority leader
Newt Gingrich	R-Ga.	House minority whip

Determination of Issue Stances

I applied the original coding rules that I used for the presidential candidates' positions, taken from the *New York Times*, to the coding of issue stances for party leaders from Congress (see Appendix 1). However, I took issue stances for the party leaders from both the *New York Times* and *Congressional Quarterly Weekly Report*.

I took the policy positions of the congressional party leaders from articles that appeared in the two publications between May of the election year and election day. I used this extended time period for three reasons. First, a party leader may attempt to influence the outcome of primaries by articulating stances that are different from the eventual winner's. This would be an indication of disagreement with the nominee's position and is important for the prospects of governing. Second, party leaders in Congress do play an important role in shaping the agenda of the party. Their attempts to set the agenda for the party point to areas of conflict between a winner of the campaign and the congressional party leaders who would work with the president. This influence assumes added meaning during a presidential election year, so a period during which party leaders articulate their positions is necessary to study the full effect of interactions between electoral and governing coalitions. Finally, the number of statements made by party leaders is smaller than the number made by presidential candidates. An extended period of study produces more issue stances that can be compared to those of the presidential candidates.

Once again I followed the coding rules reported in Appendix 1, with some modifications for *Congressional Quarterly Weekly Report,* to determine when quoted and attributed statements made by party leaders had enough policy content to be coded. The modifications are as follows:

- I coded statements by a reporter that indicate a party leader's policy stance, even if I could find no corresponding statement quoted from or attributed to the party leader.
- I coded reports of a party leader's sponsorship of, authorship of, or act of presenting a legislative action. However, I coded these instances only if the leader's actions are mentioned in the body of an article, not when they are merely included in a list at the end of an article and not when the position was listed in a comprehensive legislative report. The justification for these exclusions is similar to the justification for using the *New York Times*. The focus of this research is public policy positions taken by party leaders and presidential candidates. Conflicts that occur in public are deemed to be more serious and less susceptible to resolution. Most legislative actions are not public in the sense the mass media make the greater public aware of them. But when a party leader's actions gain sufficient notice to be reported in the mass media, the party leader would regard the report as a public pronouncement of the issue stance. Because *Congressional Quarterly Weekly Report* is a somewhat specialized media source,

it reports legislative actions in a comprehensive manner. I did not code legislative actions mentioned in *Congressional Quarterly Weekly Report* within lists or comprehensive legislative action reports because I could not safely assume that the party leader regarded the stance as significant.

• When a party leader in any way expressed support for or opposition to a piece of legislation, I did not code the various provisions of the individual piece of legislation as separate issue stances unless the party leader specifically mentioned them. Therefore I considered the various provisions together. Here the problem is inferring support or lack of support for particular provisions of legislation for which the party leader has expressed general support. The only reasonable choice was to consider all provisions as a whole when comparing the issue stances of party leaders to those of the presidential candidates. I followed this rule except when a presidential candidate made specific statements or promises that both agreed and disagreed with individual provisions of a single legislative action supported or opposed by a party leader or when the format or content of the *Congressional Quarterly Weekly Report* article seemed to warrant the separation of an action's provisions in relation to the overall party leader's support or opposition.

• When a party leader made conflicting statements, I coded the last position enunciated by the party leader.

• When a party leader took similar positions on an issue,I combined them and treated them as a single position. But if a party leader's position varied even slightly, I coded the variations separately. For example, Speaker Thomas Foley in 1992 lobbied against the Interior Committee's Old-Growth Forest Bill because of its extensive provisions protecting Pacific Northwest forests—habitat of the spotted owl—from loggers. However, he hesitantly supported a similar bill by the Agricultural Committee that had more lenient old-growth provisions for the protection of the spotted owl. Another example from 1992 involves Majority Leader Gephardt, who urged that worker-training provisions be included in the North American Free Trade Agreement (NAFTA) for workers who lose their jobs because of the agreement, to be funded through a NAFTA-provided cross-border transaction tax. Gephardt also supported purely domestic job-training programs independent of the NAFTA treaty.

• I coded issue stances reported in *Congressional Quarterly Weekly Report* between May 1 and the election date. The exceptions are those few stances when the context indicated that the positions probably were not taken within the time parameters and the party leader's current position could be different. I did not code stances taken before the time period but reported in *Congressional Quarterly Weekly Report* within the time limits. A single exception to this rule was a statement made before May 1 that I included because of its direct relevance to the presidential campaign.

Notes

Introduction: Political Parties and the Question of Democracy

1. David B. Magleby and Kelly D. Patterson, "Poll Trends: Congressional Reform," *Public Opinion Quarterly* 58 (Fall 1994): 423; see also Kelly D. Patterson and David B. Magleby, "Public Support for Congress," *Public Opinion Quarterly* 56 (Winter 1992): 539–51.
2. Poll for the Wall Street Journal/NBC News, January 23–28, 1993; see Gerald F.Seib, "Clinton Builds Positive Rating to 64% in Survey with Public Willing to Forgive Early Missteps," *Wall Street Journal*, January 29, 1993, 16A.
3. James Ceaser, "Down in the Polls When He Should Be Up, Bill Clinton Appears in Trouble," *Public Perspective* 4 (May–June 1993): 3.
4. For why divided party control would create certain problems for government see Gary W. Cox and Samuel Kernell, "Introduction: Governing a Divided Era," in *The Politics of Divided Government*, ed. Gary W. Cox and Samuel Kernell (Boulder, Colo.: Westview, 1991), 1–10.
5. David B. Magleby, *KBYU–Utah Colleges Exit Poll 1994* (Provo, Utah: Brigham Young University, 1994).
6. Newt Gingrich and Dick Armey, *Contract with America*, ed. Ed Gillespie and Bob Schellhas (New York: Times Books, 1994), 15.
7. Karlyn H. Bowman and Everett Carll Ladd, eds. "Public Opinion and Demographic Report," *American Enterprise* 4 (November–December 1993): 94–95.
8. See John R. Hibbing and Elizabeth Theiss-Morse, *Congress as Public*

Enemy: Public Attitudes Toward American Political Institutions (New York: Cambridge University Press, 1995), particularly chaps. 1 and 7.

9. Two recent examples of alarmist titles are William Lance Bennett's *The Governing Crisis: Media, Money, and Marketing in American Elections* (New York: St. Martin's Press, 1991) and H. Mark Roelofs's *The Poverty of American Politics: A Theoretical Interpretation* (Philadelphia: Temple University Press, 1992).
10. For a theoretical discussion of why this is so see Neil Postman, *Amusing Ourselves to Death: Public Discourse in the Age of Show Business* (New York: Viking Penguin, 1985).
11. See David M. Ricci, *The Transformation of American Politics: The New Washington and the Rise of Think Tanks* (New Haven, Conn.: Yale University Press, 1993), particularly ch. 4.
12. James W. Ceaser, *Liberal Democracy and Political Science* (Baltimore: John Hopkins University Press, 1990), 8.
13. Giovanni Sartori, *A Theory of Democracy Revisited* (Chatham, N.J.: Chatham House, 1987), 3.
14. Moisei Ostrogorski, *Democracy and the Organization of Political Parties, II: The United States*, Transaction editor Seymour Martin Lipset (New Brunswick, N.J.: Transaction Books, 1982); Robert Michels, *Political Parties: A Sociological Study of the Oligarchical Tendencies of Modern Democracy*, trans. Eden Paul and Cedar Paul (New York: Free Press, 1962).
15. E. E. Schattschneider, *Party Government*, ed. Phillips Bradley (New York: Holt, Rinehart, and Winston, 1942), 1.
16. Sartori, *Democracy Revisited*, 17.
17. Parties can be understood explicitly as organizations designed to win electoral office, a conceptualization that does fit nicely with the democratic theory of Giovanni Sartori. Joseph A. Schlesinger has particularly emphasized this aspect of political parties. See, for example, Joseph A. Schlesinger, "The New American Political Party," *American Political Science Review* 79 (December 1985): 1152–69.
18. Giovanni Sartori, *Parties and Party Systems: A Framework for Analysis*, vol. 1 (New York: Cambridge University Press, 1976), 49.
19. Sartori, *Democracy Revisited*, 64, emphasis in original.
20. For a thorough discussion of this point see Ibid., 58–72.
21. Ibid., 98.
22. Ibid., 102–15.
23. David R. Mayhew, *Divided We Govern: Party Control, Lawmaking, and Investigations, 1946–1990* (New Haven, Conn.: Yale University Press, 1991), 199.
24. Sartori, *Democracy Revisited*, 206.
25. For further discussion see Sartori, *Democracy Revisited*, chaps. 5 and 8.
26. Paul T. David, Ralph M. Goldman, and Richard C. Bain, *The Politics of*

National Party Conventions (Washington, D.C.: Brookings Institution, 1960), 6.

27. See Ceaser, *Liberal Democracy and Political Science*, ch. 8.

1. Party Performance and the Decline-of-Party Thesis

1. Paul Allen Beck and Frank J. Sorauf, *Party Politics in America*, 7th ed. (New York: HarperCollins, 1992), chaps. 1 and 2.
2. Some commentators refer to the lack of linkage in the three forms of the political party as party decline.
3. See, among others, Richard Hofstadter, *The Idea of a Party System: The Rise of Legitimate Opposition in the United States, 1780–1840* (Berkeley: University of California Press, 1969), and Douglas W. Jaenicke, "The Jacksonian Integration of Parties into the Constitutional System," *Political Science Quarterly* 101, no. 1 (1986): 85.
4. Some of the more prominent discussions of the role of political parties and partisanship are found in these books: Angus Campbell, Philip E. Converse, Warren E. Miller, and Donald E. Stokes, *The American Voter* (New York: John Wiley, 1960); Sidney Verba and Norman H. Nie, *Participation in America: Political Democracy and Social Equality* (New York: Harper and Row, 1972); Hofstadter, *The Idea of a Party System*; and William H. Flanigan and Nancy H. Zingale, *Political Behavior of the American Electorate*, 7th ed. (Washington, D.C.: Congressional Quarterly Press, 1991).
5. See, for example, William J. Keefe, *Parties, Politics, and Public Policy in America*, 5th ed. (Washington, D.C.: Congressional Quarterly Press, 1988).
6. One of the earliest works to argue for strengthened political parties is Committee on Political Parties of the American Political Science Association, *Toward a More Responsible Two-Party System* (New York: Rinehart, 1950). A more recent account appears in James L. Sundquist, *Constitutional Reform and Effective Government*, rev. ed. (Washington, D.C.: Brookings Institution, 1992), particularly ch. 6.
7. Gary R. Orren, "The Changing Styles of American Party Politics," in *The Future of American Political Parties: The Challenge of Governance*, ed. Joel L. Fleishman (Englewood Cliffs, N.J.: Prentice-Hall, 1982), 31.
8. See Richard G. Niemi and Herbert F. Weisberg, eds., *Controversies in Voting Behavior*, 3d ed. (Washington D.C.: Congressional Quarterly Press, 1993); Campbell and others, *The American Voter*; and Bernard R. Berelson, Paul F. Lazarsfeld, and William N. McPhee, *Voting: A Study of Opinion Formation in a Presidential Campaign* (Chicago: University of Chicago Press, 1954).
9. For institutional causes of the decline see Everett Carll Ladd, *Where Have All the Voters Gone? The Fracturing of America's Political Parties*, 2d ed. (New York: W. W. Norton. 1982), ch. 3.

10. Martin P. Wattenberg, *The Decline of American Political Parties, 1952–1980* (Cambridge, Mass.: Harvard University Press, 1984), ch. 4.
11. James L. Sundquist, "The Crisis of Competence in Our National Government," *Political Science Quarterly* 95 (Summer 1980): 183–208.
12. Wattenberg, *Decline of American Political Parties*, 4.
13. U.S. Congress, House, Democratic Caucus, *Preamble and Rules of the Democratic Caucus*, rev., 102d Cong., 1st sess., January 9, 1991, ii.
14. See part 2 of David Mayhew, *Congress: The Electoral Connection* (New Haven, Conn.: Yale University Press, 1974).
15. House Democratic Caucus, *Preamble and Rules*, Rule 1, paragraph C.
16. See Gerald M. Pomper, *Passions and Interests: Political Party Concepts of American Democracy* (Lawrence: University Press of Kansas, 1992), 118–21.
17. James W. Davis, *National Conventions in an Age of Party Reform* (Westport, Conn.: Greenwood, 1985), 19.
18. William Crotty and John S. Jackson III, *Presidential Primaries and Nominations* (Washington, D.C.: Congressional Quarterly Press, 1985), 17.
19. The elections studied in this book are not exhaustive of the elections in the age of the brokered convention.
20. Nelson W. Polsby, *Consequences of Party Reform* (New York: Oxford University Press, 1983), 34–35.
21. Ibid., 34.
22. Ibid., 35.
23. Ibid.
24. Ibid., 49.
25. Kenneth A. Bode and Carol F. Casey, "Party Reform: Revisionism Revised," in *Political Parties in the Eighties*, ed. Robert A. Goldwin (Washington, D.C.: American Enterprise Institute for Public Policy Research, and Gambier, Ohio: Kenyon College, 1980), 6.
26. Polsby, *Consequences of Party Reform*, 35.
27. Ibid., 48.
28. Ibid., 42.
29. Bode and Casey, "Party Reform," 7.
30. Pope McCorkle and Joel L. Fleishman, "Political Parties and Presidential Nominations: The Intellectual Ironies of Reform and Change in the Mass Media Age," in *The Future of American Political Parties*, 143.
31. William Crotty, *American Parties in Decline*, 2d ed. (Boston: Little, Brown, 1984), 193.
32. Ibid.
33. See James A. Reichley, "The Rise of National Parties," in *The New Direction in American Politics*, ed. John E. Chubb and Paul E. Peterson (Washington, D.C.: Brookings Institution, 1985), 175–200.
34. Pomper, *Passions and Interests*, 118.

35. David B. Truman, "Party Reform, Party Atrophy, and Constitutional Change: Some Reflections," *Political Science Quarterly* 99 (Winter 1984–85): 645.
36. Tip O'Neill and William Novak, *Man of the House: The Life and Political Memoirs of Speaker Tip O'Neill* (New York: Random House, 1987), 36.
37. See Sidney Hyman, "Nine Tests for the Presidential Hopeful," *New York Times Magazine*, January 4, 1959, 11.
38. Jonathan Alter, Mark Miller, and Eleanor Clift, "Gary's Sound-Bite Campaign," *Newsweek*, January 4, 1988, 22.
39. Ibid.
40. Stephen J. Wayne, *The Road to the White House: The Politics of Presidential Elections*, 2d ed. (New York: St. Martin's Press, 1984), 15.
41. Leon D. Epstein, *Political Parties in the American Mold* (Madison: University of Wisconsin Press, 1986), 303.
42. Frank J. Sorauf, "Political Parties and Political Action Committees: Two Life Cycles," *Arizona Law Review* 22, no. 2 (1980): 451.
43. For two excellent treatments of the efforts of the congressional party organizations to assist candidates see Paul S. Herrnson, *Party Campaigning in the 1980s* (Cambridge, Mass.: Harvard University Press, 1988), ch. 4, and David E. Price, *Bringing Back the Parties* (Washington, D.C.: Congressional Quarterly Press, 1984), ch. 9.
44. For a discussion of the role that national party organizations can play in raising money for congressional campaigns see Paul Herrnson, "National Party, Decision-Making Strategies, and Resource Distribution in Congressional Elections," *Western Political Quarterly* 42 (September 1989): 301–23.
45. Norman J. Ornstein, Thomas E. Mann, and Michael J. Malbin, *Vital Statistics on Congress, 1993–1994* (Washington, D.C.: Congressional Quarterly Press, 1994), 69.
46. Ibid., 72.
47. Darrell M. West, *Air Wars: Television Advertising in Election Campaigns, 1952–1992* (Washington, D.C.: Congressional Quarterly, 1993), ch. 5; Paul S. Herrnson, *Congressional Elections: Campaigning at Home and in Washington* (Washington, D.C.: Congressional Quarterly Press, 1995), ch. 7.
48. For further discussion of these issues see Michael J. Malbin, ed., *Money and Politics in the United States: Financing Elections in the 1980s* (Chatham, N.J.: Chatham House, 1984); Herbert E. Alexander, *Financing Politics: Money, Elections, and Political Reform*, 3d ed. (Washington D.C.: Congressional Quarterly Press, 1984); Gary C. Jacobson, *Money in Congressional Elections* (New Haven, Conn.: Yale University Press, 1980); and Herrnson, *Congressional Elections*, ch. 9.
49. An extreme example of this situation occurred during the 1986 elections

in Illinois. Two candidates from the Lyndon Larouche Party, a right-wing organization, won two places in the general election on the Democratic ballot. One individual won the Democratic nomination for lieutenant governor, and the other won the nomination for secretary of state. This probably could not happen in a congressional election because primary candidates usually have a much higher profile. However, because of the direct primary the parties can do little to prevent candidates of any ideological persuasion from contesting for a place on the ballot in the general election.

50. Crotty, *American Parties in Decline*, 232.
51. Roger H. Davidson and Walter J. Olezek, *Congress and Its Members*, 2d ed. (Washington D.C.: Congressional Quarterly Press, 1985), 173.
52. Barbara Sinclair, "The Speaker's Task Force in the Post-Reform House of Representatives," *American Political Science Review* 75 (June 1981): 397–410; and James G. Gimpel, *Legislating the Revolution: The Contract with America in its First 100 Days* (Needham Heights, Mass.: Allyn and Bacon, 1996).
53. Paul S. Herrnson and Kelly D. Patterson, "Toward a More Programmatic Democratic Party? Agenda-Setting and Coalition-Building in the House of Representatives," *Polity* 27 (Summer 1995): 619–25.
54. Kenneth A. Shepsle, *The Giant Jigsaw Puzzle: Democratic Committee Assignments in the Modern House* (Chicago: University of Chicago Press, 1978).
55. O'Neill and Novak, *Man of the House*, 282.
56. James L. Sundquist, *The Decline and Resurgence of Congress* (Washington, D.C.: Brookings Institution, 1981).
57. For a discussion of this episode see David W. Rohde, *Parties and Leaders in the Post-Reform House* (Chicago: University of Chicago Press, 1991), 22–23.
58. Melissa P. Collie and David W. Brady, "The Decline of Partisan Voting Coalitions in the House of Representatives," in *Congress Reconsidered*, 3d ed., ed. Lawrence C. Dodd and Bruce I. Oppenheimer (Washington, D.C.: Congressional Quarterly Press, 1985), 285.
59. Ibid.
60. Ibid.
61. Xandra Kayden and Eddie Mahe Jr., *The Party Goes On: The Persistence of the Two-Party System in the United States* (New York: Basic Books, 1985); Larry J. Sabato, *The Party's Just Begun: Shaping Political Parties for America's Future* (Glenview, Ill.: Scott, Foresman, 1988).
62. For example, see John F. Bibby, "Party Renewal in the National Republican Party," in *Party Renewal in America: Theory and Practice*, ed. Gerald M. Pomper (New York: Praeger, 1980), 102–15; Cornelius P. Cotter and John F. Bibby, "Institutional Development of Parties and the Thesis of Party Decline," *Political Science Quarterly* 95 (Spring 1980): 1–27; James L.

Gibson, Cornelius P. Cotter, John F. Bibby, and Robert J. Huckshorn, "Whither the Local Parties?: A Cross-Sectional and Longitudinal Analysis of the Strength of Party Organizations," *American Journal of Political Science* 29 (February 1985): 139–60; and Paul S. Herrnson, "Do Parties Make a Difference? The Role of Party Organizations in Congressional Elections," *Journal of Politics* 48 (August 1986): 589–615.

63. See Lloyd N. Cutler, "To Form a Government," *Foreign Affairs* 59 (Fall 1980): 126–43; James MacGregor Burns, *The Power to Lead: The Crisis of the American Presidency* (New York: Simon and Schuster, 1984); and Austin Ranney, *Curing the Mischiefs of Faction: Party Reform in America* (Los Angeles: University of California Press, 1975).
64. See, for example, Gary C. Jacobson, "Party Organization and Distribution of Campaign Resources: Republicans and Democrats in 1982," *Political Science Quarterly* 100 (Winter 1985–86): 603–25.
65. Ornstein, Mann, and Malbin, *Vital Statistics*, 98.
66. Herrnson, "Do Parties Make a Difference?" and Herrnson, *Party Campaigning in the 1980s*, chaps. 4 and 5.
67. Richard E. Neustadt, *Presidential Power: The Politics of Leadership from FDR to Carter* (New York: John Wiley, 1980).
68. See, for example, the essays in Richard Pious, ed., *The Power to Govern: Assessing Reform in the United States* (Montpelier, Vt.: Capital City Press, 1981).
69. For an example of this type of work see William Greider, *Who Will Tell the People? The Betrayal of American Democracy* (New York: Simon and Schuster, 1992), particularly ch. 10.
70. Lester G. Seligman and Cary R. Covington, *The Coalitional Presidency* (Chicago: Dorsey Press, 1989), chaps. 1 and 2.
71. Paul Charles Light, *The President's Agenda: Domestic Policy Choice from Kennedy to Reagan*, rev. ed. (Baltimore: Johns Hopkins University Press, 1983); Jeff Fishel, *Presidents and Promises: From Campaign Pledge to Presidential Performance* (Washington, D.C.: Congressional Quarterly Press, 1985).
72. Seligman and Covington, *The Coalitional Presidency*, 7.
73. See Nelson W. Polsby and Aaron Wildavsky, *Presidential Elections: Strategies of American Electoral Politics*, 6th ed. (New York: Charles Scribner's Sons, 1984), 97–108.
74. Lester G. Seligman, "Electoral Governing Coalitions in the Presidency: A Theory and a Case Study," *Congress and the Presidency* 10 (Autumn 1983): 125; Seligman and Covington, *Coalitional Presidency*, 8–9.
75.. Seligman and Covington, *Coalitional Presidency*, 9.
76. Ibid., 12.
77. Seligman, "Electoral Governing Coalitions," 125.
78. Ibid.

79. Michael G. Krukones, *Promises and Performance: Presidential Campaigns as Policy Predictors* (Lanham, Md.: University Press of America, 1984), 126. Krukones separates presidential elections into two groups, using 1948 as the cutoff point because of the passage of the Twenty-second Amendment and not because of any assumption he makes about the different party eras. It is the Twenty-second Amendment, he argues, that affects the rate of fulfillment of second-term presidents.
80. Fishel, *Presidents and Promises*, 42.
81. David Mayhew, *Divided We Govern: Party Control, Lawmaking, and Investigations, 1946–1990* (New Haven, Conn.: Yale University Press, 1991), 199.
82. The differences in the rates of fulfillment can be attributed to differences in measurement. Krukones does not distinguish the different kinds of promises, whereas Fishel does. Fishel creates four types of promises based on the specificity of the promise. He then examines the rate of fulfillment for each kind of promise.
83. Mayhew, *Divided We Govern*, 198.

2. Presidential Issue Stances and Party Platforms: Party Cohesion or Disintegration?

1. Paul S. Herrnson, *Party Campaigning in the 1980s* (Boston: Harvard University Press, 1988), chaps. 2 and 5.
2. Edward F. Cooke, "Drafting the 1952 Platforms," *Western Political Quarterly* 9 (September 1956): 699.
3. Paul T. David, Ralph M. Goldman, and Richard C. Bain, *The Politics of National Party Conventions* (Washington, D.C.: Brookings Institution, 1960), 407–408.
4. Martha Wagner Weinberg, "Writing the Republican Platform," *Political Science Quarterly* 92 (Winter 1977–78): 656.
5. James W. Davis, *National Conventions in an Age of Party Reform* (Westport, Conn.: Greenwood, 1983), 111.
6. Tip O'Neill and William Novak, *Man of the House: The Life and Political Memoirs of Speaker Tip O'Neill* (New York: Random House, 1987), 299.
7. Stephen J. Wayne, *The Road to the White House: The Politics of Presidential Elections*, 2d ed. (New York: St. Martin's Press, 1984), 144.
8. Davis, *National Conventions and Party Reform*, 111.
9. On differences between the Republican and Democratic parties see L. Sandy Maisel, *Parties and Elections in America: The Electoral Process*, 2d ed. (New York: McGraw-Hill, 1993), 252–53.
10. Davis, *National Conventions and Party Reform*, 120.
11. Walter J. Stone and Alan I. Abramowitz, "Ideology, Electability, and Candidate Choice," in *The Life of the Parties: Activists in Presidential*

Politics, ed. Ronald B. Rapoport, Alan I. Abramowitz, and John McGlennon (Lexington: University Press of Kentucky, 1986), 75–95.

12. A similar conclusion is reached by L. Sandy Maisel in his study of the 1992 platform-drafting process. See "The Platform-Writing Process: Candidate-Centered Platforms in 1992," *Political Science Quarterly* 108 (Winter 1993–94): 697.
13. Denis G. Sullivan, Jeffrey L. Pressman, Benjamin I. Page, and John J. Lyons, *The Politics of Representation: The Democratic Convention of 1972* (New York: St. Martin's Press, 1974), 91–92.
14. Ibid., 99.
15. Ibid., 100.
16. On Ron Brown's efforts to ensure that the platform-drafting process did not disrupt party unity, see Maisel, "The Platform-Writing Process," 671–98. For a study of the behavior of activists in presidential campaigns see Ronald B. Rapoport, "Elite Attitudinal Constraint," in *The Life of the Parties: Activists in Presidential Politics*, ed. Ronald B. Rapoport, Alan I. Abramowitz, and John McGlennon (Lexington: University Press of Kentucky, 1986), 145–63.
17. Gerald M. Pomper and Susan S. Lederman, *Elections in America: Control and Influence in Democratic Politics*, 2d ed. (New York: Longman, 1980); John D. Bradley, "Party Platforms and Party Performance Concerning Social Security," *Polity* 1 (Spring 1969): 337–58; Paul T. David, "Party Platforms as National Plans," *Public Administration Review* 31 (May–June 1971): 303–15; Ian Budge and Richard I. Hofferbert, "Mandates and Policy Outputs: U.S. Party Platforms and Federal Expenditures," *American Political Science Review* 84 (March 1990): 111–31.
18. Davis, *National Conventions and Party Reform*, 100.
19. Michael J. Malbin, "The Convention Platforms and Issue Activists," in *The American Elections of 1980*, ed. Austin Ranney (Washington, D.C.: American Enterprise Institute for Public Policy Research, 1981), 139.
20. See, for example, Joe Klein, "Plain Vanilla or Rain Forest Crunch?" *Newsweek*, July 18, 1994, 38.
21. Nelson W. Polsby, *Consequences of Party Reform* (New York: Oxford University Press, 1983), 5.
22. Thomas E. Patterson, *Out of Order* (New York: Alfred A. Knopf, 1993), 48.
23. See Appendix 1 for a discussion of the coding rules and how presidential issue stances were assembled.
24. Gerald R. Ford is included in this analysis as an incumbent presidential candidate.
25. George H. Gallup, *The Gallup Poll: Public Opinion, 1935–1971*, vol. 3 (New York: Random House, 1972), 1701.
26. Paul F. Boller Jr., *Presidential Campaigns* (New York: Oxford University Press, 1985), 297.

27. Davis, *National Conventions and Party Reform*, 150.
28. The changes in rates of agreement do not necessarily imply disagreement. A substantial number of promises are simply not mentioned in the platform.
29. The rate of agreement is computed by matching the policy positions of the candidates to the positions in the platforms of their respective parties. The number of agreements is then added and divided by the total number of positions staked out by the respective candidates. Positions not mentioned in the party platform are excluded from the figures. For a discussion of how the presidents' policy positions compared to the party platform see Appendix 1.
30. Donald Bruce Johnson, comp., *National Party Platforms, 1840–1976*, vol. 1 (Urbana: University of Illinois Press, 1978), 480.
31. Edward F. Cooke, "Drafting the 1952 Platforms," *Western Political Quarterly* 9 (September 1956): 712.
32. Ibid.
33. Stephen E. Ambrose, *Nixon: The Education of a Politician, 1913–1962* (New York: Simon and Schuster, 1987), 551.
34. Ibid., 552
35. Edward W. Chester, *A Guide to Political Platforms* (Hamden, Conn.: Archon Books, 1977), 252.
36. Congressional Quarterly, *National Party Conventions, 1831–1984* (Washington, D.C.: Congressional Quarterly Press, 1987), 107.
37. Chester, *Political Platforms*, 254.
38. Russell Baker, "Goldwater Hits Platform Accord," *New York Times*, July 24, 1960, 38.
39. Davis, *National Conventions and Party Reform*, 150.
40. Arthur M. Schlesinger Jr., *A Thousand Days: John F. Kennedy in the White House* (1965; reprint, Greenwich, Conn: Fawcett, 1967), 27.
41. Davis, *National Conventions and Party Reform*, 113.
42. See, for example, Davis, *National Conventions and Party Reform*; Wayne, *Road to the White House*; Malbin, "The Conventions, Platforms, and Issue Activists"; and Howard L. Reiter, *Selecting the President: The Nominating Process in Transition* (Philadelphia: University of Pennsylvania Press, 1985).
43. Hubert H. Humphrey, "Excerpts from Humphrey Text Dealing with Crime," *New York Times*, September 12, 1968, 36.
44. Congressional Quarterly, *National Party Conventions*, 116.
45. E. W. Kenworth, "Nixon Says Humphrey Harms Efforts of U.S. in Paris Talks," *New York Times*, September 26, 1968, 1.
46. Robert B. Semple Jr., "Nixon Scores U.S. Method of Enforcing Integration," *New York Times*, September 13, 1968, 50.
47. Johnson, *National Party Platforms*, vol. 1, 750.

48. E. W. Kenworthy, "Nixon Urges Four Steps to Curb Nation's Crime," *New York Times*, September 30, 1968, 1.
49. Robert B. Semple Jr., "Narcotics Laxity Alleged by Nixon," *New York Times*, September 17, 1968, 1.
50. See Lester G. Seligman, "Electoral Governing Coalitions in the Presidency: A Theory and a Case Study," *Congress and the Presidency* 10 (Autumn 1983): 125–46.
51. Ronald D. Elving, "Hoping to Attract More Voters, Democrats Offer Fewer Words," *Congressional Quarterly Weekly Report* 46 (June 2, 1988): 1797.
52. Johnson, *National Party Platforms*, vol. 2, 801–802.
53. Douglas E. Kneeland, "McGovern, in Jersey, Calls for $6-Billion Aid to Aged," *New York Times*, September 21, 1972, 1.
54. Johnson, *National Party Platforms*, vol. 2, 793.
55. Davis, *National Conventions and Party Reform*, 115.
56. Ibid., 116.
57. Boller, *Presidential Campaigns*, 347.
58. The Great Society comment is found in Chester, *Political Platforms*, 289; the "throwback" reference is from Congressional Quarterly, *National Party Conventions*, 127.
59. Chester, *Political Platforms*, 289.
60. Johnson, *National Party Platforms*, vol. 2, 935.
61. Ibid., 933–34.
62. Ibid., 934.
63. Ibid., 935.
64. James T. Wooten, "Carter Defends Congress and Assails Ford's Vetoes," *New York Times*, August 24, 1976, 17.
65. Johnson, *National Party Platforms*, vol. 2, 926.
66. Carter's remark about minimizing the need for abortion appears in Jimmy Carter, "Excerpts from Carter's News Conference Presenting Mondale as Choice for Vice President," *New York Times*, July 16, 1976, A-11; Carter's opposition to government financing of abortions appears in Kenneth A. Briggs, "Carter Campaign Moving to Mollify Catholics After Dispute over Democratic Party Abortion Stand," *New York Times*, August 26, 1976, 20.
67. James T. Wooten, "Carter Says Ford Lags as Reformer," *New York Times*, August 12, 1976, 1.
68. Jimmy Carter, *Keeping Faith: Memoirs of a President* (New York: Bantam, 1982), 27.
69. Phil Gailey, "Carter Urges Party to Offer a Policy Mix," *New York Times*, April 3, 1985, A-19.
70. Boller, *Presidential Campaigns*, 351.
71. What may have appeared to be purely utilitarian might also have been the result of how Carter viewed the presidency. President Carter often sought

to separate policy making from politics and saw himself as a "trustee" who was above politics. See ch. 1 in Charles O. Jones, *The Trusteeship Presidency: Jimmy Carter and the United States Congress* (Baton Rouge: Louisiana State University Press, 1988). However, even as a pure utilitarian or as a trustee, the risks to the basis of political support are the same.

72. Martha Wagner Weinberg, "Writing the Republican Platform," *Political Science Quarterly* 92 (Winter 1977–78): 655.
73. Ibid., 656.
74. Ibid., 661.
75. Congressional Quarterly, "Foreign Policy: Hub of Platform Conflict," *Congressional Quarterly Weekly Report* 34 (August 14, 1976): 2183.
76. Johnson, *National Party Platforms*, vol. 2, 983.
77. Ibid.
78. Ibid., 974.
79. Ibid., 975.
80. Ibid., 979.
81. See Weinberg, "Writing the Republican Platform."

3. Issue Stances and Issue Types: Governance Without Leaders?

1. See Jonathan Rauch, *Demosclerosis: The Silent Killer of American Government* (New York: Times Books, 1994), esp. ch. 6, and the National Academy of Public Administration, *Beyond Distrust: Building Bridges Between Congress and the Executive* (Washington, D.C.: 1992), esp. ch. 4.
2. Hart and Teeter Research Companies, *Public Perspective* 6 (June–July 1995): 57.
3. Theodore J. Lowi, "American Business, Public Policy, Case Studies, and Political Theory," *World Politics* 16 (July 1964): 677–715.
4. See David R. Mayhew, *Congress: The Electoral Connection* (New Haven, Conn.: Yale University Press, 1974), 84–105.
5. See, for example, Theodore J. Lowi, "Four Systems of Policy, Politics, and Choice," *Public Administration Review* 32 (July–August 1972): 298–310; Robert J. Spitzer, *The Presidency and Public Policy: The Four Arenas of Presidential Power* (University: University of Alabama Press, 1983); and Douglas D. Heckathorn and Steven M. Maser, "The Contractual Architecture of Public Policy: A Critical Reconstruction of Lowi's Typology," *Journal of Politics* 52 (November 1990): 1101–23.
6. Randall B. Ripley and Grace A. Franklin, *Congress, the Bureaucracy, and Public Policy*, 5th ed. (Pacific Grove, Calif.: Brooks Cole, 1991), 20–21.
7. These are difficult questions, most of which cannot be answered through strictly empirical studies. Party theorists should try to stipulate how governability can best be achieved.
8. The argument that political parties are increasingly irrelevant to voters is

made in Martin P. Wattenberg, *The Decline of American Political Parties, 1952–1988* (Cambridge, Mass.: Harvard University Press, 1984); see also Martin P. Wattenberg, "Dealignment in the American Electorate," in *Parties and Politics in American History*, ed. L. Sandy Maisel and William G. Shade (New York: Garland, 1994), 225–40.

9. The percentages reported are rounded to the nearest whole number. Percentages are computed by assigning each policy position to one of six categories. The total for each category is then divided by the total number of positions. Policy positions taken by presidential candidates are taken from a content analysis of the *New York Times*. See Appendix 1 for a discussion of the coding rules for presidential positions. Appendix 1 also contains a discussion of how issue positions were assigned to particular categories. Although this study used the competitive and protective regulatory categories, the results are not reported here. The number of competitive regulatory policies was too small to include (see Appendix 1). I omitted the protective regulatory category because I believe that the other policy types are more relevant to the argument over the decline of political parties.

10. Crowded primary fields may also induce candidates to make outrageous statements, not just redistributive statements. I have no measure of "outrageousness," but candidates must take the kinds of positions that attract supporters and get the candidates on the news. Redistributive issues are much more likely to succeed in these areas. See Thomas E. Patterson, *Out of Order* (New York: Alfred A. Knopf, 1993), ch. 4.

11. The pre-reform period is 1952 to 1968. The post-reform period is 1972 to 1992.

12. The test is a difference-in-means test. The difference reported here is significant at the .05 level.

13. The test is a difference-in-means test. The difference is significant at the .10 level.

14. E. E. Schattschneider, *The Semisovereign People: A Realist's View of Democracy in America* (Hinsdale, Ill.: Dryden Press, 1975), ch. 1.

15. Jimmy Carter and Ronald Reagan, "Transcript of the Presidential Debate Between Carter and Reagan in Cleveland: Burden of Social Security," *New York Times*, October 29, 1980, A-28.

16. Terence Smith, "Garment Workers Applaud President," *New York Times*, September 30, 1980, A-1.

17. Leslie Bennetts, "New York Feminist Unit Backs Carter and Assails Reagan," *New York Times*, October 24, 1980, A-16.

18. Charles Mohr, "Goldwater Gives a Tax-Cut Pledge," *New York Times*, September 6, 1964, 1.

19. Barry Goldwater, "Transcript of Goldwater's Address to the County Officials in Washington," *New York Times*, August 11, 1964, 14.

20. Francis X. Clines, "Reagan Attacks Mondale, Vowing Veto of Tax Rises," *New York Times*, August 5, 1984, A-1.
21. Ronald Reagan, "Transcript of Reagan's Speech Accepting G.O.P. Nomination," *New York Times*, August 24, 1984, A-12.
22. Ronald Reagan, "We will Lift America Up," *New York Times*, September 27, 1984, D-22.
23. Francis X. Clines, "President Denies Plan to Increase Tax in Next Year," *New York Times*, July 25, 1984, A-1.
24. The difference is not statistically significant at the .05 level.
25. The difference is not statistically significant at the .05 level but is at the .10 level.
26. See Appendix 1 for a full discussion of how issue stances are assigned to one of the three categories.
27. The differences between the two parties are statistically significant at the .05 level.
28. The difference between the two parties is only a little more than 6%, and the chi-square is not statistically significant at the .05 level (see table 3.5).
29. See George C. Edwards III, *At the Margins: Presidential Leadership of Congress* (New Haven, Conn.: Yale University Press, 1989), particularly ch. 10.
30. For a concise outline of why presidents are thought to have more success in the foreign policy arena see Aaron Wildavsky, "The Two Presidencies," in *The Two Presidencies: A Quarter Century Assessment*, ed. Steven A. Shull (Chicago: Nelson-Hall, 1991), 11–25.
31. See Ripley and Franklin, *Congress, Bureaucracy, Public Policy*, ch. 7.
32. Ibid., 152.
33. Ibid., 153.
34. Crisis policy is excluded from the analysis. Obviously presidential candidates cannot say what they will do during a crisis, so no promises can be categorized as crisis policies. In any event crisis policies are the most susceptible to presidential influence and are not as closely connected to the question of coalition building and governance. See Ripley and Franklin, *Congress, Bureaucracy, Public Policy*, 153, 175.
35. One party's emulation of the issue positions of the other can be explained in two ways. First, the parties seek to move toward the middle of public opinion, which is most advantageous electorally. Such a spatial interpretation of the data is most consistent with the work of Anthony Downs, *An Economic Theory of Democracy* (New York: Harper and Row, 1957), esp. chaps. 7 and 8. However, other data in this chapter seem to show that the parties, although taking the same proportion of stands, actually disagree with one another. Consequently presidential candidates need to satisfy party activists that provide resources (money, votes, workers, and so on) necessary to carry on a campaign. These differences are more compatible

with party cleavage theories. See, for example, Benjamin I. Page, *Choices and Echoes in Presidential Elections: Rational Man and Electoral Democracy* (Chicago: University of Chicago Press, 1978), chaps. 1, 4, and 10.

36. See Benjamin I. Page and Robert Y. Shapiro, *The Rational Public: Fifty Years of Trends in Americans' Policy Preferences* (Chicago: University of Chicago Press, 1992), chaps. 5, 6, and pp. 307–11.
37. The data measure only whether an issue statement was made. The frequency with which the issue statement was made or its centrality to the campaign were not measured.
38. Fendall W. Yerxa, "Goldwater and Rockefeller Exchange Praise in Albany," *New York Times*, September 26, 1964, sec. 1, p. 5.
39. See John R. Petrocik, *Party Coalitions: Realignment and the Decline of the New Deal Party System* (Chicago: University of Chicago Press, 1981), chaps. 1 and 10.
40. See Darrell M. West, *Making Campaigns Count: Leadership and Coalition-Building in 1980* (Wesport, Conn.: Greenwood, 1984), ch. 3.

4. Party Leaders and Presidential Candidates: An Old Remedy for a New Problem

1. For example, see David R. Mayhew, *Divided We Govern: Party Control, Lawmaking, and Investigations, 1946–1990* (New Haven, Conn.: Yale University Press, 1991), and Jon R. Bond and Richard Fleisher, *The President in the Legislative Arena* (Chicago: University of Chicago Press, 1990).
2. Darrell M. West, *Making Campaigns Count: Leadership and Coalition Building in 1980* (Westport, Conn.: Greenwood, 1984), chaps. 3 and 4.
3. John W. Kingdon, *Agendas, Alternatives, and Public Policies* (Boston: Little, Brown, 1984), 66.
4. See Appendix 2 for the list of party leaders used in this study and the rules by which leaders are selected.
5. Robert L. Peabody, "House Party Leadership: Stability and Change," in *Congress Reconsidered*, 3d ed., ed. Lawrence C. Dodd and Bruce I. Oppenheimer (Washington, D.C.: Congressional Quarterly Press, 1985), 258.
6. Tip O'Neill and William Novak, *Man of the House: The Life and Political Memoirs of Speaker Tip O'Neill* (New York: Random House, 1987), 273.
7. William J. Crotty, *American Parties in Decline*, 2d ed. (Boston: Little, Brown. 1984), 235.
8. Roger H. Davidson and Walter J. Olezek, *Congress and Its Members*, 2d ed. (Washington, D.C.: Congressional Quarterly Press, 1985), 200.
9. Barbara Sinclair, "The Speaker's Task Force in the Post-Reform House of Representatives," *American Political Science Review* 75 (June 1981): 397–410; Paul S. Herrnson and Kelly D. Patterson, "Toward a More

Programmatic Democratic Party? Agenda Setting and Coalition Building in the House," *Polity* (Summer 1995): 607–28.

10. Paul S. Herrnson, *Congressional Elections: Campaigning at Home and in Washington* (Washington, D.C.: Congressional Quarterly Press, 1995), 135.
11. Lewis A. Froman and Randall B. Ripley, "Conditions for Party Leadership: The Case of the House Democrats," *American Political Science Review* 59 (March 1965): 53.
12. Crotty, *American Parties in Decline*, 244.
13. Peabody, "House Party Leadership," 261. See also Paul S. Herrnson, Kelly D. Patterson, and John J. Pitney Jr., "From Ward Heelers to Public Relations Experts: The Parties' Response to Mass Politics," in *Broken Contract? Changing Relationships Between Americans and Their Government*, ed. Stephen C. Craig (Boulder, Colo.: Westview, 1996), 251–67, and Barbara Sinclair, "The Congressional Party: Evolving Organizational, Agenda-Setting, and Policy Roles," in *The Parties Respond: Changes in the American Party System*, ed. L. Sandy Maisel (Boulder, Colo.: Westview, 1990), 221–48.
14. Peabody, "House Party Leadership," 262.
15. See David E. Price, *The Congressional Experience: A View from the Hill* (Boulder, Colo.: Westview, 1992), 85–86.
16. Roger H. Davidson, "Senate Leaders: Janitors for an Untidy Chamber?" in *Congress Reconsidered* 3d ed., ed. Lawrence C. Dodd and Bruce C. Oppenheimer (Washington, D.C.: Congressional Quarterly Press, 1985), 226.
17. Ibid., 227.
18. Ibid., 236.
19. See Stephen Hess, "Live from Capitol Hill," in *Live from Capitol Hill: Studies of Congress and the Media* (Washington, D.C.: Brookings Institution, 1992), 33–61.
20. See Froman and Ripley, "Conditions for Party Leadership," 52–63. Even minority leaders are important to the president. See William F. Connelly Jr. and John J. Pitney, *Congress's Permanent Minority? Republicans in the U.S. House* (Lanham, Md.: Rowman and Littlefield, 1994), chaps. 2 and 3.
21. See Leon D. Epstein, *Political Parties in the American Mold* (Madison: University of Wisconsin Press, 1986), chaps. 1, 2, and 11.
22. See David R. Mayhew, *Congress: The Electoral Connection* (New Haven, Conn.: Yale University Press, 1974), part 1, and Richard F. Fenno Jr., *Home Style: House Members in Their Districts* (Boston: Little, Brown, 1978), ch. 7.
23. John W. Kingdon, *Congressmen's Voting Decisions*, 3d ed. (Ann Arbor: University of Michigan Press, 1989), ch. 7.
24. See Price, *The Congressional Experience*, 86–90.
25. For a description of the link between self-interest and the behavior of

members of Congress see Mayhew, *Congress: The Electoral Connection*, part 1.

26. Gary C. Jacobson, "Party Organization and Distribution of Campaign Resources: Republicans and Democrats in 1982," *Political Science Quarterly* 100 (Winter 1985–86): 603.
27. See Stanley Bach and Steven S. Smith, *Managing Uncertainty in the House of Representatives: Adaptation and Innovation in Special Rules* (Washington, D.C.: Brookings Institution, 1988), chaps. 1 and 2.
28. Recognizing that the institution often suffered at the hands of individual goals, scholars issued two reports emphasizing reforms that would moderate some of the excesses. See Thomas E. Mann and Norman J. Ornstein, *A First Report of the Renewing Congress Project* (Washington, D.C.: American Enterprise Institute for Public Policy Research and the Brookings Institution, 1992), and Thomas E. Mann and Norman J. Ornstein, *A Second Report of the Renewing Congress Project* (Washington, D.C.: American Enterprise Institute for Public Policy Research and the Brookings Institution, 1993).
29. Jeff Fishel, *Presidents and Promises* (Washington, D.C.: Congressional Quarterly Press, 1985), 17–23.
30. Observations of the author while working for the Democratic Caucus as a Congressional Fellow of the American Political Science Association.
31. The policy positions of congressional leaders are taken from the *New York Times* and *Congressional Quarterly Weekly*. I combined the issue stances from these sources into one large list and compared them to the issue stances of the presidential candidates. The complete list of party leaders whose issue stances were coded appears in Appendix 2. Appendix 2 also contains the coding rules used in assembling the issue stances of the congressional party leaders.
32. Connelly and Pitney, *Congress's Permanent Minority*, 27–32.
33. See Timothy E. Cook, *Making Laws and Making News: Media Strategies in the U.S. House of Representatives* (Washington, D.C.: Brookings Institution, 1989), ch. 1, and Stephen Hess, *The Ultimate Insiders: U.S. Senators in the National Media* (Washington, D.C.: Brookings Institution, 1986), ch. 1.
34. Robert Taft, "Robert Taft Statement on meeting with Dwight D. Eisenhower," Official File, Box 711, Dwight D. Eisenhower Library, Abilene, Kansas.
35. Robert Taft to Dwight D. Eisenhower, Official File, Box 711, Dwight D. Eisenhower Library, Abilene, Kansas.
36. "Congressional Leaders to Dwight D. Eisenhower," February 22, 1952, Ann Whitman File, Name Series, Box 14, Dwight D. Eisenhower Library, Abilene, Kansas.
37. Dwight D. Eisenhower, "Typed Notes by Eisenhower, Resume of First Year

as President," Ann Whitman File: DDE Diary Series, Box 4, DDE Personal Diary January–November 1954 (2), January 18, 1954, p. 5.

38. George C. Edwards III, "The Two Presidencies: A Reevaluation," *American Politics Quarterly* 14 (July 1986): 247–63.
39. Arthur Schlesinger Jr., *A Thousand Days: John F. Kennedy in the White House* (Greenwich, Conn.: Fawcett, 1965), 20.
40. Ibid., 21.
41. John D. Morris, "Nixon to Support Eisenhower Plan for Care of Aged," *New York Times*, May 7, 1960, 1.
42. John W. Finney, "Humphrey Urges a June Deadline on A-Test Parley," *New York Times*, October 3, 1960, 1.
43. Donald Bruce Johnson, comp., *National Party Platforms: 1840–1976*, vol. 2 (Urbana: University of Illinois Press, 1956, 1978), 599.
44. Ibid., 596.
45. Connelly and Pitney, *Congress's Permanent Minority*, 32–34.
46. Jimmy Carter, *Keeping Faith: Memoirs of a President* (New York: Bantam, 1982), 74.
47. O'Neill and Novak, *Man of the House*, 313.
48. Ibid., 203.
49. James L. Sundquist, *The Decline and Resurgence of Congress* (Washington, D.C.: Brookings Institution, 1981).
50. See Samuel Kernell, *Going Public: New Strategies of Presidential Leadership* (Washington, D.C.: Congressional Quarterly Press, 1986), ch. 1, and Bruce Buchanan, *The Citizen's Presidency: Standards of Choice and Judgment* (Washington, D.C.: Congressional Quarterly Press, 1987), ch. 1.

5. Rethinking Governability and the Study of Political Parties

1. See David Mayhew, *Divided We Govern: Party Control, Lawmaking, and Investigations, 1946–1990* (New Haven, Conn.: Yale University Press, 1991), 137.
2. See Paul Frymer, "Ideological Consensus Within Divided Party Government," *Political Science Quarterly* 109 (Summer 1994): 287–311. Frymer argues that agreement between Congress and the president can be explained by members who come from districts that are ideologically similar to the president. Consequently the tendency of voters to elect Republican presidents and Democratic Congresses does not necessarily produce ideological disagreement between the two branches of government.
3. Gary W. Cox and Samuel Kernell make a similar argument in "Introduction: Governing in a Divided Era," in *The Politics of Divided Government*, ed. Cox and Kernell (Boulder, Colo.: Westview, 1991), 4.
4. Conversely this incentive does present problems. After all, congressional leaders do receive credit or perceive that they receive credit from voters for

obstructing presidential initiatives, which seemed to be at the heart of Republican opposition to President Clinton's health reform proposal in 1994. However, rates of agreement between presidential candidates and congressional leaders, although stable, are never as high as the rates of agreement of leaders and candidates of the same party.

5. This argument is made by Albert D. Cover, Neil Pinney, and George Serra, in "Ideological Cohesion Between Congress and the President: Does the Road to the White House Matter?" Paper presented at the annual meeting of the Midwest Political Science Association, Chicago, April 14–17, 1994.
6. Mayhew, *Divided We Govern*, 160.
7. Michael G. Krukones, *Promises and Performances: Presidential Campaigns as Policy Predictors* (Lanham, Md.: University Press of America, 1984); Jeff Fishel, *Presidents and Promises: From Campaign Pledge to Presidential Performance* (Washington, D.C.: Congressional Quarterly Press, 1985); Jon R. Bond and Richard Fleisher, *The President in the Legislative Arena*, ed. Benjamin I. Page (Chicago: University of Chicago Press, 1990); Mayhew, *Divided We Govern*.
8. See, for example, David S. Broder, *The Party's Over: The Failure of American Politics* (New York: Harper and Row, 1972); James L. Sundquist, "Party Decay and the Capacity to Govern," in *The Future of American Political Parties*, ed. Joel L. Fleishman (Englewood Cliffs, N.J.: Prentice-Hall, 1982); James L. Sundquist, "The Crisis of Competence in Our National Government," *Political Science Quarterly* 95 (Summer 1980): 183–208; James MacGregor Burns, *The Power to Lead: The Crisis of the American Presidency* (New York: Simon and Schuster, 1984); and Demetrios Caraley, "Elections and Dilemmas of American Democratic Governance: Reflections," *Political Science Quarterly* 104 (Spring 1989): 19–40.
9. The most notable of the calls for reform is found in the American Political Science Association's "Toward a More Responsible Two-Party System: A Report of the Committee on Political Parties," *American Political Science Review* 44, Supplement (September 1950). Discussions of specific reforms also appear in some of the more recent literature. See, for example, David E. Price, *Bringing the Parties Back* (Washington, D.C.: Congressional Quarterly Press, 1984), and Larry J. Sabato, *The Party's Just Begun: Shaping Political Parties for America's Future* (Glenview, Ill.: Scott, Foresman, 1988).
10. See, for example, Michel Crozier, *The Trouble with America* (Berkeley: University of California Press, 1984), and Michel Crozier, Samuel P. Huntington, and Joji Watanuki, *The Crisis of Democracy: Report on the Governability of Democracies to the Trilateral Commission* (New York: New York University Press, 1975).
11. Evron M. Kirkpatrick, "Toward a More Responsible Two-Party System:

Political Science, Policy Science, or Pseudo Science?" *American Political Science Review* 65 (December 1971): 965–90.

12. Alan Ware, *Citizens, Parties, and the State: A Reappraisal* (Princeton, N.J.: Princeton University Press, 1987), 1. A similar point is made by James W. Ceaser, *Presidential Selection: Theory and Development* (Princeton, N.J.: Princeton University Press, 1979), 310. Exceptions are cited in Gerald R. Pomper, *Passions and Interests: Political Party Concepts of American Democracy* (Lawrence: University Press of Kansas, 1992), and Ware, *Citizens, Parties, and the State*.
13. Clearly political parties can perform vital functions. If critics agree that one function is achieving governability, and a consensus on this point certainly seems to have occurred, scholars should use the concept to organize a theory of parties; the concept also could be the basis of empirical studies about political parties. See Theodore Lowi, "Toward Functionalism in Political Science: The Case of Innovation in Party Systems," *American Political Science Review* 57 (September 1963): 570–83.
14. Nancy Landon Kassebaum, Lloyd N. Cutler, and C. Douglas Dillon, foreword to *Reforming American Government: The Bicentennial Papers of the Committee on the Constitutional System*, ed. Donald L. Robinson (Boulder, Colo.: Westview, 1985), xv. The Committee on the Constitutional System is a private organization composed of individuals from a wide variety of disciplines and occupations. Its members include academics, elected officials, and former members of the executive branch. The committee's purpose is to study the operation of the constituional system and find ways to ameliorate its operation.
15. Edward H. Lehman defines *polity* as "society's overall system of political power. It includes both 'upward' participation processes through which nonstate actors seek to convert intermember power into political power and 'downward' control processes through which state authorities use political power to dominate intermember power." See Lehman, *The Viable Polity* (Philadelphia: Temple University Press, 1992), 48–49.
16. Ibid., 50.
17. Ibid., 50–51.
18. Ibid., 85–86.
19. See Joseph A. Schlesinger, "The New American Political Party," *American Political Science Review* (December 1985): 1152–69.
20. R. Kent Weaver and Bert A. Rockman, "Institutional Reform and Constitutional Design," in *Do Institutions Matter? Government Capabilities in the United States and Abroad*, ed. Weaver and Rockman (Washington, D.C.: Brookings Institution, 1993), 474.
21. See David W. Rohde, *Parties and Leaders in the Post-Reform House* (Chicago: University of Chicago Press, 1991), chaps. 3, 4, and 5, and Paul S. Herrnson and Kelly D. Patterson, "Agenda Setting and Coalition Building

in the House: Toward a More Programmatic Democratic Party?" *Polity* (Summer 1995): 607–28.

22. See Pomper, *Passions and Interests*, 35–46.
23. Giovanni Sartori, *Parties and Party Systems: A Framework for Analysis*, vol. 1 (Cambridge, England: Cambridge University Press, 1976), chaps. 1 and 2.
24. Ralf Dahrendorf, "Effectiveness and Legitimacy: On the Governability of Democracies," *Political Quarterly* 51 (October–December 1980): 393–410.
25. Ibid., 396.
26. This bifurcation suggests another important problem with which party theorists should grapple: which measure of effectiveness is really the more important, policy making or policy delivery? The two are by no means mutually exclusive, but it seems plausible that one could occur without the other.
27. Dahrendorf, "Effectiveness and Legitimacy," 397.
28. Ibid., 401.
29. Alan Ehrenhalt, *The United States of Ambition: Politicians, Power, and the Pursuit of Office* (New York: Times Books, 1991).
30. Dahrendorf, "Effectiveness and Legitimacy," 401–402.
31. For a discussion of party competition see Ware, *Citizens, Parties, and the State*, ch. 3.
32. Paul Goodman, "The First American Party System," in *The American Party Systems: Stages of Development*, eds. William Nisbet Chambers and Walter Dean Burnham (New York: Oxford University Press, 1981), 59.
33. Richard P. McCormick, "Political Development and the Second Party System," in *The American Party Systems*, eds. Chambers and Burnham, 109.
34. Ibid., 106.
35. David M. Ricci, *The Tragedy of Political Science: Politics, Scholarship, and Democracy* (New Haven, Conn.: Yale University Press, 1984), 294.
36. Sartori, *Parties and Party Systems*, 43
37. Lehman, *The Viable Polity*, 48–52.
38. Several studies have explored some plausible connections. See, for example, John P. Bradley, "Partly Platforms and Party Performance Concerning Social Security," *Polity* 1 (Spring 1969): 337–58; Paul T. David, "Party Platforms as National Plans," *Public Administration Review* (May–June 1971): 303–15; and Gerald M. Pomper and Susan S. Lederman, *Elections in America: Control and Influence in Democratic Politics*, 2d ed. (New York: Longman, 1980).
39. See Steven E. Rhoads, *The Economist's View of the World: Government, Markets, and Public Policy* (Cambridge, England: Cambridge University Press, 1985), ch. 11.
40. See James L. Sundquist, *Constitutional Reform and Effective Govern-*

ment, rev. ed. (Washington, D.C.: Brookings Institution, 1992); for a discussion of congressional reforms see Richard Pious, "Congressional Power," in *The Power to Govern: Assessing Reform in the United States*, ed. Pious, (Montpelier, Vt.: Capital City Press, 1981), 45–61.

41. Even here there is a question of how public opinion should be measured and expressed. See Benjamin Ginsberg, *The Captive Public: How Mass Opinion Promotes State Power* (New York: Basic Books, 1986).

42. Leon Epstein, *Political Parties in the American Mold* (Madison: University of Wisconsin Press, 1986), 345.

43. The uniquely candidate-centered electoral system in the United States is surely a product of constitutional design. See Gordon S. Wood, *The Creation of the American Republic, 1776–1787* (New York: W. W. Norton, 1972), ch. 5.

44. Morton White, *Philosophy, the Federalist, and the Constitution* (New York: Oxford University Press, 1987), chaps. 12 and 13.

45. Everett Carll Ladd makes a similar argument in "Party Reform and the Public Interest," *Political Science Quarterly* 102 (Fall 1987): 355–69.

APPENDIX 1: IDENTIFICATION OF ISSUE STANCES

1. Gerald M. Pomper and Susan S. Lederman, *Elections in America: Control and Influence in Democratic Politics*, 2d ed. (New York: Longman, 1980), 237. The two categories I excluded are "Rhetorical Pledges" and "General Pledges." For a more detailed discussion of the rules, verbs, and language used to identify issue stances, see pp. 236–37.

2. Lester G. Seligman, "Electoral Governing Coalitions in the Presidency: A Theory and a Case Study," *Congress and the Presidency* 10 (Summer 1983):131.

3. Darrell M. West, *Making Campaigns Count: Leadership and Coalition Building in 1980* (Westport, Conn.: Greenwood, 1984), 80–83.

4. Randall B. Ripley and Grace A. Franklin, *Congress, the Bureaucracy, and Public Policy*, 5th ed. (Pacific Grove, Calif.: Brooks Cole, 1991).

Bibliography

Alexander, Herbert E. *Financing Politics: Money, Elections, and Political Reform,* 3d ed. Washington, D.C.: Congressional Quarterly Press, 1984.

Alter, Jonathan, Mark Miller, and Eleanor Clift. "Gary's Sound-Bite Campaign." *Newsweek,* January 4, 1988, 22.

Ambrose, Stephen E. *Nixon: The Education of a Politician, 1913–1962.* New York: Simon and Schuster, 1987.

Bach, Stanley and Steven S. Smith. *Managing Uncertainty in the House of Representatives: Adaptation and Innovation in Special Rules.* Washington, D.C.: Brookings Institution, 1988.

Baker, Russell. "Goldwater Hits Platform Accord." *New York Times,* July 24, 1960, 38.

Beck, Paul Allen and Frank J. Sorauf. *Party Politics in America,* 7th ed. New York: Harper Collins, 1992.

Bennett, William Lance. *The Governing Crisis: Media, Money, and Marketing in American Elections.* New York: St. Martin's Press, 1991.

Bennetts, Leslie. "New York Feminist Unit Backs Carter and Assails Reagan." *New York Times,* October 24, 1980, A-16.

Berelson, Bernard R., Paul F. Lazarsfeld, and William N. McPhee. *Voting: A Study of Opinion Formation in a Presidential Campaign.* Chicago: University of Chicago Press, 1954.

Bibby, John F. "Party Renewal in the National Republican Party." In *Party Renewal in America: Theory and Practice.* Ed. Gerald M. Pomper, 102–15. New York: Praeger, 1980.

Bode, Kenneth A. and Carol F. Casey. "Party Reform: Revisionism Revised."

In *Political Parties in The Eighties*. Ed. Robert A Goldwin, 3–19. Washington, D.C.: American Enterprise Institute for Public Policy Research, 1980 and Gambier, Ohio: Kenyon College, 1980.

Boller, Paul F. Jr. *Presidential Campaigns*. New York: Oxford University Press, 1985.

Bond, Jon R. and Richard Fleisher. *The President in the Legislative Arena*. Chicago: University of Chicago Press, 1990.

Bowman, Karlyn H. and Everett Carll Ladd, eds. "Public Opinion and Demographic Report." *American Enterprise* 4 (November–December 1993): 73–96.

Bradley, John P. "Party Platforms and Party Performance Concerning Social Security." *Polity* 1 (Spring 1969): 337–58.

Briggs, Kenneth A. "Carter Campaign Moving to Mollify Catholics After Dispute Over Democratic Party Abortion Stand." *New York Times*, August 26, 1976, 20.

Broder, David S. *The Party's Over: The Failure of Politics in America*. New York: Harper and Row, 1972.

Buchanan, Bruce. *The Citizen's Presidency: Standards of Choice and Judgment*. Washington, D.C.: Congressional Quarterly Press, 1987.

Budge, Ian and Richard I. Hofferbert. "Mandates and Policy Outputs: U.S. Party Platforms and Federal Expenditures." *American Political Science Review* 84 (March 1990): 111–31.

Burns, James MacGregor. *The Power to Lead: The Crisis of the American Presidency*. New York: Simon and Schuster, 1984.

Campbell, Angus, Philip E. Converse, Warren E. Miller, and Donald E. Stokes. *The American Voter*. New York: John Wiley, 1960.

Caraley, Demetrios. "Elections and Dilemmas of American Democratic Governance: Reflections." *Political Science Quarterly* 104 (Spring 1989): 19–40.

Carter, Jimmy. "Excerpts from Carter's News Conference Presenting Mondale as Choice for Vice President." *New York Times*, July 16, 1976, A-11.

——. *Keeping Faith: Memoirs of a President*. New York: Bantam, 1982.

Carter, Jimmy and Ronald Reagan. "Transcript of the Presidential Debate Between Carter and Reagan in Cleveland: Burden of Social Security." *New York Times*, October 29, 1980, A-28.

Ceaser, James W. *Presidential Selection: Theory and Development*. Princeton: Princeton University Press, 1979.

——. *Liberal Democracy and Political Science*. Baltimore: John Hopkins University Press, 1990.

——. "Down in the Polls When He Should Be Up, Bill Clinton Appears in Trouble." *Public Perspective* 4 (May–June 1993): 1–6, 33–34.

Chester, Edward W. *A Guide to Political Platforms*. Hamden, Conn.: Archon Books, 1977.

Clines, Francis X. "President Denies Plan to Increase Tax in Next Year." *New York Times*, July 25, 1984, A-1.

——. "Reagan Attacks Mondale, Vowing Veto of Tax Rises." *New York Times*, August 5, 1984, A-1.

Collie, Melissa P. and David W. Brady. "The Decline of Partisan Voting Coalitions in the House of Representatives." In *Congress Reconsidered*, 3d ed. Ed. Lawrence C. Dodd and Bruce I. Oppenheimer, 272–87. Washington, D.C.: Congressional Quarterly Press, 1985.

Committee on Political Parties. American Political Science Association. "Toward a More Responsible Two-Party System: A Report of the Committee on Political Parties." *American Political Science Review* 44 (1950): supplement.

Congressional leaders to Dwight D. Eisenhower. February 22, 1952, Ann Whitman File, Name Series, Box 14. Dwight D. Eisenhower Library, Abilene, Kansas.

Congressional Quarterly. "Foreign Policy: Hub of Platform Conflict." *Congressional Quarterly Weekly Report* 34 (August 14, 1976): 2183.

——. *National Party Conventions, 1831–1984*. Washington, D.C.: Congressional Quarterly, 1987.

Connelly, William F. Jr. and John J. Pitney Jr. *Congress' Permanent Minority? Republicans in the U.S. House*. Lanham, Md.: Rowman and Littlefield, 1994.

Cook, Timothy E. *Making Laws and Making News: Media Strategies in the U.S. House of Representatives*. Washington, D.C.: Brookings Institution, 1989.

Cooke, Edward F. "Drafting the 1952 Platforms." *Western Political Quarterly* 9 (September 1956): 699–712.

Cotter, Cornelius P. and John F. Bibby. "Institutional Development of the Parties and the Thesis of Party Decline." *Political Science Quarterly* 95 (Spring 1980): 1–27.

Cover, Albert, Neil Pinney, and George Serra. "Ideological Cohesion Between Congress and the President: Does the Road to the White House Matter?" Paper presented at the annual meeting of the Midwest Political Science Association, Chicago, April 14–17, 1994.

Cox, Gary W. and Samuel Kernell. "Introduction: Governing a Divided Era." In *The Politics of Divided Government*. Ed. Gary W. Cox and Samuel Kernell, 1–10. Boulder, Colo.: Westview, 1991.

Crotty, William. *American Parties in Decline*, 2d ed. Boston: Little, Brown, 1984.

Crotty, William J. and John S. Jackson III. *Presidential Primaries and Nominations*. Washington, D.C.: Congressional Quarterly Press, 1985.

Crozier, Michel. *The Trouble with America*. Berkeley: University of California Press, 1984.

Crozier, Michel, Samuel P. Huntington, and Joji Watanuki. *The Crisis of Democracy: Report on the Governability of Democracies to the Trilateral Commission*. New York: New York University Press, 1975.

Cutler, Lloyd N. "To Form a Government." *Foreign Affairs* 59 (Fall 1980): 126–43.

Dahrendorf, Ralf. "Effectiveness and Legitimacy: On the Governability of Democracies." *Political Quarterly* 51 (October–December 1980): 393–410.

David, Paul T. "Party Platforms as National Plans." *Public Administration Review* 31 (May–June 1971): 303–15.

David, Paul T., Ralph M. Goldman, and Richard G. Bain. *The Politics of National Party Conventions*. Washington D.C.: Brookings Institution, 1960.

Davidson, Roger H. "Senate Leaders: Janitors for an Untidy Chamber?" In *Congress Reconsidered,* 3d ed. Ed. Lawrence C. Dodd and Bruce I. Oppenheimer, 225–52. Washington D.C.: Congressional Quarterly Press, 1985.

Davidson, Roger H. and Walter J. Oleszek. *Congress and its Members,* 2d ed. Washington, D.C.: Congressional Quarterly Press, 1985.

Davis, James W. *National Conventions in an Age of Party Reform,* Westport, Conn.: Greenwood, 1983.

Downs, Anthony. *An Economic Theory of Democracy*. New York: Harper and Row, 1957.

Edwards, George C. III. "The Two Presidencies: A Reevaluation." *American Politics Quarterly* 14 (July 1986): 247–63.

——. *At the Margins: Presidential Leadership of Congress*. New Haven, Conn.: Yale University Press, 1989.

Ehrenhalt, Alan. *The United States of Ambition: Politicians, Power, and the Pursuit of Office*. New York: Times Books, 1991.

Eisenhower, Dwight D. "Typed Notes by Eisenhower, Resume of First Year as President." Ann Whitman File: DDE Diary Series, Box 4, DDE Personal Diary January–November 1954 (2), January 18, 1954.

Elving, Ronald D. "Hoping to Attract More Votes, Democrats Offer Fewer Words." *Congressional Quarterly Weekly Report* 46 (June 2, 1988): 1797–98.

Epstein, Leon D. *Political Parties in the American Mold*. Madison: University of Wisconsin Press, 1986.

Fenno, Richard F. Jr. *Home Style: House Members in Their Districts*. Boston: Little, Brown, 1978.

Finney, John W. "Humphrey Urges a June Deadline on A-Test Parley." *New York Times,* October 3, 1960, 1.

Fishel, Jeff. *Presidents and Promises: From Campaign Pledge to Presidential Performance*. Washington, D.C.: Congressional Quarterly Press, 1985.

Flanigan, William H. and Nancy H. Zingale. *Political Behavior of the American Electorate,* 7th ed. Washington, D.C.: Congressional Quarterly Press, 1991.

Froman, Lewis A. and Randall B. Ripley. "Conditions for Party Leadership: The Case of the House Democrats." *American Political Science Review* 59 (March 1965): 53.

Frymer, Paul. "Ideological Consensus Within Divided Party Government." *Political Science Quarterly* 109 (Summer 1994): 287–311.

Gailey, Phil. "Carter Urges Party to Offer a Policy Mix." *New York Times* April 3, 1985, A-19.

Gallup, George H. *The Gallop Poll: Public Opinion 1935–1971*, 3 vols. New York: Random House, 1972.

Gibson, James L., Cornelius P. Cotter, John F. Bibby, and Robert J. Huckshorn. "Whither the Local Parties?: A Cross-Sectional and Longitudinal Analysis of the Strength of Party Organizations." *American Journal of Political Science* 29 (February 1985): 139–60.

Gimpel, James G. *Legislating the Revolution: The Contract with America in its First 100 Days*. Needham Heights, Mass.: Allyn and Bacon, 1996.

Gingrich, Newt and Dick Armey. *Contract with America*. Ed. Ed Gillespie and Bob Schellhas. New York: Times Books, 1994.

Gingsberg, Benjamin. *The Captive Public: How Mass Opinion Promotes State Power*. New York: Basic Books, 1986.

Goldwater, Barry. "Transcript of Goldwater's Address to the County Officials in Washington." *New York Times*, August 11, 1964, 14.

Goodman, Paul. "The First American Party System." In *The American Party Systems: Stages of Development*. Ed. William Nisbet Chambers and Walter Dean Burnham, 56–89. New York: Oxford University Press, 1981.

Greider, William. *Who Will Tell the People? The Betrayal of the American Democracy*. New York: Simon and Schuster, 1992.

Hart and Teeter Research Companies. "Survey for the Council for Excellence in Government, March 16–18, 1995," *Public Perspective* 6 (June–July 1995): 57.

Heckathorn, Douglas D. and Steven M. Maser. "The Contractual Architecture of Public Policy: A Critical Reconstruction of Lowi's Typology." *Journal of Politics* 52 (November 1990): 1101–23.

Herrnson, Paul S. "Do Parties Make a Difference? The Role of Party Organizations in Congressional Elections." *Journal of Politics* 48 (August 1986): 589–615.

——. *Party Campaigning in the 1980s*. Cambridge, Mass.: Harvard University Press, 1988.

——. "National Party, Decision-Making Strategies, and Resource Distribution in Congressional Elections." *Western Political Quarterly* 42 (1989): 301–23.

——. *Congressional Elections: Campaigning at Home and in Washington*. Washington, D.C.: Congressional Quarterly Press, 1995.

Herrnson, Paul S. and Kelly D. Patterson. "Toward a More Programmatic

Democratic Party? Agenda-Setting and Coalition-Building in the House of Representatives." *Polity* 27 (Summer 1995): 607–28.

Herrnson, Paul S., Kelly D. Patterson, and John J. Pitney Jr. "From Ward Heelers to Public Relations Experts: The Parties' Response to Mass Politics." In *Broken Contract? Changing Relationships Between Americans and Their Government*. Ed. Stephen C. Craig, 251–67. Boulder, Colo.: Westview, 1996.

Hess, Stephen. *The Ultimate Insiders: U.S. Senators in the National Media*. Washington, D.C.: Brookings Institution, 1986.

——. "Live from Capitol Hill." In *Live from Capitol Hill: Studies of Congress and the Media*. Washington, D.C.: Brookings Institution, 1992.

Hibbing, John R. and Elizabeth Theiss-Morse. *Congress as Public Enemy: Public Attitudes Toward American Political Institutions*. New York: Cambridge University Press, 1995.

Hofstadter, Richard. *The Idea of a Party System: The Rise of Legitimate Opposition in the United States, 1780–1840*. Berkeley: University of California Press, 1969.

Humphrey, Hubert H. "Excerpts from Humphrey Text Dealing with Crime." *New York Times*, September 12, 1968, 36.

Hyman, Sidney. "Nine Tests for the Presidential Hopeful." *New York Times Magazine* January 4, 1959, 11.

Jacobson, Gary C. *Money in Congressional Elections*. New Haven, Conn.: Yale University Press, 1980.

——. "Party Organization and Distribution of Campaign Resources: Republicans and Democrats in 1982." *Political Science Quarterly* 100 (Winter 1985–86): 603–25.

Jaenicke, Douglas W. "The Jacksonian Integration of Parties into the Constitutional System." *Political Science Quarterly* 101, no. 1 (1986): 85–107.

Johnson, Donald Bruce, comp. *National Party Platforms, 1840–1976*, 2 vols. Urbana: University of Illinois Press, 1978.

Jones, Charles O. *The Trusteeship Presidency: Jimmy Carter and the United States Congress*. Baton Rouge: Louisiana State University Press, 1988.

Kassebaum, Nancy Landon, Lloyd N. Cutler, and C. Douglas Dillon. Foreword. In *Reforming American Government: The Bicentennial Papers of the Committee on the Constitutional System*. Ed. Donald L. Robinson, xi–xvi. Boulder, Colo.: Westview, 1985.

Kayden, Xandra and Eddie Mahe Jr. *The Party Goes On: The Persistence of the Two-Party System in the United States*. New York: Basic Books, 1985.

Keefe, William J. *Parties, Politics, and Public Policy in America*, 5th ed. Washington, D.C.: Congressional Quarterly Press, 1988.

Kenworthy, E. W. "Nixon Says Humphrey Harms Efforts of U.S. in Paris Talks." *New York Times*, September 26, 1968, 1.

——. "Nixon Urges Four Steps to Curb Nation's Crime." *New York Times*, September 30, 1968, 1.

Kernell, Samuel. *Going Public: New Strategies of Presidential Leadership.* Washington, D.C.: Congressional Quarterly Press, 1986.

Kingdon, John W. *Agendas, Alternatives, and Public Policies.* Boston: Little, Brown, 1984.

——. *Congressmen's Voting Decisions* 3d ed. Ann Arbor: University of Michigan Press, 1989.

Kirkpatrick, Evron M. "Toward a More Responsible Two-Party System: Political Science, Policy Science, or Pseudo-Science?" *American Political Science Review* 65 (December 1971): 965–90.

Klein, Joe. "Plain Vanilla or Rain Forest Crunch?" *Newsweek,* July 18, 1994, 38.

Kneeland, Douglas E. "McGovern, in Jersey, Calls for $6-Billion Aid to Aged." *New York Times,* September 21, 1972, 1.

Krukones, Michael G. *Promises and Performance: Presidential Campaigns as Policy Predictors.* Lanham, Md.: University Press of America, 1984.

Ladd, Everett Carll. *Where Have All the Voters Gone? The Fracturing of America's Political Parties,* 2d ed. New York: W. W. Norton, 1982.

——. "Party Reform and the Pubic Interest." *Political Science Quarterly* 102 (Fall 1987): 355–69.

Lehman, Edward W. *The Viable Polity.* Philadelphia: Temple University Press, 1992.

Light, Paul Charles. *The President's Agenda: Domestic Policy Choice from Kennedy to Reagan,* rev. ed. Baltimore: John Hopkins University Press, 1991.

Lowi, Theodore J. "Toward Functionalism in Political Science: The Case of Innovation in Party Systems." *American Political Science Review* 57 (September 1963): 570–83.

——. "American Business, Public Policy, Case Studies, and Political Theory." *World Politics* 16 (July 1964): 667–715.

——. "Four Systems of Policy, Politics, and Choice." *Public Administration Review* 32 (July–August 1972): 298–310.

Magleby, David B. *KBYU–Utah Colleges Exit Poll 1994.* Provo, Utah: Brigham Young University, 1994.

Magleby, David B. and Kelly D. Patterson. "Poll Trends: Congressional Reform." *Public Opinion Quarterly* 58 (Fall 1994): 419–27.

Maisel, L. Sandy. *Parties and Elections in America: The Electoral Process,* 2d ed. Ed. Stephen J. Wayne. New York: McGraw-Hill, 1993.

——. "The Platform-Writing Process: Candidate-Centered Platforms in 1992." *Political Science Quarterly* 108 (Winter 1993–94): 671–98.

——. "Conventions, Platforms, and Issue Activists." In *The American Elections of 1980.* Ed. Austin Ranney, 99–141. Washington, D.C.: American Enterprise Institute for Public Policy Research, 1981.

Malbin, Michael J., ed. *Money and Politics in the United States: Financing Elections in the 1980s.* Chatham, N.J.: Chatham House, 1984.

Mann, Thomas E. and Norman J. Ornstein. *A First Report of the Renewing Congress Project*. Washington, D.C.: American Enterprise Institute for Public Policy Research and the Brookings Institution, 1992.

——. *A Second Report of the Renewing Congress Project*. Washington, D.C.: American Enterprise Institute for Public Policy Research and the Brookings Institution, 1993.

Mayhew, David R. *Congress: The Electoral Connection*. New Haven, Conn.: Yale University Press, 1974.

——. *Divided We Govern: Party Control, Lawmaking, and Investigations, 1946–1990*. New Haven, Conn.: Yale University Press, 1991.

McCorkle, Pope and Joel L. Fleishman. "Political Parties and Presidential Nominations: The Intellectual Ironies of Reform and Change in the Mass Media Age." In *The Future of American Political Parties: The Challenge of Governance*. Ed. Joel L. Fleishman, 140–68. Englewood Cliffs, N.J.: Prentice-Hall, 1982.

McCormick, Richard P. "Political Development and the Second Party System." In *The American Party Systems: Stages of Development*. Ed. William Nisbet Chambers and Walter Dean Burnham, 90–116. New York: Oxford University Press, 1981.

Michels, Robert. *Political Parties: A Sociological Study of the Oligarchical Tendencies of Modern Democracy*. Trans. Eden Paul and Cedar Paul. New York: Free Press, 1962.

Mohr, Charles. "Goldwater Gives a Tax-Cut Pledge." *New York Times*, September 6, 1964, 1.

Morris, John D. "Nixon to Support Eisenhower Plan for Care of Aged." *New York Times*, May 7, 1960, 1.

National Academy of Public Administration. *Beyond Distrust: Building Bridges Between Congress and the Executive*. Washington, D.C.: National Academy of Public Administration, 1992.

Neustadt, Richard E. *Presidential Power: The Politics of Leadership from FDR to Carter*. New York: John Wiley, 1980.

Niemi, Richard G. and Herbert F. Weisberg, eds. *Controversies in Voting Behavior*, 3d ed. Washington, D.C.: Congressional Quarterly Press, 1993.

O'Neill, Tip and William Novak. *Man of the House: The life and Political Memoirs of Speaker Tip O'Neill*. New York: Random House, 1987.

Ornstein, Norman J., Thomas E. Mann, and Michael J. Malbin. *Vital Statistics on Congress, 1993–1994*. Washington, D.C.: Congressional Quarterly Press, 1994.

Orren, Gary R. "The Changing Style of American Party Politics." In *The Future of American Political Parties*. Ed. Joel L. Fleishman, 4–41. Englewood Cliffs, N.J.: Prentice-Hall, 1982.

Ostrogorski, Moisei. *Democracy and the Organization of Political Parties.*

Volume II: The United States. Ed. Seymour Martin Lipset. New Brunswick, N.J.: Transaction Books, 1982.

Page, Benjamin I. *Choices and Echoes in Presidential Elections: Rational Man and Electoral Democracy*. Chicago: University of Chicago Press, 1978.

Page, Benjamin I. and Robert Y. Shapiro. *The Rational Public: Fifty Years of Trends in Americans' Policy Preferences*. Chicago: University of Chicago Press, 1992.

Patterson, Kelly D. and David B. Magleby. "Public Support for Congress." *Public Opinion Quarterly* 56 (Winter 1992): 539–51.

Patterson, Thomas E. *Out of Order*. New York: Alfred A. Knopf, 1993.

Peabody, Robert L. "House Party Leadership: Stability and Change." In *Congress Reconsidered*, 3d ed. Ed. Lawrence C. Dodd and Bruce I. Oppenheimer, 253–71. Washington D.C.: Congressional Quarterly Press, 1985.

Petrocik, John R. *Party Coalitions: Realignment and the Decline of the New Deal Party System*. Chicago: University of Chicago Press, 1981.

Pious, Richard M. "Congressional Power." In *The Power to Govern: Assessing Reform in the United States*. Ed. Richard Pious, 45–61. Montpelier, Vt.: Capital City Press, 1981.

Polsby, Nelson W. *Consequences of Party Reform*. New York: Oxford University Press, 1983.

Polsby, Nelson W. and Aaron Wildavsky. *Presidential Elections: Strategies of American Electoral Politics*, 6th ed. New York: Charles Scribner's Sons, 1984.

Pomper, Gerald M. *Passions and Interests: Political Party Concepts of American Democracy*. Lawrence: University Press of Kansas, 1992.

Pomper, Gerald M. and Susan S. Lederman. *Elections in America: Control and Influence in Democratic Politics*, 2d ed. New York: Longman, 1980.

Postman, Neil. *Amusing Ourselves to Death: Public Discourse in the Age of Show Business*. New York: Viking Penguin, 1985.

Price, David E. *Bringing Back the Parties*. Washington, D.C.: Congressional Quarterly Press, 1984.

——. *The Congressional Experience: A View from the Hill*. Boulder, Colo.: Westview, 1992.

Ranney, Austin. *Curing the Mischiefs of Faction: Party Reform in America*. Los Angeles: University of California Press, 1975.

Rapoport, Ronald B., Alan I. Abramowitz, and John McGlennon, eds. *The Life of the Parties: Activists in Presidential Politics*. Lexington: University Press of Kentucky, 1986.

Rauch, Jonathan. *Demosclerosis: The Silent Killer of American Government*. New York: Times Books, 1994.

Reagan, Ronald. "Transcript of Reagan's Speech Accepting G.O.P. Nomination." *New York Times*, August 24, 1984, A-12.

——. "We will Lift America Up." *New York Times*, September 27, 1984, D-22.

Reichley, James A. "The Rise of National Parties." In *The New Direction in American Politics*. Ed. John E. Chubb and Paul E. Peterson, 175–200. Washington, D.C.: Brookings Institution, 1985.

Reiter, Howard L. *Selecting the President: The Nominating Process in Transition*. Philadelphia: University of Pennsylvania Press, 1985.

Rhoads, Steven E. *The Economist's View of the World: Government, Markets, and Public Policy*. Cambridge, England: Cambridge University Press, 1985.

Ricci, David M. *The Tragedy of Political Science: Politics, Scholarship, and Democracy*. New Haven, Conn.: Yale University Press, 1984.

——. *The Transformation of American Politics: The New Washington and the Rise of Think Tanks*. New Haven, Conn.: Yale University Press, 1993.

Ripley, Randall P. and Grace A. Franklin. *Congress, the Bureaucracy, and Public Policy*, 5th ed. Pacific Grove, Calif.: Brooks Cole, 1991.

Roelofs, H. Mark. *The Poverty of American Politics: A Theoretical Interpretation*. Philadelphia: Temple University Press, 1992.

Rohde, David W. *Parties and Leaders in the Post-Reform House*. Chicago: University of Chicago Press, 1991.

Sabato, Larry J. *The Party's Just Begun: Shaping Political Parties for America's Future*. Glenview, Ill.: Scott, Foresman, 1988.

Sartori, Giovanni. *Parties and Party Systems: A Framework for Analysis*, vol. 1. New York: Cambridge University Press, 1976.

——. *The Theory of Democracy Revisited*. Chatham, N.J.: Chatham House, 1987.

Schattschneider, E. E. *Party Government*. Ed. Phillips Bradley. New York: Farrar and Rhinehart, 1942.

——. *The Semisovereign People: A Realist's View of Democracy in America*. Hinsdale, Ill.: Dryden, 1975.

Schlesinger, Arthur M. Jr. *A Thousand Days: John F. Kennedy in the White House*. 1965. Reprint, Greenwich, Conn.: Fawcett, 1967.

Schlesinger, Joseph A. "The New American Political Party." *American Political Science Review* 79 (December 1985): 1152–69.

Seligman, Lester G. "Electoral Governing Coalitions in the Presidency: A Theory and a Case Study." *Congress and the Presidency* 10 (Autumn 1983): 125–46.

Seligman, Lester G. and Cary R. Covington. *The Coalitional Presidency*. Chicago: Dorsey, 1989.

Semple, Robert B. Jr. "Nixon Scores U.S. Method of Enforcing Integration." *New York Times*, September 13, 1968, 1.

——. "Narcotics Laxity Alleged by Nixon." *New York Times*, September 17, 1968, 1.

Shepsle, Kenneth A. *The Giant Jigsaw Puzzle: Democratic Committee Assignments in the Modern House*. Chicago: University of Chicago Press, 1978.

Sinclair, Barbara. "The Speaker's Task Force in the Post-Reform House of Representatives." *American Political Science Review* 75 (June 1981): 397–410.

——. "The Congressional Party: Evolving Organizational, Agenda-Setting, and Policy Roles." In *The Parties Respond: Changes in the American Party System*. Ed. L. Sandy Maisel, 227–48. Boulder, Colo.: Westview, 1990.

Smith, Terence. "Garment Workers Applaud President." *New York Times*, September 30, 1980, A-1.

Sorauf, Frank J. "Political Parties and Political Action Committees: Two Life Cycles." *Arizona Law Review* 22, no. 2 (1980): 445–63.

Spitzer, Robert J. *The Presidency and Public Policy: The Four Arenas of Presidential Power*. University: University of Alabama Press, 1983.

Stone, Walter J. and Alan I. Abramowitz. "Ideology, Electability, and Candidate Choice." In *The Life of the Parties: Activists in Presidential Politics*. Ed. Ronald B. Rapoport, Alan I. Abramowitz, and John McGlennon, 75–95. Lexington: University Press of Kentucky, 1986.

Sullivan, Denis G., Jeffrey L. Pressman, Benjamin I. Page, and John J. Lyons. *The Politics of Representation: The Democratic Convention of 1972*. New York: St. Martin's Press, 1974.

Sundquist, James L. "The Crisis of Competence in Our National Government." *Political Science Quarterly* 95 (Summer 1980): 183–208.

——. *The Decline and Resurgence of Congress*. Washington, D.C.: Brookings Institution, 1981.

——. "Party Decay and the Capacity to Govern." In *The Future of American Political Parties: The Challenge of Governance*. Ed. Joel L. Fleishman, 42–67. Englewood Cliffs, N.J.: Prentice-Hall, 1982.

——. *Constitutional Reform and Effective Government*, rev. ed. Washington, D.C.: Brookings Institution, 1992.

Taft, Robert. "Robert Taft Statement on Meeting with Dwight D. Eisenhower." Official File, Box 711, Dwight D. Eisenhower Library, Abilene, Kans.

Truman, David B. "Party Reform, Party Atrophy, and Constitutional Change: Some Reflections." *Political Science Quarterly* 99 (Winter 1984–85): 637–55.

U.S. Congress. House. Democratic Caucus. *Preamble and Rules of the Democratic Caucus*, rev. 102d Cong., 1st sess., January 9, 1991.

Verba, Sidney and Norman H. Nie. *Participation in America: Political Democracy and Social Equality*. New York: Harper and Row, 1972.

Wall Street Journal/NBC News. *Wall Street Journal/NBC News Poll*, January 23–28, 1993.

Ware, Alan. *Citizens, Parties, and the State: A Reappraisal*. Princeton, N.J.: Princeton University Press, 1987.

Wattenberg, Martin P. *The Decline of American Political Parties, 1952–1988*. Cambridge, Mass.: Harvard University Press, 1984.

——. "Dealignment in the American Electorate." In *Parties and Politics in American History* Ed. L. Sandy Maisel and William G. Shade, 225–40. New York: Garland, 1994.

Wayne, Stephen J. *The Road to the White House: The Politics of Presidential Elections,* 2d ed. New York: St. Martin's Press, 1984.

Weaver, R. Kent and Bert A. Rockman. "Institutional Reform and Constitutional Design." In *Do Institutions Matter? Government Capabilities in the United States and Abroad.* Ed. R. Kent Weaver and Bert A. Rockman, 462–82. Washington, D.C.: Brookings Institution, 1993.

Weinberg, Martha Wagner. "Writing the Republican Platform." *Political Science Quarterly* 92 (Winter 1977–78): 655–62.

West, Darrell M. *Making Campaigns Count: Leadership and Coalition-Building in 1980.* Westport, Conn.: Greenwood, 1984.

——. *Airs Wars: Television Advertising in Election Campaigns, 1952–1992.* Washington, D.C.: Congressional Quarterly, 1993.

White, Morton. *Philosophy, the Federalist, and the Constitution.* New York: Oxford University Press, 1987.

Wildavsky, Aaron. "The Two Presidencies." *The Two Presidencies: A Quarter Century Assessment.* Ed. Steven A. Shull, 11–25. Chicago: Nelson Hall, 1991.

Wood, Gordon S. *The Creation of the American Republic, 1776–1787.* New York: W. W. Norton, 1972.

Wooten, James T. "Carter Says Ford Lags as Reformer." *New York Times,* August 12, 1976, 1.

——. "Carter Defends Congress and Assails Ford's Vetoes." *New York Times* August 24, 1976, 17.

Yerxa, Fendall W. "Goldwater and Rockefeller Exchange Praise in Albany." *New York Times,* September 26, 1964, sec. 1, p. 5.

Index